MEGILLAT TIKVAH

FAITH, HOPE AND SURVIVAL
The Journey of Rabbi Tzvi Elimelech Roszler

Published by
Myer Roszler
MIAMI BEACH, FLORIDA
myerroszler@yahoo.com

ISBN: 978-0-578-93567-6

Cover and Interior: Gary A. Rosenberg • www.thebookcouple.com
Editing: Erica Rauzin

Printed in the United States of America

Contents

Introduction

This was not meant to be a book. In March 1985, my father, our family's Zeidy, Rabbi Tzvi Elimelech Roszler, decided to record the story of his life using a cassette tape recorder. Whenever he had a chance over the next eight years, he dictated his life story. He often waited months between recording sessions, but he finished in 1993. He would record varying lengths of his history at various times. He collected and stored all the tapes in a box until 2013. He then had the foresight to realize that technology had changed drastically, and he had all the tapes digitized and transferred to thumbnail drives so we could listen to them on our computers. One of his buddies from the morning minyan at Beth Jacob Congregation in Beverly Hills did the transfer for him. He then gave the thumb drives to his children and some of his grandchildren, where they languished in our desk drawers for five years. Sadly Zeidy passed away in 2017.

In 2018, I went to part time status as a physician and found myself with free time. I consulted with my sisters and decided to try to turn Zeidy's dictations into a book. I really had no idea how to do this. Luckily for me, our daughter Rachel once worked at a transcription/translation service in Miami where they do translations, dubbing, and subtitles for foreign movies and soap operas. So my family suggested that I get the tapes professionally transcribed and see if I could turn the results into a book. Luckily Rachel's company had a branch in Israel where they found someone familiar with English, Hebrew and Yiddish to do the transcriptions. I was pleasantly surprised when I received the transcriptions to see that they revealed a well thought-out story. However, since Zeidy's narrative was unscripted and done in spurts over eight years, there were redundancies, diversions and tangents from a scripted story.

As with many transcription services I worked with over the years, the accuracy of the transcript was very good, but far from perfect, so some parts of the story had words missing or wrongly transcribed. Some of these problems may be have been due to the quality of the original cassette tapes. Also, although Zeidy's English was excellent, I discovered that there's a big difference between oral free style dictation and a written history book.

The next step was for me to compare the dictated tapes and the transcribed product to check for accuracy and to make sure no portions were skipped. As I did this, I also tried to edit the transcripts to improve the syntax, make them more understandable, omit redundancies, and move tangents to the appropriate timeline. While doing this, I tried to preserve Zeidy's style of storytelling and maintain fidelity to his exact words and context. I had retired during the 2020 Covid Epidemic and was able to devote a significant amount of time to editing the book. It has taken over 2 years of time.

Unfortunately, my editorial skills and English grammar dexterity were not sufficient to produce a well written work. So I asked my good friend and neighbor Erica Meyer Rauzin, who is a professional editor, to edit the manuscript, and get it ready for publication. She did a terrific job.

Generally in the text, parentheses signify an English translation of a Hebrew, Yiddish, or German word. In some places, set off in brackets, you'll find background explanations I've written about a person or place. I borrowed heavily from Wikipedia and other sources I found on the internet. Almost all the chapters are directly Zeidy's words and descriptions. However, in the last chapter, I summarized some portions for brevity. My sister Esther wrote the chapter about Zeidy's life from 1988 onward and the one about Grandma Maureen. My son Amichai wrote the chapter on the history and function of the Ebensee concentration camp, which he visited in 2016. He also assisted with computer issues, Hebrew typing, and tombstone translations. My sisters Raizel and

Elizabeth in Cleveland sorted through thousands of photographs and documents from my parents' belongings, and some of those appear in this book.

My cousin, Rifka Weiss of Modiin, Israel, (Daughter of Rabbi and Mrs Richtman, who played such an integral role in Zeidy's early life in the United States) was very helpful supplying photographs and identifying long lost relatives. My cousin Rabbi Binyomin Dovid Ruttner, the son of the Shomkpter Rav (who played such an important role for Zeidy in the Displaced Person Camp in Germany) and currently the Rav of the Maareh Yecheskel Shtieble in Brooklyn, donated a number of photographs.

The layout of the book is in a different sequence than the order of the tapes. The book is mostly chronological; however, I placed the chapters about Zeidy's relatives and his *yichus* (lineage) as separate appendices at the end of the book. They make for interesting reading, but they added complexity to the main story. I completely rewrote the chapter on yichus to make it more understandable. His stories about his relatives conclude in the late 1980s, and he did not get to update most of them.

Amichai provided the name of the Book. Our ancestor the Tosefoth Yom Tov, in the 1700s wrote a short book on his trials and tribulations, from exile to redemption and called it "Megillat Eivah" (The scroll or story of animosity). Amichai used a play on words and a more positive tone in calling the book, "Megillat Tikvah", Faith, Hope and Survival, the Journey of Rabbi Tzvi Elimelech Roszler.

My sisters, Raizel, Esther, and Elizabeth dedicated a good portion of their time and energy to take of care of our parents during the final years of their lives. Since I was working and living in Miami, my involvement was minimal. I hope that this book can somehow compensate them for their Chessed Shel Emes.

Zeidy recorded two excellent documentaries about his life in Europe before coming to America. One is with the University of Southern California Shoah Foundation: https://vhaonline.usc.edu/viewingPage?testimonyID=45087&returnIndex=0

He made another documentary with the Simon Wiesenthal Museum, hosted by United States Holocaust Museum: https://collections.ushmm.org/search/catalog/irn513297

I encourage all his relatives and descendants to view these videos since they provide extra and new information that may not be in the book. Throughout his memoir, Zeidy pleads with his survivors to remember the Nazis' evil, horrific destruction of the European Jewish way of life and their decimation of his family.

Al Tisckach—Do not forget.

Chapter 1

I am Tzvi Elimelech Roszler. I was born on November 16, 1929, *13 Heshvan 5690*. Today is Sunday March 4, 1985. It's the 10th day of Adar 5745 in the Jewish calendar, the month of Purim. The weekly Torah reading is *Ki Sesa*. Today, at age 56, I decided at last to record some of my family's history.

Background

We are from Romania's Transylvania region, which was called Sieben-bürgen in Yiddish. This region changed hands back and forth between Romania and Hungary a number of times. Prior to the First World War, it was part of the Austro-Hungarian Empire. After the war, it became Romanian, which it remained until 1940. From 1940 to 1944, the Germans gave half of Transylvania to their ally Hungary. It received our area, the city of Borgo Prund, and also Cluj (Klausenberg) and the city of Bistritz, where our close relatives lived. After 1945, the region was ceded back to Romania, and it remains under the Romanian government to this day.

We lived in Borgo Prund until May 1944 when we were deported to a ghetto in Bistritz. We stayed there about a month. Then we were deported to Auschwitz, Poland, where the Germans killed my parents, my younger brother Yecheskal (Chezki), age 10, and my younger sister Sarah (Suri). I was 14 when the Nazis sent me with my older brother Yitzchak Shmuel to the Mauthausen concentration camp and then to the subcamp Ebensee, also in Austria. He died there six days before liberation. I had an older sister, Chava, who was born after Yitzchak Shmuel and before me, but she died in early childhood.

Zeidy's birth certificate—He thought that he needed his birth certificate to immigrate to the USA in 1947. Although he was in Germany in the DP camp, he was somehow able to get someone from Borgo to send it to him.

People sometimes call me Hersh-Melech, instead of Tzvi Elimelech. Our surname now is Roszler. It was Rössler in Romania, where it was pronounced *ressler*, but since English has no umlaut, it became Roszler in America.

My wife's name is Malke, in English, Maureen. Her maiden name was Bloomberg. Her parents, Yosef (Grandpa George) and Tzirel (Grandma Sarah) Bloomberg, were active in the San Francisco Jewish community and, later, in the community in Los Angeles.

We have four children. Our oldest daughter Raizel was named after my mother. At this point and after the name of every family member who is gone, I always whisper *aleya hasholem* in their memory. Our son Chaim

Meir was named after my grandfather, Chaim Ressler, and my father, Meir Ressler. My middle daughter Esther Sarah was named after my wife's grandmother and after my sister Sarah *aleihem hasholem*. And my youngest daughter is Yetta Rivka, named after my father-in-law's mother and my paternal grandmother.

Family photo at Esther Kandel's home in Beverlywood, in about 2013.

I received *smicha* (Rabbinic ordination) at Yeshivas Torah Vadaas in Brooklyn, New York. Two great rabbis (*gedolim*), Rav Schnider and Rav Kushilevitz *aleihem hasholem* signed my ordination.

Zeidy's Rabbinical Ordination from 1952—At 22, he was one
of the youngest *musmachim* at the time of his ordination from
Yeshiva Torah Vadaas in Williamsburg, New York City.

I spent several months in *chinuch* (teaching) in New York after
graduation, and I also continued my secular education at Brooklyn College.
Then, I left New York City and became *Rav* (rabbi) in Hornell, in
upstate New York, near the Rochester and Buffalo area. It was a small
community, but we had a number of Jewish people and a number of
synagogue members. After four years in Hornell, I became *Rav* in Duluth,
in northern Minnesota. I served at a *mechabdik* (honored) congregation,

with a very fine synagogue with a balcony. When we arrived, the city had *talmidei hachamim* (religious scholars). Unfortunately, the community deteriorated in later years because, at that time, it had no *yeshiva katana* (day school) to educate its children. As a result, we left also because we wanted to have a day school for our children when they reached school age. In 1961, we moved to Los Angeles.

My Immediate Family

My oldest brother was Yitzhak Shmuel. He was actually a genius in both learning and business. He learned for a short time in Borgo Prund where we lived, and then he went for a short time to the Vishnitz yeshiva in the city of Grosswardein. This city is about 400 kilometers from Borgo Prund, which in Europe was considered a great distance.

Yitzhak Schmuel had a mind for everything. He was very smart, a tremendous learner, and a big businessman. He would help my father *alav hasholem* a lot in the lumber business. He actually sort of managed the business while he was home and learning in Borgo Prund.

Many times when the public school teacher would get stuck with some mathematical problem, he would help her along. He had beautiful handwriting. When I was a child, he was everything to me. He used to make the forms for lead *dreidels* (spinning tops children play with at Hanukkah), and he used to make rubber stamps; he could make anything. He was ambidextrous and could write with both hands. The rabbis would praise him for his learning. He died in the concentration camp. He died *yod-zayin Iyar,* the 30th of April, 1945, six days before the Americans liberated us. I will come back to him later on when we speak of the concentration camp.

My oldest brother was three and a half years older than I am, and my sister, Suri, was two years younger. I have a picture of her. She attended *Beis Yaakov* (House of Jacob girls school) in Burgo Prund and had her beginnings there. For a few years, a teacher came down and taught at *Beis Yaakov,* and then one of the *shochet's* (ritual slaughterer's) daughters became the teacher. And, of course, Suri also went to public school. She was a smart girl at the age of twelve when she was taken to the concentration camp where the Germans killed her.

My younger brother Chezki, whom I loved very much, was killed by the Germans when he was ten. He started wearing glasses when he was about seven or eight. I was his big brother, four years older, but I had tremendous love for him. Of course, I loved my sister and my other brother too, but Chezki especially because he was the youngest. He was killed by the Germans in Auschwitz.

Suri, his sister—Zeidy had only this one picture of his sister (bottom left) and none of his brothers.

My Father

My father was Meir Ressler, who also was killed in Auschwitz in 1944 at the hands of the Germans. He learned under the city rabbis of Borgo and Bistritz.

My father grew up as a child in Mureşenii and was sent to learn in Borgo Prund. I believe he also learned in Bistritz in a *yeshiva* (Jewish school), and he was a very good student, a very good *talmid hacham*. I remember him as an adult learning late at night even though he was in business, and it was very difficult. But he practically never failed to study at least the *Choke Lyisrael*. [A book that broke down the portion of the week along with relevant material from the Mishna and Gemarah, and Kabbalistic commentary. Interestingly, it was mainly a book for Sefardim.]

He had to get up early, about 4 o'clock in the morning, because in the lumber business, the early bird catches the worm! He would get up and hire a driver to go 20 kilometers to buy wholesale lumber, which the peasants would bring, sometimes in one wagon, or three or four wagons, filled with fresh-cut lumber from trees in the forest. He would send it to the lumber mills or to the factory for processing into boards of various sizes for use as building materials. Merchants from all over the country would come and purchase from us and various other local lumber manufacturers. My father was a very shrewd businessman.

During the First World War, he was called up to the Austro-Hungarian army. He ended up in Turkey, since Turkey was one of the allies of the Austro-Hungarians. He spent several years working at a hotel in Turkey. When he came back from Turkey, he brought a number of *sfarim* (books). They were very well bound and had many *perushim* (commentaries). They were somewhat like the *Mikruess Gaddoles* [*a very popular, standard set of Chumashim*] with the *mefarshim* (commentary), I believe, from the Ramban, Evan Ezra, and so on. He also brought back a huge rolled picture of Constantinople, where he was either a receptionist or a guard at a hotel, I can't remember exactly. The only thing I recall is that he used to tell us bread is called "eckmeck" in Turkish.

When my father came back from the army, he moved to Borgo Prund. My mother's family members who lived in Borgo Prund at that time included my cousin Eddie's father, Zalman Leib Kahan, who was married to my mother's sister, my aunt who was also Helen Baum's mother. He was the *shadchan* (matchmaker) between my father and my mother who lived in Cluj (Klausenburg). My father started establishing himself as a lumber merchant, a lumber wholesaler, and by the summer the *shidduch* (the match) happened, and my mother *aleya hasholem* moved to Borgo Prund, where we were born.

My father was a wonderful man; he was very sympathetic. Though many times he was also strict, he was a wonderful, very loving man. He also was concerned for poor people. We would have one, two or even three *orchim* (visitors) at our table *kimat* (almost) every *Shabbes*. In those days, many people were poor, and they would come just to collect money for themselves and their families. They would come Friday night to shul, and my father *alav hasholem* and my mother, who was his helper, always sat them at the table. Especially during the war, the Second World War, we tried to help out many people.

People would come around practically every day, and we would give *tzedakah* (charity). As *cheder* (school) boys we would go around to collect various things and, naturally, we tried our best. Times were very bad during depression years; business was very bad. Yet, we still tried to do as much as possible, though the situation economically and financially was very bad at that time. Today it is a big *yichus* (an important thing) to eat whole wheat bread, while in Europe whole wheat bread was the bread of the poor. And we had to eat the whole wheat because the flour was cheaper, that is how bad our situation was.

Raizel, his mother—(right) Raizel Kahana before her marriage.
(center and left) Her niece Chana Kahana Richtman and nephew
Joe Kahn, who both moved to the US before WW2.

Even at that time we tried to always pay the *schar limud* (payment to the rabbi at our boys' school) for teaching *Torah*. My father and my mother *aleihem hasholem* always made sure that there would be money to pay the *rebbe* because the community did not pay. We had no central committee, so it was up to the individual people who tried to chip in. Besides that, we also tried to donate the lumber remnants, which could have been sold. We provided some of that lumber for heating the *chadarim* (schools), which, of course, had no central heating. In later years, we would send lumber by train to my grandparents in Klausenburg when we had business shipments going there.

Zeidy's mother, Raizel, after she married—She is wearing a wig and a hat since Chasidic women followed the custom of shaving their heads.

My father was a very good man, but sadly he died early, I don't know exactly at what age,. I think he was born in 1893. I've heard 1883, but I'm very doubtful of that. I would say most likely 1893, which means that during the First World War—which broke out in 1914 in Europe—he was about 21 years old. *[According to his birth certificate his father was 45 at the time of Zeidy's birth in 1929, which would mean he was born in 1883 or 1884].* Of course, he died at a very young age. He was killed by Hitler together with my mother, my brother Chezki, and my sister Suri in the gas chambers. They all died together, *Hashem yikom damam* (May God avenge their souls).

He would often come to *cheder* when we little ones were studying. This was his nature. Sometimes when we were not listening exactly at what he said, or when we broke things, he was quite strict about that, but his love for us was boundless. It was tremendous love for us children and for our mother and for the whole family. He also would try to help his brothers and sisters. Especially in the early 1940s, when business was good—before they took us to the concentration camps—he would try to help them financially. This was his family. This was his character.

I really didn't get to know my father all that well—and that is too bad—because when he died in the concentration camp, in Auschwitz, I was only 14. Unfortunately, as much as he wanted to spend time with us, as much as he tried, he did not have much time since life in Europe was very difficult. It was not like here, where you have time to sit down with your children and spend time with them, and so on. He had to do a job, and we had to go to *cheder*. We would come and help with the business, too. My elder brother *alav hasholem* and I would help also with the billing. We did not have the modern conveniences of an adding machine. If we'd had that, it would have been such a tremendous labor saving device!

My mother *aleya hasholem* had to do many things, although we bought bread at the bakery. At times during the war, we couldn't go to the bakery. So we had to bake. She had to darn socks, to wash our clothes; everything was a chore. Yet, I would say, my parents were happily married. Well not, "I would say;" I know they were very happily married. They constantly worried about their children, constantly worried about anti-Semitism, and so on. And yet, I was not old enough when my parents were murdered to have really had the chance to get to know them as deeply as our children know us, possibly because of their difficult life.

The only things we saw as children were a nice life and family unity during every *simcha* (holiday gathering). Of course, I remember walking with my father *alav hasholem* to *shul* (synagogue), being with my mother when she prepared for *Pesach* or got ready for *Shabbes*. All these things naturally rubbed off on us children. But, yet again, I must emphasize, I could not learn as much from them as I would have liked. Of course, I would have liked to have known more about my father and my mother, too. But I believe I did get some insight and some knowledge of their life.

My father *alav hasholem* wore a *shtreimel* (a Chassidic fur hat) and a *kappatta* (long coat) in the house on *Shabbes*. He was called a modern *Hasidic* Jew, and we were what was called a modern *Hasidic* family. He was a businessman, and weekdays he would wear like a three-quarter jacket, a long jacket, like a uniform of a modern *Hasidic* Jew who was a business-man. He wouldn't necessarily wear black clothes, but he did wear a black hat. As a child, I wore *payos* (side curls) behind my ears, and my brother *alav hasholem* also had *payos* behind his ears. My father had a beard, but it was cut. He kept it very nicely trimmed because he was a businessman, and he sometimes had to deal with government officials, peasants, lumber manufacturers, merchants, and so on. So he was a modern *Hasidic* Jew.

He was naturally very religious. He *davened* (prayed) with his *Tallis* (prayer shawl) over his head and with a *gartel* (a special string used by Hasidic custom like a belt). When he prayed, he would use a *Likutey Tzvi siddur* (a prayerbook, now out of print), which was published for more learned Jews in that it had more commentary on the prayers. Even today, the *Likutey Tzvi* is a very fine type of *siddur* to have. *[I looked for it but could not find a copy except on auction sites].*

My father put on both Rashi and Rabbenu Tam *tefillin* (black leather boxes holding prayers that are strapped to the head and arm while pray-ing). They vary in that the head piece of the tefillin holds four pieces of parchment which can be arranged in two different orders. Most men use the order of Rashi, but Hasidic Jews use both. They have a second pair with the parchment arranged according to Rashi's grandson Rabbenu Tam, so they put on two sets of tefillin in the morning.

He was very respected by the *Rav* in town since, of course, we were distant relatives of the Maareah Yecheskal, as my mother's side descended from him.

The townspeople also respected him, and he used to do *toves* (favors) for people, especially during the war years, when he had a license to operate a lumber processing business, and other people did not have one. So he was well known in the community and well respected for his knowledge and his status. There were some distant relatives who did not get along well with him, but they made up in later years and everything was forgotten.

I am just trying to think out loud, trying to recall here things about my father *alav hasholem*. I remember that from time to time he would take me along with him to the lumber mills. Various peasants delivered our lumber to the mills, some smaller mills and some larger ones. Occasionally when I was a young child, age three or four, my father would take me to walk along with him to see how his lumber was being processed and to see the operator of the mill. Sometimes he took me to see the *goyim* (non-Jews), the peasants from whom we bought the lumber. Of course, I was not always the best-behaved child, and many times my father did not want to take me because he had important matter to transact, and I would have been in the way—like many children. I insisted, and my father said, "no." I insisted, and my father even tried to bribe me sometimes, to give me some money, and I said, "no!" I would scream and yell as children do. But my father would always act with love; sometimes he won and sometimes I won.

Once, when I was about five years old, he took me on a trip. We went with a driver about 15 or 20 kilometers to go to the forest to see the lumber or to buy lumber, I cannot recall exactly. For some reason, we had to walk back. I don't know what happened to the driver. There was a narrow gauge railroad all along the way, but no trains running, and we had to walk back. I recall what an ordeal it was. My father said, "Soon, soon we will be home." This was one of the most interesting events of my childhood, walking so far with my father. Of course, we always walked together to *shul*, to *daven*.

Our city had no eruv (a wall within which observant Jews can carry items on *Shabbes*), so in winter, he would wear his *tallis* on his shoulder, under his coat, and walk to *shul* that way. I recall wintertime. Snow covered the ground, which was frozen. It was very cold where we lived. I can still visualize the *Shabbes*, when I would walk to *shul* with my father and both my brothers, my youngest brother Chezki and my eldest brother Yitzchak Shmuel.

My sister sometimes came later on to *shul*. Women did not necessarily come to *shul* every *Shabbes*, but they would come sometimes, and little girls would come with them and play in the *shul* yard where we boys used to love to play with our friends and make a lot of noise. I can still recall winter days, how we walked in the snow and over the frozen ground. I can still hear the noise and see the snow on the street; the sun would shine on it, but it stayed frozen. During the wintertime, the farmers used sleds to transport lumber or other things, even people.

When we come around to talking about school, I will explain why it was so difficult, the difficult life we had as Jews and specifically as Jewish children. Life was difficult as it was, but as Jewish children, we suffered anti-Semitism and problems with *Shabbes* at school because we were forced to go there.

This will conclude for the time being this short review of my father's life. I know it is very little, but after all these years, even the things I knew are fading. I am forgetting, and I find it really very difficult to recall many things that I once knew. I don't remember many details from my childhood, or many details about my father and my mother *aleihem hasholem*, who were killed in 1944. Now it's 1986, so that happened 42 years ago, and that is why I have decided to record many of these things so that there should be a record because people forget.

His father, my grandfather Chaim Ressler, was also a *Rav*—a *goan* (great rabbinical scholar) in Vaslui, in north Romania near Jassy. He was an expert in *Niglah v Nistar*, the revealed and secret aspects of the Torah. He learned Torah *yomam va'lelea* (day and night). He also had great knowledge of the mystical Jewish teachings called *Kabbalah*. He served as a *dayan* (judge) in the city of Dorna Vatra, Transylvania. In around 1940, he was asked to come to Vaslui—now a city of around 100,000 people—to mentor a young rabbi, Rabbi Halpert, and to teach him how to become a competent Rav.

[In the 1950s, Rabbi Halpert moved to Israel and became the Rabbi of North Tel Aviv. His son Shmulkie (Samuel) became a member of the Knesseth for the Agudah party.]

The Jews of the Jassy area were not deported during the war, so my grandfather Chaim survived there and died in 1949. Because of the war, the deportations and the change in jurisdiction of his hometown from Rumanian to Hungarian rule, he never saw his family again.

Borgo Prund

Borgo Prund was a nice Jewish community, the county seat for all the smaller Borgos villages, and the head seat for all the Borgos. There was lower Borgo, middle Borgo, upper Borgo, and Russian Borgo—I don't know why it was called Russian Borgo. These small scattered communities included Mureşenii Borgo (Mureşenii Bârgăului), where my grandparents lived.

The courthouse was in Borgo Prund and so was the market, which usually took place during *Shabbes* so the Jews could not participate. The main business district of the Borgos was in Borgo Prund, our community of four or five thousand people, maybe six thousand. Borgo's Jewish population alone was approximately 150 to 200 families.

It was a compact little town with Jews from all

Entry sign to the shtetel of Borgo Prund— Borgo Prund was the main town and county seat of the smaller little Borgo villages. It is in a valley in the Carpathian mountains and looks like a Swiss hamlet.

walks of life. There were *Hassidic* Jews and non-*Hassidic* Jews. The whole Jewish community was Orthodox. No Jewish-owned store or business was open on *Shabbes* in the days before the Hungarians arrived in 1940. After that certain businesses were open on *Shabbes* by law. That created many, many difficulties, so Jews hired non-Jews to keep their business open. If you closed, you were not only penalized—you were put in jail.

Borgo Prund had some Jewish store owners, but its main industry was lumber. And, of course, the majority of people were non-Jewish Romanians. The town was the industrial and business seat of all the Borgos, a cluster of villages extending for a distance of about 40 to 50 kilometers, all the way to the border of Bukovina, the neighboring state next to Transylvania. It was Romanian until World War II and now is part of Ukraine.

Borgo Prund is in the Carpathian Mountains, and it's surrounded by hills, with huge mountains in the distance. It actually sits in a valley in between the huge Carpathians, and it looks like a village in Switzerland. In the winter, of course, it was very cold, and it would snow there. In the summer, which was nice and pleasant, the air was very clear.

I remember that I had a very nice childhood. Until I was five years old, we had an apartment that wasn't very big, two or three rooms. At the time, we knew it was for a smaller family. We rented the apartment from a *Chassidic* family named Marmarush. Some of the Marmarush children who survived the Holocaust live in Israel and some in New York.

[Ed: When Myer was in Israel in 1976, he and Zeidy went to visit one of the Marmarush sons in the Tel Aviv post office, where he was a night clerk. He later wrote a commentary about the Kli Yakar, one of the commentators on the Bible. And, to tell another story with a Marmarush connection, when we went back to Borgo in 1997, we went to the small Jewish cemetery just outside town. It was in excellent condition considering that no Jews had lived there for 50 years. We went to look for the matzevah (headstone) of Zeidy's sister Chava, who died when she was very young, prior to the Holocaust. Either we could not find it, or they did not have the custom of putting up matzevahs for young children. However, we found a very ornate 1944 matzevah for the father of this Mr. Marmarush. Zeidy remembered the funeral, which happened just before they were deported.]

There was no hospital in Borgo Prund when I was born. I was delivered at home by a Jewish *masha* (midwife). Her name was Fruma. She had a son named Aku, who was not exactly the most prominent person in the community. People sort of looked down him because of the way he conducted himself.

I remember as a child—I must have been five or six years old—I had pneumonia, which was a very serious sickness in those days. It is serious even today, but then there were no antibiotics. I still recall lying in bed and wearing a vest that was sent from America. It was a big deal to get a vest from the United States or, indeed, any garment.

And I remember my parents *aleihem hasholem* were very worried about what was going to happen. They used to sort of bribe us children and give us money, and during the depression years money was not so readily available. I had a very large sum of money by those standards, given to pacify me and make me feel better. So I had pneumonia, and I can still recall the doctor coming to take my temperature. And he talked about the crisis, and when the crisis was going to come. As I said, pneumonia was a very serious illness, and many people died of it because there were no antibiotics. And I remember the day when the doctor said that the crisis was over, and I would be alright.

In most instances, when a woman was pregnant, it was not a doctor, but a midwife who delivered the baby. I believe our Jewish midwife, Fruma, delivered all of us. She was a very interesting personality. She was an old-fashioned lady who lived on the main street in town in a one-room house. You can imagine the sanitary conditions that existed when she had to deliver a baby. She may have washed her hands—I really don't know. She had to boil water, since there was no hot water. You had to boil it on the wooden stove. Everything had to be done at the house. We did not have the comfort of a huge house, nobody did. So it was amazingly miraculous, even the number of children who survived childbirth because of the unsanitary conditions. The woman giving birth would stay in bed for a long time—that was the custom, maybe a week, maybe two weeks.

The night before the *bris* (circumcision ceremony), the children gathered and went to the home of the baby and read *Kriat Shma* and said some special *Shir Hamaalot* (Psalms). [This was the *Vacht Nacht*—literally the night watch—done the night before a bris.] The children would get nuts and candy, so during a *bris* there was always something to look forward to. The *bris* also often took place in the house, though sometimes it took place in the shul. I would say most people were invited. The children would go, too.

It was not a formal thing, like a wedding, but in general the community was very close knit. It was different from the bigger cities where they had more of a spread between various groups. Our community's *shohet* (ritual meat slaughterer) was also its *moel* (the one who performed the circumcision).

In 1943, or maybe in January 1944, I remember a difficult night. I was in Muresenni, and my father's younger sister Feiga *aleya hasholem* was having some complications from her pregnancy, and her baby was coming. She had married a man who was hiding from the authorities. He was a *tamim vnealam* (disappeared), which means he was hiding in order not to be sent to the labor camps, because they took Jews to the labor camp and sent many to the front. This happened to some of my uncles who never returned. Feiga's husband was hiding in Klausenburg most of the time, but before she gave birth, he came stealthily and was hiding in Mureșenii. Nobody could know he was there.

When it was time to get the doctor for Feiga, I went myself to get a driver, because my grandmother *aleya hasholem* was an old lady, and there was no one else to get the driver. We sent the driver Friday night to get the doctor in Borgo, Doctor Fisch. He came and delivered the baby.

You see the difficulties. It was very cold, and there were no taxis in Borgo Prund. You had to go six miles by horse and wagon. This was quite a ride with a horse and buggy. It took an hour at least. Later on, Feiga had some complications, and I had to go get the doctor again. So I had to borrow somebody's bicycle. It was January. I remember the streets were frozen; there was snow. I went to get the driver to fetch the doctor from Borgo. The next week, the *moel* came and stayed for *Shabbes* at the house. It was quite a big *bris,* and we invited everybody in town. The difficulty was you had to bake yourself and cook yourself for all of these people, but yet it was a happy occasion.

Not far from Borgo Prund, there is a little town called Tihuta. It is also called Tihuța Pass, Pasul Tihuța, Pasul Bârgău, Borgói-hágó or, in Hungarian, Burgó. It is a high mountain pass in the Romanian Bârgău Mountains (the Eastern Carpathians) connecting Bistritz (Transylvania) with Dornei Vatra (Bukovina, Moldavia), where my paternal grandfather served as a *dayan*.

[The pass was made famous by Bram Stoker's novel Dracula, *where, it was called "the Borgo Pass." It was the gateway to the realm of Count Dracula. Stoker most likely found the name on a contemporary map. He never actually visited the area. Today the pass is home to Hotel Castel Dracula, a small ski resort built in 1974. The hotel, which looks like a medieval villa, has become quite an attraction due to its architectural style and the beauty of its location. We visited it in 1997.]*

The Joint Distribution Committee (JDC) maintained a summer camp in Tihuta for underprivileged Jewish children. In the summer, children would come from various places, many from large cities and, of course, some from Borgo Prund and other small towns nearby. The JDC could bring impoverished Jewish children to the summer camp, where they would receive sufficient good food to fatten them up a bit.

As a child, I looked forward to summertime when these different children arrived by train from various cities, and I would make new acquaintances. They were transferred to Borgo by train or truck. A smaller railroad, a narrower rail line, used to run from Borgo to Tihuta. One time, as a matter of fact, my brother Itzhak Shmuel *aleya hasholem* went to the camp for a summer. My parents sent him because they felt that he was undernourished. The JDC did beautiful things for those children.

People would come to Borgo Prund from big cities to relax and visit relatives during the summertime. As children—even before I was five—we liked to go to climbing in the hills; it was very pleasant.

Before I reached the *cheder* (school) age of three, I would *schlep* along with my brother, even when I was two and a half or two and three-quarters. At three, I started *cheder*. There was no specific nursery school as we know it today. From three years of age, we were all together with other children. Up to age 18, we were practically in one room, just called *cheder* [literally room in Hebrew].

So, I started at the age of three, learning the *alef beit*. Of course, it was customary to drop candies for children as they started learning *alef beit*. I did it for my children. In some situations, they would take a child and wrap him in a *tallit* and take him to *cheder* for the first time. I do not recall specifically if this happened to me, but I recall that when I first started learning the *alef beit,* they dropped some candy drops or raisins or something sweet, to make the learning the *Torah* sweet. They did this so I would have *cheshek*, willingness to learn *Torah.*

I caught up and learned to read very fast because I was taught by the European method, not like nursery schools here or day schools that teach the *aleph beis* first. Instead, they first taught us the vowels—like ooh, aah, eh—then the letters (the *otiyot,)*. We would learn the vowels separately, the *kamatz* and *patach,* the *segol,* the *hirik,* and the *shuruk,* and so on. Then we would learn the *alef beis,* and we would apply the vowels. I would say *kamatz alef, auh* or *kamatz beis bauh, patach alef, patach beis,* and so on.

In *cheder,* I became one of the fastest readers. Sometimes I would even pray too fast in the *Siddur* (prayer book). By age three, we had already spent quite a bit of time in the *cheder* learning. At about age four or so, we started learning a little bit of *Chumash* (Torah). At five, we already learned the regular *parsha* (portion) of the week and, on *Shabbes,* we even learned a little bit of *Mishnayes.*

Now, of course, I had one deficiency. My handwriting was not the most beautiful at the time. I always had trouble with my handwriting, I just could not print letters nicely, especially not Hebrew letters. It was customary, in those days, to have children write on a little blackboard. Every child had a little blackboard with him, and he would write with a thin piece of chalk. And as long as you wrote on that little blackboard, instead of writing with a pencil in a notebook, you were not considered as being a big boy.

So, since my handwriting was very bad, very poor, the teacher would try to make me write things over and over again. But after a while, I was very tired of it, and I actually talked back to the teacher. That was a terrible, terrible sin, to talk back like that to the *rebbi;* it was a very grave sin. a child should never, never talk back to the *rebbi,* for the sake of *derech eretz* (respect). Of course, my parents always agreed with the *rebbi.*

One time, I was really so angry that I did not want to copy the writing on my little blackboard. I thought of myself as already big enough to be able to write in a notebook, but apparently that was not my *rebbi's* opinion. I screamed and yelled, making a very unpleasant situation. Possibly as a result, even today my handwriting is not the most desirable…let's put it that way.

When I was a child, most of the Jews lived on the main street. Our original house was at 24 Main Street. We lived there until I was about five years old, then we moved to a private house which we rented. We always thought that we would buy this house.

Zeidy in 1997 in front of his house in Borgo—The Roszlers rented this house from a Jewish family. When we visited in 1997, the house was occupied by the town thieves, the Gutchka family, who claimed they bought it from the Roszlers.

The owner was a very old lady, a Jewish woman, but very sick. She had delusions, and she would see all kinds of giants, and so on. She was very mentally disturbed, and her distant relatives would bring her food.

It was a nice house, with very large rooms, very big rooms. Though the house itself was not very large, it had a big kitchen, which also served as a dining room during the week. On *Shabbes,* we used one of the other rooms, a sort of a dining room, office, and living room. It also had a large bed, which we used at night. We had another large bedroom, my parent's bedroom, in which they had beautiful furniture, gorgeous furniture, especially bought for them after they were married.

We had a huge yard. Later on, when business was very good in the years 1940 to 1943, we also used it as a warehouse. We had several other warehouses that we rented for the storage of lumber for building. We also stored it in the lumber yards, the lumber factory, and the mills. We used several other yards that we rented from neighbors, and we kept lumber in various places.

Chapter 2

I remember from my childhood that next to the yard, we had a beautiful garden, a very wild garden. In the garden, we had various trees—several apple trees, pears, cherries, apricot trees, and also plums. Part of the garden was planted with vegetables, so we could grow our own. Since that time, I take great pleasure in seeing things grow.

Often as children, we would play in our yard. Children would come, various friends, to play hide and seek, thieves and cops, cops and robbers, and various other games. It was a beautiful yard, very fresh, with grass in it. My father also had someone build a swing, table, and benches in the yard. Often the family had a chance to sit out there together.

Shavuous mornings are a particular, pleasant memory. We would be up very early in the morning, since we stayed awake learning all night. Before we went to shul, I learned in the garden with my brother *alav hasholem* or sometimes my father *alav hasholem* and enjoyed the fresh beautiful air. In the summertime, in the afternoons after we came back from learning in *cheder,* we would play in the yard.

However, our home had some inconveniences which were not exactly pleasant. There was no electricity or light in our house or any other homes, except a very few. There was no plumbing, except for the homes of maybe one or two families who owned businesses.

The streets of Borgo Prund were not paved. In the early 1940s, they laid a sort of pavement on the main street, but it was rocks, not exactly cement or asphalt. I believe it was finally paved during World War II because the Hungarians, who were Germany's allies, needed to use it. Borgo Prund was on the main road leading to Romania and the Russian front line.

At one time, the city did install some streetlights. I believe it was toward the end of the Romanian rule in 1938-39, or maybe during the Hungarian rule, possibly in 1940, in order to make Borgo Prund into more of a city, but that was a very cruel hoax.

Since the town had no electricity, the lights were lit with petroleum or kerosene. Light poles were set up every block or so, and a person who lived in that area had the duty of lighting the lamp every night, though it gave only a very little light. But it was an official order, which again, let's not forget, came from the dictatorial state; whether it was Hungarian or Romanian, it was not a democracy. We couldn't get away with anything. The people had no input as far as protesting in any way that would actually help. So, when the city or town council decreed that you had to light your own kerosene lamp, it was quite a problem if you didn't.

Another problem that created a very difficult situation in summer-time was the tremendous dust throughout the town, particularly since the main street was not paved or, later, was covered only with rocks. Ditches ran on both sides of the main street, and there were ditches all through the town. Eventually the ditches led to one of the rivers. The town diverted water from the river into the ditch on one side of the street. So, instead of the city washing the streets or spraying the streets with water during the summer to control the dust, every person was obliged to water down the street in front of his property and spray it to eliminate some of the dust.

Now you can imagine the difficulty involved in that. Let's say we lived on one side of the street, but the water was in the ditch on the other side. We still had to spray the street, but, of course, we had no hoses, and there was no running water. So, we had to take a pan across to the other side of the street and bend down and take that water and spray it across the entire property in front of our house. Sometimes the ditch did not hold enough water. And if you did not water every day, and if the police passed by and found out that you did not water the front of your street, you could be arrested. Such was life in a dictatorial state.

My parents *aleihem hasholem zichronam livracha* were very devoted. They loved their children very much and would worry about us if we had even the slightest sickness. There were maybe two or three physicians in our community, and only one was Jewish, Doctor Fisch, who incidentally lived through the Holocaust. Once in Tel Aviv, I talked to him on the telephone, as he was also a very distant relative of ours. Our parents worried constantly about us and our welfare. They were always encouraging us to learn. Of course, *Torah* was the main thing.

They tried to dress us to the best of their ability; they also tried to feed us well. They always paid the *schar limud* (cheder school fee). In the depression years, it was difficult to pay this cost and everything else.

They would encourage giving *tzedakah* as much as possible, since there were always poor people around, and our home was open to the *orchim* (visitors) particularly on *Shabbes*. The townspeople were also very poor, but when outside *orchim* such as a *magid* (visiting preacher) would pass by, we would give him a couple of dollars or invite him for a meal.

Other emergencies arose in later years. When the Germans already had a foothold in Hungary in the 1940s, we had an organization similar to the United Jewish Appeal (UJA), and everyone participated in giving. Also, in that time, Jewish young men were taken to join the Hungarian labor force instead of being taken to the army. Many were stationed in or near our town, and we always tried to invite these young people of army age to come to our house so we could try to feed them. I remember that one *Pesach*, we set up a very big party.

Of course, food was very scarce. We tried to do the best we could, with *matzos*, potatoes, and so on to feed these people. They had very little food in the labor camp. However, the army labor camps were not concentration camps; this happened before that time. Instead of taking Jews to the army, the government actually employed them in labor camps, though it paid them next to nothing. The camps sometimes had kosher kitchens, though not always, but the food was very meager. We would try, alongside some other people in the community, to feed them and do the best we could for them.

In our yard, we had a well, although it was contaminated. *[When we went back to Borgo in 1997 the well was still there.]* So, we would get water from the well of our neighbor across the street. We paid a woman to come every day to bring water from across the street and put it into a big barrel we had in the kitchen. The house had no running water.

This woman would help us every day. We had a maid, not that we were rich, but labor was very, very cheap. And, of course, since my mother had four children, it was very difficult for her to do everything by herself. She was a housewife, but every job was very much more difficult than it is today.

Take, for example the wash, which was a major undertaking. My mother *aleya hasholem* had to make a big wash every three or four weeks to wash the linen. She needed to heat the water and leave the laundry overnight to simmer in a big barrel. The next day the maid would take it out, rinse it in the river, and hang it to dry. Of course, since we had no electricity, no running water, and no gas, this was done manually. Everything had to be heated with wood. *[In 1997, the people of Borgo Prund were still washing the laundry by the banks of the river, however, you could see that by then they had detergent, which turned part of the water white.]*

In the kitchen was a huge wood stove, and we had another stove in one of the other rooms. When the air was very cold in wintertime, we would heat the stoves with wood. It helped that we were in the lumber business. At night, before we went to sleep, my father *alav hasholem* would put a big chunk of wood in the kitchen oven, so it would stay hot longer and keep the house warm during the night. In the morning, of course, there was a problem because you had to remake the fire.

The other problem was the plumbing. Everyone had outhouses, and actually it was not very pleasant to have to go to the outhouse at the other end of the yard. They also occasionally had to be emptied and cleaned. *[In 1997, many inhabitants of Borgo still had outhouses.]* The trash disposal was also a big problem. In our city we did not have trash pickups, so we had something like a trash bin at the other end of the yard. This had to be emptied every so often.

It was a very hard life, but if you had sufficient food and clothing, at least you could momentarily forget some of the difficulties. It was pleasant, and the children were happy.

The parents were happy when the authorities left them alone. We were always afraid when a policeman passed by, and everybody had to stand at attention—and there was some anti-Semitism involved.

While we lived under Romanian occupation, the anti-Semitism was extreme, specifically in the years of about 1938 and 1939. In 1940, when the fascist Hungarian government ruled Transylvania, things became very dangerous. They were very fierce, and the times were fearful for Jews.

Jews actually took their lives in their hands, for instance, when they took the trains, since the Hungarians would throw off Jews from the trains, literally killing them. Such terrible occurrences were why Chaim Ressler, my paternal grandfather *alav hasholem,* who was *rav* in the city of Vaslui deep in Rumania, could not travel to return to his wife and daughter who lived in the little town of Mureşenii, six kilometers north of Borgo Prund [then part of Hungary].

The Romanians were bad, especially the later years, but the situation worsened later when the Hungarians came in. Their police were called the Tollakshov (which means feathers), since they used to wear feathers in their hats. Jews would tremble when they passed by because the Tollakshov were very anti-Semitic.

But Borgo Prund was a nice little town, and life was good and pleasant under the circumstances. During the war years—the first years of the war—even though we suffered under the Hungarians, our business was good. Though, unfortunately, we did not know exactly what was happening in Poland.

Czechoslovakia had already deported the Jews to Auschwitz and to different concentration camps. Refugees came from Poland and Czechoslovakia, and they told us all kinds of stories about what was happening. For some reason or another, we refused to believe that these things were really happening. Life seemed to go on normally.

As a matter of fact, Jews were hiding in Klausenberg, in Cluj. Some of my uncles and aunts from my mother's side were hiding because they did not have Hungarian citizenship, and they had to live on their false identification cards. We knew this, yet still we refused to believe that these things were really happening, because our life went on practically normally.

As mentioned, anti-Semitism did exist in Borgo. Here is one specific example: My father's business was that he would buy lumber from the farmers who owned the forest some 20 or 30 miles away, and they would bring it down to Borgo. Sometimes he would buy 50 to 100 cubic meters, sometimes 20 cubic meters, sometimes 10 cubic meters of raw lumber, and we would have it processed at the mills. Borgo and the surrounding area had many lumber mills. Some were old-fashioned water mills, and some were mechanical mills, operated with electricity.

After the Hungarians occupied Transylvania in 1940, they required Jewish merchants to have special licenses in order to conduct business. So all Jewish merchants, specifically lumber merchants, and some others, had to submit their licenses for review. They were left hanging in the air as whether they'd get their licenses back.

I remember this specific incident when my mother *aleya hasholem* once went to the city of Bistritz, the capital of the county, to ask the commission officials about the license. Bistritz was a very Jewish, very religious city, about 20 kilometers from Borgo Prund. Some of my uncles and their families lived there. In order not to be obvious, and to show that we were not rich or wealthy people, she borrowed old clothes from my aunts. The commissioner would have construed any nice dress or a nice coat as showing how the Jews were well off and, of course, the commissioner himself could have been anti-Semitic.

My mother *aleya hasholem* pleaded with the commissioner, telling him that my father should have special privileges since he was a veteran of the German army in World War I.

Thus, when my mother came to the commissioner, she appealed to him that he should restore my father's business license, since my father was a war veteran, and that entitled him to special privileges. The commissioner, who was quite anti-Semitic, told my mother *aleya hasholem* about this fellow Béla Kun, a Jewish Communist who lived during the First World War. The commissioner said to my mother that this Béla Kun was also a war veteran. As if to say, you Jews may be war veterans, but today you are all like traitors to the Hungarian state.

[Béla Kun, 1886–1938, born Béla Kohn, was a Hungarian Jewish Communist revolutionary and politician who was the de facto leader of the Hungarian Soviet Republic in 1919. Following the fall of the Hungarian revolution, Kun emigrated to the Soviet Union, where he became an organizer and an active participant of the Red Terror in Crimea (1920–1921). He was executed in Stalin's Great Purge in 1938.]

I can still recall that when she came home from Bistritz, from seeing this commissioner, she was very sad. Let us not forget our whole livelihood depended on us getting back this license. Without a license, you couldn't do business. But, fortunately, though it was sometime later—I can't recall exactly how long it took—the license was restored to us. I don't remember if that had anything to do with my father being a war veteran or not. With that, we were able to do business for several years.

Also with this license, my father *alav hasholem* was able to take some other Borgo merchants who were denied licenses *tahat knafav* (under his wings). He was able to help them out because when they did business, he let them do it under the auspices of our license. The Hungarians would fine you for the slightest irregularities, and they would fine you tremendous amounts. And the taxes were exorbitant on every little thing. But yet, we existed and life went on semi-normally.

When *Shabbes* and *Yom Tov* came, we made our lives happy.

In Borgo Prund, the central place of Jewish life, of course, was the *shul*. The big *shul* was a very nice *shul*, built probably 100 years earlier. We also had a small *beit hamidrash* (library and place of study). The *rav* was Rav Friedlander, a tremendous *talmid hacham* and a friend of the family. He was also our distant relative because his family descended from Maareah Yecheskal, who had been the chief rabbi of Transylvania 150 years earlier.

Rav Friedman was also a descendant of the *Lisker geza*.

[Lisker is the name of a Hasidic dynasty founded by Rabbi Tzvi Hirsch Friedman. It takes its name from the Yiddish name for Olaszliszka, a village in Hungary.]

All day and night, he sat and learned. He had a library full of *sfarim* and, of course, in those days people had lots of *shayles* (questions about Jewish law). He would answer *shayles* dealing with slaughtered chickens, if the chickens were kosher or not, and he also sat as a *Dayan* (a judge).

Rav Chaim Ressler, Muresenii or Marosborgo

My grandmother *aleya hasholem*, and my aunt *aleya hasholem*—the wife, and daughter of Rav Chaim Ressler, my grandfather *alav hasholem,* who could not travel from Vaslui—all lived in Mureşenii.

My grandfather, as mentioned, was a big *talmid hacham,* at one time the leading citizen of Mureşenii. He was a *Baal Mekubal.* He knew *Kabbalah*; he sat *yomam va'lelea* (day and night) and learned. He was a tremendous *yira shamaim* (fearful of the heavens or fearful of the Lord), and that's how he raised his children.

I would visit there once in a while and spend *yomtovim* (holidays) there. I believe that the last time I saw my grandfather was in 1936. In the early 30s, perhaps even the late 20s, he was sought after to go to various communities to become *rav* and *dayan* (judge). That's how he actually died far away from his family in Vaslui, in old Romania, which we visited in 1983 [and 1999]. We visited his *kever* (grave) there, and we have pictures of his *matzevah* (headstone). In the picture, we have the *yichus* (family history) describing how great he was.

Light of Peace
Righteous one, who knew his creator from his youth;
Ran constantly to serve his lord;
The Rabbi Gaon, son of the holy ones, "bows when he enters and when he leaves and labors in Torah" (b. Sanhedrin 88b with minor changes);
Constantly "holding back the many from sinning" (Malachi 2:6);
Rabbi Chaim the son of Rabbi Tzvi Elimelech Z"l
Grandson of the holy ones: The *Kedushat Levi* (Rabbi Levi Yitzchok of Berditchev), The *Pri Kodesh Haliluim* (Rabbi Tzvi Hirsh Eichenstein of Zidichov), and The *Bnei Yissaschar* (Rabbi Tzvi Elimelech Spira of Dinov), their memory should protect us.
Died: 26 of Tishrei 5709 (1949)
May his soul be bound up in the bond of everlasting life

Matzeva of grandfather Rav Chaim Roszler in Vaslui,
Romania—He survived the war and died in 1949.

Before he was a *dayan* in the city of Donavatra, a resort city about 25 to 30 kilometers away from the Borgos, and he was very well known to the *Satmar Rabbi*. When his children or any member of the family came to visit the *Satmar Rabbi*, he would always sit them next to him, in the first seat next to *Satmar Rabbi*, because of the great reverence, love, and respect that he had for my grandfather Chaim Ressler *alav hasholem*.

Mureşenii

Of course, going six miles to Mureşenii was a big trip for us because you had to rent a horse or wagon. Very seldom, you could find a taxi, but there weren't that many cars around Borgo Prund. It had very few automobiles before the Second World War. So, we would have to hire a horse and buggy and, sometimes in the winter, a sleigh. It was always fun.

Mureşenii was a small, little town, a village, and there were, I don't know exactly, maybe 30, possibly 40, Jewish families. They had a small shul, but it was adequate for the people.

The land for the shul was donated by my great-grandfather, Tzvi Elimelech, who moved there prior to the First World War (I'm not certain exactly when). He was from somewhere in Galicia (Poland), but I really don't know how he came to Mureşenii. Of course, I am named after him, and he was named after the *Bnei Yisascharr*.

At the time, our area of Transylvania was part of the Austro-Hungarian empire. So, if you were a citizen of, let's say, Galicia, where certain areas also were part of Austro-Hungary, then it was easier to move from one part of the Empire to the other. I'm not speaking about it being physically easier, but it was easier in terms of what your citizenship allowed.

Tzvi Elimelech married, but I don't know if he married in Galicia or when he lived in our area. And he had several sons, though I am not familiar with all his children. He also had several brothers and sisters who lived in the area until they moved away to Marosvásárhely and other places. Like my great-grandfather, who learned constantly, they were all *talmidey hachamim* (Torah scholars).

פֿנ
איש אמונים תֿח וישֿ
חסיד ועניו
מֿה **צבי אלימלך** זֿל
בֿן מֿה בנימין זֿל נכֿד בעל
קדושת לוי ובעל עטרת צבי
בעל בֿני ישֿשכֿר ועֿוד צדיקֿים
נפֿטר ליֿל דֿ יתֿרו כֿא שבט
ונקבֿר למחרתו
שנת עֿטרֿת לפֿק
תֿ נֿ צֿ בֿ הֿ

Here is buried
A man of great faith, a scholar and had the fear of heaven
Our teacher the **Rav Tzvi Elimelech** Z'L
The son of our teacher Rav Binyomin Z'L
Great grandson of the Kedushat Levi (Rabbi Levi Yitchak of Berditchiv)
The Ateret Tzvi (Tzvi Hirsh of Zidichov)
And the Bnei Yissachar (Tzvi Elimelech of Dinov)
And other righteous relatives
Departed the evening of Wednesday of Parashat Yitro 21st of Shvat
And was buried the next day
Of the year of the crown
May his soul be bound up in the bond of everlasting life

Matzeva of great grandfather R' Tzvi Elimelech Roszler in Bistritz,
Transylvania—Zeidy was named after this great-grandfather.

Here is buried
The righteous Rebitzen with lineage from the holy
Sarah Roszler peace be on her
The daughter of the great and righteous teacher
Rabbi Meir Z'L, Chief of the Bais Din of the holy community of Pautik
Direct descendent of the Chacham Tzvi (Rabbi Tzvi Ashkenazi) and
The Baal Levushim (Rabbi Mordecai Yoffe), may their memory protect us
Wife of our teacher and Tzadik Rabbi Tzvi Elimelech
Departed the 21st of Tishrei 1929
May her soul be bound up in the bond of everlasting life
Tombstone refurbished by her great grandchildren
Rabbi Tzvi Elimelech and Malka Roszler

Matzeva of great grandmother Sara Roszler
in Bistritz, Transylvania.

My great-grandfather owned a large, huge piece of land. He donated part of it for in Mureşenii's *shul,* which stood until the end of Second World War. He had a huge house, even by the standards of today, with a number of bedrooms, a store, and also an inn. His inn was not like a motel; it mainly sold spirits and wine. In his store, he sold all sorts of groceries, candies, textiles, and so on. This is how he made a living, and he was recognized as one of the most important members of the community.

Some other Jews lived there, and in that village they were all *shomer Shabbes* (Shabbat observant) without exception. The people of Mureşenii made their living from various things: some were tradesmen, some had stores, and some bought lumber from the people of Borgo Prund. There were handymen and artisans, practitioners of various occupations. Most of them, unfortunately, were not rich. In fact, I would say most of them were quite poor. However, my family made a fairly good living.

I always had *rachmones* (pity) for one of my teachers who came from Mureşenii, since he had to come to Borgo every Sunday and go back to Mureşenii every Friday, and he would not see his family for a whole week.

The house my grandmother lived in had a huge, big yard and a big garden which extended all the way to a river. As a child, it was always a good experience to go there and run around in the garden. I enjoyed myself. I would go to the river, which the people also used in the summertime as a *mikve* (ritual bath).

I do not recall Mureşenii having a *mikve,* so the women actually had to come to the *mikve* in Borgo Prund. It was quite an ordeal for all these women in wintertime, because it was very difficult to travel, and it was snowy, frozen, and cold, and yet it was important for them to come to the *mikve.*

My father's youngest sister, my aunt *aleya hasholem* who lived in Mureşenii, was named Feiga. She was married to a man named Sholem Friedman. My father *alav hasholem* arranged her wedding and paid for most of it. We rented a truck, because there was no railroad anymore. We once had a narrow-gauge railroad, but the Romanians removed it in 1939. There was no bus transportation either after 1939 or 1940. So, actually, the only transportation we could use was a horse and wagon, or a truck or car, which were scarce.

Aunt Feiga gave birth to a son in 1943, during the war. Her husband was in hiding, because Jewish males were being drafted to labor camps. Some were being sent to the Russian front to assist in the war, to dig the trenches, and do all kinds of dirty work with very little food. Many of them died there. My uncle was what they called in those days a *tamim vnealam* (literally, pure and hidden, but actually meaning disappeared), because he was a draft dodger. He hid under an assumed name in Gross Verdin, where the Vishnitzer Rebbi lived. He had false papers. When his wife gave birth, he snuck back home, but he had to be very cautious not to be seen by anyone.

In my grandparents' home, the kitchen was huge, with a big oven as described in the song *Ofen Pripipchick*. They used it to make *cholent* (a stew that cooks overnight) for *Shabbes*, and it took up six, eight, ten feet like a commercial baker's oven. They baked large loaves of bread in it. If necessary, you could also use it to make *matzos*. I do not remember if they made their own *matzos* for *Pesach* or if they purchased them from Borgo Prund. On top of the oven, we would store things or, in wintertime, people would want to sleep on top of the oven.

In the inn, there was a huge hall where the non-Jews would come and buy spirits and wine, and they would drink to make themselves happy. Sometimes the inn had a gypsy orchestra, too. Although I don't remember if the inn functioned any more in my day, my grandmother and my aunt *aleihem hasholem* ran a general store from which they made a living.

My grandmother, my aunt and uncle (her husband) *aleihem hasholem* stayed in Mureșenii until they were deported to Auschwitz in 1944. There, unfortunately, they were killed.

Cluj

Now, we will talk about my mother's family. They lived in the city of Cluj or, in Yiddish, Klausenburg, the capital city of Transylvania. Klausenburg was a modern city, and it was always a great thrill to go to there. The distance from Borgo Prund to Klausenburg was approximately 120 kilometers, about 60 miles. However, in those days, from before or even during the Second World War until 1944, going to Klausenburg was considered a major trip—like, for example, going today from Los Angeles to at least New York or maybe even to Israel.

You would have to pack, because it took about four hours by train. In the Romanian regime they had a train called Malaxa after the name of the manufacturer; it was a bit faster, like a diesel train, but it was still considered a major trip. My mother *aleya hasholem* sometimes took all or one or two of the children to visit my grandparents *aleihem hasholem* in Klausenburg.

Klausenburg had a population of approximately 120,000 people at the time, or perhaps even more. That was a large city, already, a nice-looking city, a beautiful city. You could see the difference between the people of a large city compared to those of a small town, like Borgo Prund or Mureșenii Borgo or Tihutsa. You could see the differences in the big city people's manners and dress. In Yiddish we have the expression *klein shtetl,* meaning people from a small town. You could tell they were different based on their manners, conduct, language, clothes, and so on.

The town had a big park called in Hungarian "Cetățuia," which means a special walkway. Klausenburg also had theaters, large stores with elevators, and many multi-story buildings, many mini-skyscrapers, I don't know how tall the tallest building was at that time, maybe five or six stories. Later on, during the Hungarian time, they had a department store. It was not by any means a Macy's, but it was a variety store where you could buy many different things and, to us, this was a great thrill.

Of course, it was also a thrill to see the family, which was the most important thing: my grandparents *aleihem hasholem,* all my uncles and aunts, cousins, and various distant relatives. We all established friendships.

Klausenburg also had a number of *shuls* and *beit midrashim.* There were two large ones. The Ashkenazishe Shul and the Nutzach Sfard Chassidic great shul.

The Ashkenazishe Shul followed the Ashkenazi *minhag* (customs). At the time, its Chief Rabbi was Rabbi Glazer, a tremendous *talmid hacham* and *mechaber* of *sfarim* (author of books). He was a *shem davor* (a famous name). Since he was the *Ashkenazi* rabbi, perhaps the *Chassidim* may not have looked at him as an authority, as they would a Sefardi Chassidic Rebbi, but he was a great *gaon* (genius), a great *talmid hacham* (scholar) and a very *frum* (religious) man. His son has lived in Los Angeles for the last 25 years.

The town also had the yeshiva where some members of my family learned, like my cousin Eddie Kahn.

Rav Yekusiel Yehudah Halberstam was the chief rabbi of the Nutzach Sfard Chassidic *shul*. He survived the Holocaust, but he lost his wife and 11 children in Auschwitz. Rav Halberstam was one of the first to come from Germany to the United States after the war to apprise people of what actually happened in the Holocaust. He gathered money and used it to establish yeshivas (schools) in German Displaced Persons Camps. He subsidized the Felderfing Displaced Persons Camp, where I lived prior to coming to the United States. Rav Halberstam underwrote some of our religious facilities, including a kosher kitchen. He saved many boys in the mixed-up world after the war. Their religious affiliations did not matter to him. To a large degree, he was responsible for bringing religion back to the people, including the 4,000 Jews at Felderfing, where my cousin Rabbi Ruttner *alav hasholem*, the *Shunktover Rav,* was the chief rabbi.

The Germans also killed my cousin Yishay Kahan *alav hasholem,* the son-in-law of my uncle Aizik Kahan, who lived in the United States in the 1930s. My cousin had been the secretary—today you would call him the executive director—of the *Sfaradic Kehila*. Each of these ravs had his own *kehila* (community), his own *mikve* and his own *shul*.

The Ashkenazi community used the city *mikve* in Klausenburg, a delightful place for everyone because it had so many amenities, or desirable things, that we did not have at the *mikve* in Borgo. For example, if I recall correctly, it had a *schwitz* (steam bath). It also had beds, so we could lie down and take a rest and nap after we went to *mikve* on Friday afternoon. There was also a pool, a very modern thing by our standards.

Klausenburg had new modern buildings. In some places, it had indoor plumbing, which to us coming from Borgo Prund was a luxury we just could not imagine, since we had none. We had to use outdoor facilities in the winter, during the winter days, and especially at night, when it was sometimes 20 or 25 degrees below zero. Where my grandparents lived in Klausenburg, they also did not yet have indoor plumbing.

However, they did have electricity. I will not speak of the wiring, how it was done, because it was very dangerous. The codes were lax, and people had open wires that could electrocute them. They also had gas for cooking, as well as a water pump with a faucet in the common yard. Although they had a sink in the kitchen, it had no faucet. In Cluj, it was a big pleasure to go to the yard and get as much water as you wanted. Another advantage of the faucet was that it sat above a well, which people used as a sort of refrigerator during the summer.

My uncle Yosef Yehezkel Kahana *zichrono livracha* and his family lived in Klausenburg, and they had a sort of indoor plumbing. There was no door directly from their apartment to the bathroom. You went out of one door from the apartment and then into another door, but it was indoor plumbing, and this was a great luxury to us. One of my cousins, Chaim Kahan, also moved to one of the apartments in that courtyard. He was the son-in-law of my uncle Yitzchak Issik, who moved to the United States.

The whole idea of being in the big city was a marvelous experience for us children. First of all, the streets were already paved or covered with cobblestone. Of course, there were more cars in the city. Trucks picked up the trash and garbage once or twice a week. In Borgo Prund, you had to take things to a big garbage bin in the yard, and that had to be emptied from time to time by a contractor or a peasant who would come with his horse or ox and wagon and haul it away somewhere.

In Klausenburg, we could buy anything in the store, like milk. In Borgo, you would have to go a few doors away to the farmer who had a cow or several cows. You would have to watch the farmers milk the cow, since the milk needed to be *chalav Yisroel* (kosher). So, one of us, a member of the family, would have to go practically every morning early to get the milk because there was no refrigeration. Then we would take the milk home and boil it. In Klausenburg, you could just go to a grocery store.

One of the proprietors was named Schwarz, and he sold kosher butter. In Borgo Prund, buying butter was difficult. We had to buy from a Jewish farmer, and because he was far away, he came only once a week to sell his butter. He also made cottage cheese. Making hard cheese or American-type cheese was more difficult, because it had to be made with kosher rennet, which was available only in the summertime. In Klausenburg, we could buy cheese and butter and all kinds of vegetables in the store. In Borgo Prund, we had to depend on what the nearby farmers had or on our garden. In the big city, you had all these things. You could, for example, buy textiles, different clothes, ready-made clothes, ready-made shoes. In the big city, you could find such things easily.

Klausenburg had approximately 20,000 Jews and a number of *beit hamidrashim.* My grandparents lived on 33 Golomb Utca Street. Golomb means birds, but I cannot recall how to say it in Romanian.

In 1983, we visited the house they had rented, but no one was at home. Of course, it had changed, the whole house, the outside, and the gates, and the people had put up an iron fence so we couldn't go in. A funny incident happened during that visit. When we told the driver we hired that the name of the street was Golomb Utca. He said that now it was called Strada Parungu, which means birds in Romanian. Of course, I was not familiar with this name, and I insisted it couldn't be, but he insisted it was—and, of course, he was right.

We have a picture of my grandfather, a great *talmid hacham.* His name was Arieh Leibich Kahana, but he was called the *Apahida Rebbi,* and his father was Itzhak Aizik Kahana. He was actually a *kadosh*—a holy Jew—who sat day and night, and all he did was learn. He had a *beit hamidrash,* which had several *minyanim* (prayer groups of at least 10 men), perhaps two or three, maybe more. People would start there early in the morning and stay until about 11 o'clock, when they would be done. He depended

upon a sort of membership fee, or donation, that people would make; he was
not a rich man by any means.

My grandfather was the great-grandson of the Baal Kuntras Hasefekos who
was the Rav of Sziget, and he traced his
lineage to the Tosfos Yom Tov. He was
grandson of the Maareah Yecheskal,
the chief Rav of Transylvania. My
great-grandmother—the mother of my
grandfather—who was named Chava,
was the Maareah Yecheskal's daughter. Many miracles are told about the
Maareah Yecheskal, and he was a tremendous, great *gaon*. He was *mechaber*
(author) of many *sfarim* (books), and we
have some of them, including *Shaarey*

Rabbi Aryeh Leib Kahana—
Zeidy's grandfather, the Apahida
Rebbe, had a *beis hamidrash* in
Cluj (Klausenburg). A rebbe in a
small village of Apahida, he moved
to Cluj after World War I

Grandparents Henya Leah Kahana (left) and Rabbi Aryeh Leib Kahana.

Matzeva of his maternal grandparents, who are buried in Cluj

Tzion, Sheilas and Tshuves (questions and answers about Jewish practice), and a *haggadah* (Passover seder prayer book).

Henya Leah was my grandmother, my mother's mother, *aleya has-holem.* She also was from distinguished *yichus* (ancestry). My grandparents had an apartment next to my grandfather's *beit hamidrash.* He wrote a *sefer* (book) that I think was called *Yad Haari,* but it is not still in print, for some reason. [*During the 1980s, one of Zeidy's cousins from the Ruttner side tried to publish it and collected some money, but for whatever reason, it still was not published*].

הרב הגאון המפורסם כהן לאל עליון
דרכי ד' הודה
חסיד בן בתו של מראה יחזקאל
ונכד לבעל קונטרס הספיקות
מגזע תוספות יום טוב
תלמוד לבעל ייטב לב ולדודו בעל מעגלי צדק
מורנו הרב אריה ליבוש כהנא בן מורנו הרב יצחק אייזיק זצ"ל
שהיה הרב דקהל הקדש אפהידא והגליל
הניח אחריו כתב יד ספר יד אריה
נפטר בשנה טובה י"א לחודש מרחשוון תש"ג לפרט קטן
תנצב"ה

The great and famous Rabbi and Kohen to the Almighty
Went in the path of God with praise
Hassid. The son of the daughter of the *Mar'eh Yeḥezkel* (Rabbi Yeḥzkel Paneth)
The grandson of the author of the *Kuntres ha-sefekot* (Rabbi Yehudah Kahana Heller)
Descendent of the *Tosefot Yom Tov* (Rabbi Yom Tov Lipmann Heller)
A student of the *Yetev Lev* (Rabbi Yekusiel Yehuda Teitelbaum) and his uncle, the author of the *Ma'agalei Tzedek* (Rabbi Menaḥem Mendel Paneth)
Our teacher, **Rabbi Aryeh Leibish Kahana**, the son of our teacher, Rabbi Yitzhak Izaak, of blessed memory;
Who was the rabbi of the community of Apahida and its neighboring areas
He leaves after him the manuscript of the book *Yad Aryeh*
Died: 11 of Ḥeshvan 5703 (1943)
May his soul be bound up in the bond of everlasting life

Wording from the matzeva of R'Aryeh Leib Kahana

How did my grandparents come to Klausenburg in the first place? My grandfather, the Apahida Rebbi, had been a rebbe and *shochet* (ritual slaughterer) in Apahida, a village not far from Klausenburg. In 1917 or 1918, I believe, toward the end of the First World War, the Hungarians had to flee and cede Transylvania to Romania. I am not certain if it was the Romanians or Hungarians that sort of caused a partial pogrom, but they robbed the Jewish people, and took practically everything from them. So my uncle Itzhak Aizik Kahana *alav hasholem*, the eldest son, decided to move to Klausenburg, along with my grandparents and the whole family.

People would come to my grandfather and give him *kvitilach* (notes that were supplications for him to pray for them) and *nedava'a* (money for his prayers). They had *shayles* (questions) and people who had problems came to discuss them with him. They asked him to pray for them, for their

האישה הצנועה הצדקת
הניה לאה ע׳ה עטרת בעלה
אשת הצדיק מורנו הרב אריה ליבוש כהנה ז׳ל
היתה עמדתה נאמנת
לשמש את בעלה
למען יוכל להגות בתורה יום ולילה
זה היתה חלקה מכל עמלה
לגדל בניה ובנותיה לתורה
זכת לדור בשער בת רבים יהללוה
מי ימלל פאר מעשיה ומידותיה
נפטרה ט׳ו לחדש טבת תש׳ד
תנצב׳ה

The modest righteous woman
Henia Leah, peace be upon her, the crown of her husband
Wife of our righteous teacher, Rabbi Aryeh Leibish Kahana, of blessed memory
Her trusted position to attend to her husband
In order that he delve into Torah day and night
This was her portion from all her effort
To raise her sons and daughters in Torah
She merited to dwell in the gates of the multitude hallelujah
Who can praise the splendor of her works and attributes
Died: 15 of Tevet 5704 (1944)
May her soul be bound up in the bond of everlasting life

Wording from the matzeva of Zeidy's grandmother, Henya Leah Kahana

children, and for their families. People would also come to learn from time to time. He would have hundreds of people join him on the high holidays. He was the *baal tkekeah* (shofar blower) on *Rosh Hashanah*, but he would have his grandson Reb Shimshon—who was later killed by the Germans—stand by just in case

So, my uncle and his children and the whole family from my mother's side settled in Klausenburg. My uncle *alav hasholem* bought a complex of several apartments with a shared central yard. In other words, you opened the gate and entered a *hatzer* (courtyard), and several apartments surrounded it. The front was the *beit hamidrash*, which was furnished with a few benches. Of course, it had a tremendous number of *sfarim* (books) including a *shas* (Talmud).

Next to this there was another apartment, sort of attached, where my cousin Yishay Kahana *zichrono livracha* lived with his wife and his children. His wife's name was Chavi, but she was known as Chavita. Three or four children of her children were killed in the concentration camps. My Uncle Yitzchak Issik had a house there as well, and he lived there before moving to the United States in the 1930s.

The next apartments were separated by the outhouses, because that complex did not yet have any plumbing. There was an apartment at the back of the yard where a family named Pollack lived. Mr. Pollack was studying at a *yeshiva* in Romania at that time, and he was a big *talmid hacham.* The Pollacks had two sons and two daughters. The younger son was Buchi, and the older son was Yonason. The older daughter was named Yitti, but they called her Chittu, and the younger one was Rifki. Their mother was wonderful. She helped raise my cousin's children, and she was like *bat bait* (family) at my grandparents' home and the homes of our other relatives.

What we can say about her is an interesting observation: we were told that when they took my cousin Yishay and his family to the concentration camp, Auschwitz, that when they came to the selection by a Nazi doctor *yimach shmo* (may his soul burn forever), he pointed that women with children should go on one side, and women without children should go to the other side, to life. As they were marching together, this Mrs. Pollack sort of held on to the children, and she pushed this cousin of mine, Chavi, to other side, to go to the work camp, not to concentration camp. My cousin didn't make it and she died, but that's how important the Pollaks were to my family.

My grandparents' yard was separated by what seemed at the time to be a huge fence. It must have been about 15, 16 feet high, maybe 12 feet high, maybe it just seemed bigger to me than it really was because I was a child. The neighbors on the other side of the fence were named Berger, and they had a vegetable garden in the back yard. They would plant kohlrabi. So, from time to time, when we were visiting, we would just jump the fence and help ourselves to the kohlrabi.

In Klausenburg, we also had distant relatives, first cousins of my grandparents. I used to meet them from time to time. I will mention just a few I recall who were close to my family. The leader of the family was Mr. Lieberman, my cousin's brother-in-law. He lives in Vienna, Austria, and he visited us once in Los Angeles. His daughter married into the Nissel family here in Beverly Hills. I also remember the Hellman family, relatives of the Liebermans. My cousin Chaim Kahana worked for the Hellmans as sort of a controller, bookkeeper, or accountant. They had a huge bakery called the Hellman Bakery. They were, of course, very *frum* people.

This cousin, Chaim Kahan, and his wife and children lived at that time in an apartment in this bakery complex. He had a telephone in his office. Because very few people had telephones, it was a big deal to talk on a real telephone. It was a very costly thing, to have a telephone.

At lunch time when nobody was at the office we would sneak in, and we would dial all kinds of numbers. We had the number of a competing bakery, but why we had the number I do not recall. We would call, and they would get very angry; they started screaming and yelling into the telephone. To us, of course, it was a very big joke. It didn't bother us; we were not bothered by those things.

Prior to that, my cousin lived in an apartment on the river; it's called the Szamos river. Incidentally, the last time when we were in Romania in 1983, it was very polluted and smelled terribly.

Klausenberg had a big Jewish community. They also had clinics and a Jewish hospital. I recall one episode from when I was very young, maybe five or six years old. We were very close to my cousin Eddie Kahn, who would come to Borgo to visit and often stayed in our house. We are still very close even today. He is the closest cousin I have. He is my first cousin, my mother's sister's son. Eddie would build a tremendous *sukkah*, at least it seemed tremendous in those days, a large *sukkah* with a *shluck*, in Yiddish, that means something like a roof. So, if it rains, you would pull a rope, and the sort of roof would cover the *Sukkah*.

One day when we were there before *Rosh Hashana*, I fell on a rusty nail. The reason I fell that was I loved to climb, and Eddie, of course, would let me climb, because he was busy, and while I was climbing, I wouldn't bother him. Somehow I fell—or someone caused me to fall—on a rusty nail, and they had to drag me to the Jewish hospital, one of the most outstanding hospitals in that country.

The city of Klausenburg also had a clinic owned by a Jewish doctor named Mattiash. My mother *aleya hasholem* once took me there because I was quite heavy, and my parents were very concerned about my weight. This doctor was a specialist; people would come to him from all over the world. He was a *shem davar* (great name), but not a religious Jew, by any means, though he had great respect for my grandfather who was a rabbi. My mother *aleya hasholem* took me to him, and she asked him about my obesity. What could be done? He said most likely I would outgrow it. Unfortunately, I may be a little heavy today, but when I came out of the concentration camp I weighed approximately 50 pounds, so I certainly grew out of that obesity!

All these urban things did not exist in a small town, in small communities, especially in Borgo Prund. Perhaps there may have been a hospital in Bistritz (a small city), about 20 miles from us. But these were things that existed in the big city, what we call today civilization. They also had bus transportation, but in Borgo you walked or went by horse and wagon. In Cluj, when somebody arrived at the railroad station, they had taxis. In Yiddish, we called them *yachas*, a luxurious kind of horse-drawn wagon with springs. I still recall that the noise of the wagon on the cobblestone streets was very pleasant. In the train station, we would hire one of these horse-drawn wagons to take us to my grandparents' house.

One of the big things that they had was a Jewish elementary school, a tremendous advantage because Jewish children did not have to go to a *goyish* public school, which I will speak about later on. They also had a Jewish high school, but the *Chassidic* Jews would not send their children there. It was very modern and, perhaps, some of the teachers had even been indoctrinated in *haskalla* (enlightenment) philosophy, which is contrary to *Torah*.

The city had a big university, and the *goyish* (non-Jewish) students there were known as being very anti-Semitic. From time to time, they would cause *pogromim*; they would find Jewish people for no reason except to rob them, hit them, and beat them.

Speaking of some of the relatives we had in the city, my mother had a cousin, Chaim Kahana, who had a herring factory. He did very well financially; he was quite well off. He would ship his herring to different parts of Romania and Hungary, and he made a very nice living. He too would come and daven at my grandparents' *beit hamidrash*.

In the center of Cluj, that is, Klausenburg, there was a nice statue of King Matthias, Matthias Corvinus, whom we studied in secular school. He was part Hungarian, part Romanian. My uncle Rav Izik Kahana *alav hasholem* used to joke about it. He said that from time to time, they had to take him down so he could use the bathroom. It was a joke for us because in our small town, we'd never seen a statue. Some places in Klausenburg also had central heating. We'd never seen such a thing and, of course, it was a revelation to us to have radiators.

In Borgo, if you had to telephone someone in a distant city, you had to go to the post office and let them know. Then a mailman would come later and tell you to come to the post office and get ready for a call at a certain hour. So you can see how business had to be done and how difficult it was without having a home telephone. Later, some people in Borgo had phones, but we did not. We tried to get one during the war years when business was going better, but it was very difficult to get it. For Jews, it was even more difficult.

Sometimes when someone would come from a big city to visit us in Borgo Prund, we would kind of look up to him. I always wanted to live in the big city. We thought city people had more adventures than we had, but we had different kinds of adventures. We had country living, and beautiful hills and mountains, and climbing, and so on, which they did not have in the big city.

My uncle Friedman *alav hasholem* had a printing business in Klausenburg with his family. They printed *sfarim* (books), and other things, like stationery. It was called *Iparon,* which means pencil in Hebrew.

Klausenburg also had a conservative temple, *Shtates Knob,* which was still standing in 1983. I don't know what the name means, maybe status or state. I would call it conservative for that time, but it was almost like an orthodox synagogue today. I am not sure if it had an organ. Doctor Weinberg was the rabbi; modern Jews attended there, though they were mostly *Shomer Shabbes* (religious). Still, the more Orthodox Jews looked down on them.

Sometimes we would get a copy of a Hungarian Jewish paper named *Új Kelet.* The editor of the newspaper survived World War II, and it continued to be published from Israel, but I don't know if it still exists. Whenever we got a copy in Borgo Prund, we shared the paper and passed it from person to person. It was very Zionistically inclined, but it still had a religious outlook. We did not have any access to any of the newspapers from Poland, although the Jewish community there published many Yiddish papers.

The only time I came in contact with Yiddish papers, which were also a revelation to me, was when I was a small child, and we rented an apartment from the Marmarush family. Mr. Marmarush was in the paper business. He bought recycled paper and, from time to time, I would come across Yiddish papers from Chernovitz. I saw one issue with little poems. It was very interesting to me because I had never seen a Yiddish paper. When the Hungarians took over Transylvania, we were forced to subscribe to a daily newspaper, but, of course, it was propaganda, and it was anti-Semitic. I recall reading it when I was 12, 13, 14, reading every day, and seeing what the paper told us about the frontlines of the Second World War. It was the only source of real news about what was happening during the war.

So, this is a little bit about Klausenburg and Mureșenii. Maybe I will come back to discussing these places if I can recall any more details. Let us not forget, they took us from our home to the concentration camp in May of 1944. So today it is June 1985, so all of this happened 41 years ago, and there are so many things I have forgotten and I cannot recall.

Chapter 3

Cheder

Let us first start with the *cheder* (Jewish school). The *cheder* was the most important institution in our community, in our lives and in our parents' lives. Parents would bring a child at the age of three, an age when he could hardly talk, to *cheder* and introduce him to the *rebbe,* or *lehrer* (teacher). We would address him as *Herr Lehrer* (mister teacher). The teacher had an important function in the community. Sometimes he was an advisor, and he had knowledge of different things. Like, for example, one teacher whose name was Stober brought his knowledge of how to make beer. He would teach the parents how to make beer. As a result, we had beer for *Shabbes.* My mother *aleya hasholem* would make bottled beer, just for the house, not for sale. And it was quite an event. It was really very good.

However the life of a *rebbe* was not enviable. Most of the *rebbeim* came from very poor homes. Many of them were married and had to leave their families behind. I'll give you an example of several *rebbes* that I learned from or knew. One of the earliest *chedarim* that I recall attending was practically next door to where we lived, and the *rebbe*'s name was Glazer. There were two *rebbeim*, this fellow Glazer and one more *rebbe* who was brought in from out of town, I believe his name was Yerucham. Incidentally, most of the *rebbeim* who came to us from out of town were from the county of Máramaros, which is today in Romania, in Transylvania. It's called a state, and it had a lot of very fine religious Jews, good Jews. Many of them were very poor; some of them were well-to-do, but a good majority were very poor.

A European *cheder* background is far superior to many of our day schools, even high schools, *yeshivos*. A boy who learned in the *cheder* until the age of 13 or 14 could almost learn all by himself a *blatt* (page) of *Gemarrah* (Talmud) with *Tosafoth* (commentary). We started learning *Gemarrah* at the age of six or seven, with very long hours of learning. So a boy like this would have a very good background in *Gemarrah, Shulchan Aruch* (Code of Law), *Chumash* (Torah), and *Rashi* (commentary), sometimes a little *Navi* (Prophets), too, depending on if the *rebbe* taught it. It was a very extensive education.

Even the greatest *am haaretz* (ignorant person) in Europe knew how to *daven* (pray) very well and could *daven* for the *amud* (pray for and lead the congregation), learn *Chumash* and *Rashi* and even *Mishna,* too, and *Pirkei Avot* (Ethics of the Fathers), because this was started at *cheder*. Practically all the children attended *cheder*, even if they came from the outlying villages and had to walk every day. I recall there were boys and some girls, but boys, specifically, who walked sometimes miles every day to *cheder*. It was very cold, but they did not have any transportation. As a result, even children from the villages, even though they were not great *talmidei hachamim,* (Talmud scholars) had a very good educational background. They were able to learn *Shulchan Aruch*. So even if they attended *cheder* till the age of 12, 13 or 14, they accomplished the equivalent of a modern *yeshiva* education by the age of 18.

In that group we had two *rebbeim,* Yerucham and Glazer. I believe I ended up with Glazer for a reason; I believe it was due to my brother Itzhak Schmuel *alav hasholem,* who was three-and-a-half years older than me. He was a very brilliant boy in every facet of life, in business and in learning. He was accepted to Yerucham's class, but I was much younger, and I was not accepted. My parents were very upset, because they wanted me to learn from a good *rebbe*. As a result, we ended up at Glazer's *cheder,* and he was a very good *rebbe*, but apparently not the caliber of this Yerucham.

Other *rebbeim* were known as a *dardeke, rebbeim* for little children. One of the *chedarim* was held in the backyard, in a huge garden known as being "of the Weizmanns." The Weizmann family, Eddie's grandparents, and other families lived in the front of that garden, which was very large. This *cheder* was a remote little house, partitioned in two, and it had a wooden floor. It was heated with wood, which the parents would contribute for the winter. In the summertime, we had a wooden table and some benches so we could sit outside. It was very fresh air; the air was delightful. The students' ages would begin practically from the age of five going up to 18 or 19, and I was in the older class. The *rebbe* had different classes. When I was at this *cheder,* I was about eight or nine already, or ten, perhaps, and the *rebbe* was named Tovel. Prior to this Rabbi Tovel, we had a Rabbi Stober.

Let me give you an idea of the schedule—let's say the winter schedule. At the age of seven or eight years old, you would come to *cheder* at 5:45 in the morning. It was bitter cold, but the cold did not matter, because you had to come to the class in the morning because we learned *Gemarrah* in the morning. Then after learning, about 7:15 to 7:20, we had to *daven* (pray). When we were pre-*Bar Mitzvah* we would *daven* at *cheder*. And we would rush home after *davening* at about 7:30 and eat some breakfast. It was, unfortunately, not an American kind of breakfast. It was coffee with pieces of bread broken into it, what was called *brokalach* and sometimes some other little thing. And rush off...

We rushed to public school, let's say from eight to eleven. And at eleven we would go directly back to *cheder*. Wintertime, this was some-times a challenge. We would come through the main street in Borgo, and the school was on the hill. The peasants would bring down the lum-ber, which they cut in the forest down the hill. The merchants like my father would buy this lumber and transport it to Borgo to the mill. These peasants would come down in wintertime on sleds, with oxen or horses drawing the sleds. These were very long pieces of lumber, and when we got out of school, we would sit on these pieces of lumber and get a ride, if the peasant let us.

Sometimes the driver would use his whip to get us off the wood, but sometimes the merciful ones would let us sit on these lumber pieces, and give us a ride, or a lift, a hitch, to *cheder*. We got to *cheder* about 11:15 or 11:20. The *cheder* was about a half kilometer, or three quarters of a kilometer, from the school. It was quite a distance from our house, but still we had to walk every day to school and back from school. As I said, it was very cold, but it had to be done.

We would be at *cheder* till about 1 o'clock. At 1 o'clock, we would rush home and eat lunch. The main meal was a *fleishig* (meat) meal. I will describe later what we ate for lunch. We then rushed back, because at 2 o'clock, we had to be at school again. It was a very foolish schedule, to break up the day like this. It was very difficult for Jewish children, especially, having to go to public school twice a day. I have already mentioned the distance. It was very difficult, too, for learning in *cheder,* because it disturbed the day. At 2 o'clock, we were there again until 4 o'clock, and at 4 o'clock, we left school and went to *cheder* again. We used to take along a snack; we called it in Yiddish *yozen.* We had that snack when we came back to *cheder* at 4 pm. And we would learn until 7 o'clock, sometimes later.

Of course, it was very dark, and we had lanterns with a candle. We used to walk together. Sometimes the snow was fresh. I can still hear the crispness of the snow when we walked on it. The cold wasn't very pleasant. At 7 o'clock, we did some homework. Maybe until 7:30. Mainly we finished very fast the Romanian or Hungarian homework. As a matter of fact, both my brother *alav hasholem* and I and some other Jewish boys would be among the smartest at the school. The peasants were not always the smartest. Some of them were all right, but many of them were not the brightest. When we finished our homework, we would help them, and as a result they gave us all kinds of gifts, like apples, or they would make us up little pencil holders and other things in order to pay us for helping them with homework. This was during the Romanian times.

When Hungary occupied this part of Transylvania, I was about 10. At that time, there was a split between the Hungarian school system and the Romanian school system. [*He attended a Hungarian School.*] When the school system changed, classes would be from 8 to 1 o'clock. Five hours, which created much better conditions for Jewish learning. We were able to spend more time at *cheder* with more intensive and constructive learning.

So the schedule would be: We got up and got to *cheder* at 5:30 to

5:45 in the morning. We learned until about 7:15 to 7:20, then we would *daven* for about half an hour. Then we would rush home, eat breakfast, and run to school to get there at 8 o'clock. In Hungarian school, at that time, we were there from 8 am until 1 pm. And at 1 o'clock, we would go home, eat our lunch, and perhaps take a little rest if it was possible until 2 o'clock. At 2, we had to be at *cheder* already and start learning. And the learning and *davening* at *cheder* would go until about 7 to 7:30.

So we spent the whole day learning, but we would have about 15 minutes, sometimes about half an hour break in the afternoon. And we used to play all kinds of games in *cheder*. On *Shabbes,* we would go to shul at 8 in the morning and, unfortunately, we had to go to public school on *Shabbes* as I will describe later. I also will describe the aggravation we would have every *Shabbes* in the secular school.

On *Shabbes* afternoon in wintertime, we would go to *cheder* for an hour or so, say *Borchei Nafshei* (a long prayer said on *Shabbes* afternoon) and learn a little bit. In summertime, we would go there for extensive learning in *Pirkei Avot* and then go to shul *Shabbes* afternoon and *daven Mincha* (afternoon prayers). And after the *shalosh seudous* (third meal of the *Shabbes* day), we would play in the courtyard.

I started *cheder* by the age of three, and Rav Betzalel, an elderly man, is among the earliest *rebbeim* I can recall. Our *cheder* was like a rented room, and it was run by only one *melamed* (teacher). One *melamed* would handle little children from the age of three and teach them up to age 18 or even older. They had different sized classes, maybe two or three in a class or four in a class. The *melamed* had a very difficult job. It was very hard to work from the hours of 5:30 or 5:45 am until 7:30 or 8:00 at night, with the exception of an hour or so for lunch. There were also short breaks in the morning and a break in the afternoon. Rav Betzalel was an elderly man and, of course, some of the children were wild. We used to make fun of him, sometimes, especially the older children.

I recall an episode that happened on a winter night. Some of the children—I may have been with them at the time, too—went outside. The *rebbe* was somewhere, in another room, and he fell asleep because he was so tired. It was wintertime, and it was snowing and cold. But there was a little creek, and we went out of *cheder* and went sliding on the ice.

These are some of the things that the *rebbe* unfortunately, had to contend with from us children. Most of the *rebbeim* came from very poor families. Sometimes a man became a *rebbe* because it was an escape or, perhaps, he had a family and he had to support them. Many of the *rebbeim* came from the county of Máramaros, which is full of small villages and little towns where it was very difficult to get established in a business or profession. But the *rebbeim* had already learned in the *yeshiva* for a number of years, and teaching was a way they could make a living. So we had to bring in these *rebbeim* from Máramaros, and some of them were very good, very smart.

Of course, their educational methods were not something to be proud of, but yet they were able to instill in us *yiras shamaim* (fear of heaven). And also teach us. In most cases, they did it the hard way. That is, with a rod. It was definitely not with a carrot; it was with the stick. If you did not know your work, let's say on Thursday at the oral examination, you had *tzoros* (problems), and that meant you would get beaten.

I would say one thing to the credit of our parents. Unlike here, where we jump on the teachers right away, the parents actually cooperated with the teachers who believed that hitting the child is crucial for teaching. Learning *Torah* was of such a high degree of importance that whatever the teacher said was law.

As children, we talked back, and the more we talked back, the more we got hit. Of course, these teachers had no formal instruction in education; they had no idea that they shouldn't teach this way. But they were interested, and they took it to heart that children should learn.

So elderly Rav Betzalel had his various classes. And he had a grey beard. Sometimes children were very nasty. One time this *rebbe* fell asleep, so one of the boys bought some glue and put some on his beard and on the table, so when he woke up his beard was dried to the table. Some of the children were not exactly angels.

Another *rebbe* was Weissberger, although he was not my *rebbe*. He mainly had the younger children. The small cottage was divided into two rooms with Weissberger on one side, and Stober was on the other side. Later, when Stober left, there was another *rebbe* named Tovel.

Weissberger lived in a town not far from Borgo, about six miles, or ten kilometers away. It was the same town in Mureşenii (Marosborgo) where my grandfather's family lived.

Weissberger would come every Sunday morning with his brother-in-law who worked at the lumber yards. Many times they would have to walk if they couldn't get a ride with someone who had a horse and buggy. They travelled that six miles every Sunday morning, rain or sun, cold or hot. And then on Friday afternoon, at 12 o'clock when *cheder* was finished, he sometimes got a ride and went home for *Shabbes*. Weissberger was in a sense fortunate compared to the others because he was able to go home for *Shabbes*. But many of the *rebbeim* lived at a great distance of 100, 200, or 250 miles from Borgo. They stayed in Borgo for the whole semester, or half a year. They stayed from after *Pesach* until two weeks before *Rosh Hashana*. And then they would come again after Succoth and return to their home only before *Pesach*.

They would not see their families for practically half a year; in a sense, it was tragic. And these *rebbeim* did not have separate apartments. Some of the *rebbeim* that I remember, let's say, Glazer, Weissberger, Tovel, and some of the others, would actually have a bed in one room of the *cheder*. Because *cheder* was their whole life, they actually lived there. Whatever clothing they had, they kept it somewhere at *cheder*. They hadn't too many suits or too many possessions, of course. They would save most of their money and send it to their families, so the families could live on it.

The wages were not very big. Although, I must say to the credit of our parents and, of course, all Jews in Romania and Hungary, in eastern Europe, that one of the first things people would think of was *schar limud* (tuition). It was most important to pay for the *cheder* and the *yeshiva*. It was very important to be able to pay for the *rebbe*. Of course, the wages were very low. But still, for many people, it was difficult to pay *schar limud,* especially during the depression years.

Since we were in the lumber business, we also donated the lumber remnants—which amounted to a great deal of wood—to the *cheder* to heat it in the wintertime when it was very cold.

In addition, we also had the *rebbe* come eat with us at least one day a week. The *rebbeim* would generally not eat at the *cheder*; they brought only some snacks. But meals were supplied by different *balhabiate* (families) each day, by different *balabustas* (women in the family), different parents. So the *rebbe* would eat out three times a day. Now, this was a good thing and also a bad thing for the children. The good thing was that there was rapport between the parents and the *rebbe* so the *rebbe* could give them a report. The *rebbe* would give a report of our behavior and good progress, so, in a way, it was a good thing. But sometimes his report about the children was not always glorifying, and this was not received very well among the parents, because the parents wanted the children to learn.

This Mr. Weissberger, I don't know exactly what his background was, but since he taught smaller children, I would say he had a weak background. Rabbi Glazer was from a different place. He also lived at the cheder and came from Máramaros. Some of these *rebbeim* were, of course, merciless. They would hit us very badly. For example, we had another *rebbe*, Stober. In *Yiddish* it rhymed with robber. I remember that when I was a child, he was very strict, although he was a very good *rebbe*. And he worked so hard. And this Stober was called to Bistritz to become a teacher, a *melamed*. He had a heart attack and died, I believe, before the concentration camps.

Prior to the concentration camps, six months or even a year before, we had a problem with being able to obtain *rebbeim* because the young people had been taken to the labor force or the army. As a result, only two of the *rebbeim* were left. One was Tovel, but they took him to be in the labor force, and we remained without a *rebbe*. After that, we had the son of the *rabbi* of the city. His name was Moishe Friedland, and he was also killed, I believe, in the Holocaust. I cannot recall if he taught full time or not. But those were very disturbed days, days of fear from the Hungarian and German Nazis, and it was a very sad situation.

I still remember my fear as a child, fear of not knowing when it came to taking an oral test. I don't know if I should blame the teachers for hitting us. They were so interested that the child should know, and there was no such thing as flunking. If you didn't know, you were beaten. And it did not concern the parents, because they were interested in the child learning. Some of the parents resented the beatings, but in a way, perhaps, they had no choice because they felt that the child's main purpose in being in *cheder* is learning. Some of the rebbeim, unfortunately, were very cruel. I don't know. I'm not condemning them, but it was not very pleasant for us children.

Cheder was six or seven days a week, because we had *cheder* on *Shabbes* afternoon too, especially in the summertime, when we learned *Pirkey Avot*. But looking back at the *cheder,* there were also happy times. In a sense, it was a relief to go to *cheder,* because we went to Romanian or Hungarian school in the morning. And in the afternoon, we were not among strangers. We were among our own people, our own children, Jewish children, and a Jewish *rebbe*. Whereas, in the morning, when we went to secular school, the teachers were even crueler. They would hit us for the slightest things, and they beat us. And, of course, they could call you "dirty Jew" or send you home because you had *payot* (side curls) or would not write on *Shabbes*.

But, really, all in all, I would say it was a nice time, because we looked forward to our breaks at *cheder,* to be with our friends. At our break at the afternoon, we would play all kinds of games. In the summertime, after we finished *cheder,* let's say after 7 o'clock, we would go home and eat. And then we would play all kinds of games for an hour or so on the main street or on the sides of the street. So, all in all, it was not really bad at *cheder*, especially compared to the Hungarian or Romanian school where we suffered from anti-Semitism. We were constantly being called dirty Jews and beaten, and being told that we have no rights in Romania and Hungary, and so on.

There was nothing like preschool or nursery school; we started *cheder* at the age of three, So the *cheder* served like a kind of nursery school. At five, we already started *Chumash* (bible). At six, *Mishna*. At seven, we started learning *Gemarrah*. There was a lot of stress because we had to memorize lots of things. The *Tefilas* (prayers), *Pesukim* (sentences from the Bible), and especially *Gemarrah* (Talmud). There was a lot of stress memorizing *Gemarrahs*, not so much *Tosafot* (commentaries), but mainly *Gemarrah*. We also learned how to write, mainly in *Yiddish*. We used a *bifshteler*—an instruction book on how to write letters, and so on. Some people started learning *Yordea Deah* (codes of law), at an early age. This was not in order to get *smicha* (ordination), but to get acquainted with *Halacha* (the law).

Public School

In public school, the anti-Semitism was indescribable, both during the Romanian regime and the Hungarian regime. They were very anti-Semitic. I recall that my father used to bribe some of them with lumber and wood, and so on. He tried to do anything possible to make them more lenient. But, in general, whenever they had a chance to take a dig at a Jew, they did it. The literature we read at public school was also anti-Semitic. Specifically I recall one poem that was called in Romanian *Kinyale Yevreya Lur*, which means even dogs should walk in front of the Jew, poking fun at the Jew. The Romanian holidays were all Christian. It was a Christian country, and Christianity was taught and practiced in the school. It was a very difficult period for us Jews.

In earlier times, sometimes Jewish people came to teach us. It was like a release hour, an hour of Jewish religion. But both in Hungarian and Romania schools, they said prayers before and after classes. They were religious Christian Catholic prayers which we, the Jews, of course, could not say. And in the classroom we had to sit without *yamulkas*; we were not allowed to sit with a hat on.

Outside we were persecuted by our *goyish* (non-Jewish) so-called friends. Some of them were nice because we helped them with homework. Most of the Jewish boys—I don't want to be prejudiced—but they were smarter than *goyish* boys. And we used to help them with their homework, so they gave us apples and all kinds of things as rewards. But the teachers would hit us and, sometimes, we had terrible fights with the students. So we would often skip school, and I would try to stay out of school anytime I could. For example on *Shabbes,* because we had to go to school six days a week. *Shabbes* was the worst day at school, because we wouldn't carry things on *Shabbes.* Some of us had a *Shabbes goy* or a *sheygets* (non-Jewish male). In our case, this was a Christian who would pass by my house, and I would offer him a piece of *challah* (traditional soft bread) or a cookie. And he would carry my books to school.

Later, during the Hungarian times, it became very anti-Semitic. Some of the teachers would try to make us write on *Shabbes,* and if we didn't, they would throw us out, kick us out, and beat us. We had all kinds of sorrows.

So you can imagine how it was to be at school on *Shabbes.* Even on normal days, when everybody else was writing, you could see the hatred of the *goyish* teacher. All the teachers we had were *goyim,* and you could see their hatred toward us because we would not do certain things on *Shabbes.* We would not carry books or do things that are forbidden—and we had to face the mere fact that we couldn't go to *shul* on *Shabbes.* I can still see in front of me the last *Shabbes, Shabbes shira* ("Shabbat of Song," the Shabbat in late January or early February when we read the Torah portion that covers the crossing of the Red Sea and Moses's song). I tried to ditch school often on *Shabbes,* but, somehow, it was impossible. We had a problem on *yom tovim* (Jewish holidays), on *Rosh Hashanah* and *Yom Kippur* and other holidays like *Pesach.* We had to bring a letter from the city rabbi, Rav Friedman, saying that these are official Jewish holidays, so permit us to stay out of school.

When we were absent from public school, it was also a tragedy, because they would hit you and beat you for being absent. These are all the kinds of things that happened to a person who lived in a totalitarian country. These teachers were not answerable to anybody. They could do as they willed. They could do practically anything they wanted. Sometimes you found a teacher who was nice or who defended Jews. In Romanian time, we had this teacher named Dumbrava. He was a music teacher. We tried to bribe him. Even after all these bribes, he was still a great anti-Semite. And there was the teacher Butach. He had a wife named Florica. She was my teacher at the secular school. Her husband was more liberal, and he taught my brother *alav hasholem* one class. She was a great anti-Semite, but he was a more liberal man. We also tried to bribe him. So, all along, you can see the life that we lived.

In Romania, we used to have separate classes for each grade because there was only one system, the Romanian system in the public school. There was a separate school for boys, and a separate school for girls. There were some other schools. There was one more, I don't know if everybody could get in there; it was called Skola De Meseriya, a sort of trade school. Very few Jews went to that school.

In the public school, there were eight grades. In Romania, we started at the age of seven, and school was compulsory until about the age of 15. My brother *alav hasholem* was one of the smartest pupils in the whole public school. He graduated from the eighth grade in the Romanian school in 1939. He had a problem with the teacher in mathematics because he used to show the teacher the right way to do the work. He was an extremely bright fellow. Yet when the teachers gave grades, which was really a joke, they gave him all failing grades. But that was just an act of anti-Semitism. He graduated right before the time that the Hungarians took over that part of Transylvania, at the height of the Cuza-Goga (a very anti-Semitic leader in Rumania) regime, the fascist regime. They hated the Jews. Even the teacher whose name I cannot recall gave my brother all failing marks, even though he was the A1 student of the whole school. This shows the anti-Semitism that existed in those days.

The majority of the inhabitants of Borgo were of Romanian stock. But at the end of 1939-1940, and in the early 1940s, the town's huge paper factory attracted many Hungarian residents who wanted jobs there. I don't know where they came from. I guess many of them came from Hungary, their motherland, because half of Transylvania, where we lived, was ceded to Hungary, so many of them came from there. And as a result, we had a two-tier school system. There was a Hungarian school system that began in September 1940, and then there was the Romanian school system.

All Jewish children went to the Hungarian school system. A number of Hungarian children were there, too. But since there was either not enough school money or children, there were not separate elementary schools for boys and for girls, so they combined the classes from fourth or fifth grade to eighth grade. There was only one teacher for the lower grades and one teacher for the upper grades. This teacher for the lower grades had come from deep in Hungary. Apparently, she had contact with Jews and she was quite liberal. But the other teacher—although she was used to Jewish people since she came from Klausenburg, called Kolozsvár in Hungarian—she was a terrible anti-Semite. I will elaborate. Later I will explain how this teacher used us for her purposes, to cut wood and do all kinds of menial jobs in her home. This is the power that a Hungarian or Romanian teacher had. They could do anything with the students if they really wanted to.

The peasants' children were privileged though, unfortunately, many of them were not educated. They were very simple. Of course, they had no encouragement at home. And most of the Jewish children did very well, I think.

I will not dwell too long on this matter. I just want to mention an incident that happened in the eighth grade. I graduated from that grade just before they took us to the ghetto. At the time, we did not know exactly what was waiting for us, whether they would take us to the ghetto or to Auschwitz. I don't believe we had a formal graduation, but we were given certain prizes for outstanding scholarship. And I was given a book about Hungarian authors, I believe, but there was a top prize that the school gave to someone else. My father *alav hasholem* said this prize definitely belonged to me because I was such a good student. He did not hide his dissatisfaction with the prize, although he himself was not such an ardent person when it came to secular education. He just cared for his children whom he always loved.

It is really very difficult to describe a *Shabbes* at home. Most *Shabbesim,* I would say, we would also have an *oreach*, a guest with the family, one, two, sometimes three *orchim* at the table, because there were a lot of poor people in Romania and Hungary at the time. They would come; some of them traveled from place to place. Some would sell some *sfarim* (books); some would sell nothing and just came to collect money. These people would gather in the shul for *Shabbes*. They would sleep in a room which belonged to the Jewish community. It was part of the complex where the *shochet* (the ritual slaughterer) lived.

The actual preparation for *Shabbes* started Thursdays. One of the great rabbis in the Gemorrah would start on Sunday purchasing things *lekavod Shabbes* (in honor of *Shabbes*). We started getting ready in the middle of the week. We had to make sure we had chicken or meat for *Shabbes*. Usually my mother *aleya hasholem* would bake *challah* at home.

At other times we would actually buy bread from the bakery. Of course this was a *kosher* bakery. The baker, who was named Shvaintoch, was *shomer Shabbes* (Sabbath observant). The Shvaintoch family not only had that bakery; they also had a sort of soda pop factory. They would make seltzer, and they would also make a flavored kind of seltzer like we would have today, let's say raspberry or strawberry. This in itself was quite an event.

Chapter 4

I have described the *simcha* (celebratory) occasions, but the neighbors would always participate on sad occasions, too. They helped with cooking and baking, and so on. It was a very difficult situation because you had to make everything from scratch. Nothing was ready made. It was a small community, and we did not have all the ready-made products we have today.

Take a *chassuna* (wedding) dinner, for example: There was no wedding hall. The wedding would take place in the house, usually in the home of the bride, the *kallah*. The family would have to clean out the rooms and take out the furniture. They had to bake for weeks or perhaps even months before the wedding and preserve the food. Let's say if we had 200 or 300 people, it was quite an event.

Usually with weddings in Borgo, the *chuppah* (both the wedding ceremony and the canopy over the bride and groom) took place on Friday afternoon, and the meal and wedding party would take place on *motsey Shabbes* (Saturday evening after the Sabbath). That was very common. The *chuppah* generally would be in the *shul* yard. The *chuppah* belonged to the shul. We would have four people holding the poles of the *chuppah* or sometimes they would use a *tallis* (prayer shawl) as the canopy for the *chuppah* itself. The *chuppah* celebration was extravagant just like the parties we have today, with flowers and all kinds of decorations. The tables were set with tablecloths. The family would borrow tables from the neighbors, whoever had tables. We had music, usually gypsy music.

We also usually had a *grahmer*, someone who would say rhymes to entertain the people and make the *chasson* (groom) and *kallah* happy. At my Aunt Feiga's wedding, cousin Eddie was the entertainer, or the *grahmer*. He entertained the guests by reciting rhymes. He would say all kinds of praises of the *chassan* and *kallah* and the family. I still recall how he sang this tune in *Yiddish:*

"My dear friends, I will tell you something that is very dear to me. This is my uncle Rav Meir…" [That was my father *alav hasholem*] He went on and on, entertaining us; it was very lively. However, when I brought this to Eddie's attention recently, he could not recall it, but I recall it very vividly.

And finally there was a *levaya* (a funeral). They would put the deceased on a table for *tehara* (ceremonial washing of the body). There was a special place for the *tehara* in a little house on the side of the cemetery. For some reason they would show the body to the family before the funeral. They would open the *aron* (casket) and show the family the deceased. I don't know whether this is still done today or not. When someone passed away, it was a terrible tragedy. Today we take it for granted. You go to a funeral with self-respect, nobody sheds a tear. I can recall several *levayas*. One in particular was for Zalke Gottlieb, who had a store in Borgo. He was a nice man, a bearded man, a very fine person. He must have been in his seventies. I can recall the crying and the screaming and the carrying on. He was not so young; he was about 70. Forty or fifty years ago, a man in his seventies was considered very old. Here today, it is taken for granted that it is natural that every man will die, but it was considered such a tragedy, such a terrible tragedy then, that people should die.

I recall a similar situation with a lady named Marmarush who was once our landlady. She was also an elderly woman, and she passed away. The *levaya* was held in the shul courtyard. I remember the crying and the goings on and the wailing. Mourning was something unbearable, compared to today. We had more of a community feeling and more sympathy from people than a deceased person's family gets today. Then, perhaps due to the wars, the Holocaust, all the things we went through, maybe we don't have the feelings for human beings anymore the way people used to have in those days.

The only things we could buy on *erev Shabbes* (Friday before the Sabbath begins) were vegetables from a community called the Saxons, a German ethnic group. Incidentally, they were big anti-Semites. They would bring different vegetables that they had grown. They were known for growing vegetables in the summer. Friday afternoon, they would put them out to sell, so we could buy many types of vegetables.

All along the main street and some side streets, Borgo had a number of stores. Of course, there were no department stores. Some stores sold a little bit of hardware, but most of them were groceries. They had what you needed to live in a dictatorial country, a fascist country.

A big paper factory was the largest employer in Borgo. The paper factory and the lumber mills were the major employers. This huge paper factory, the largest one in Transylvania, had several thousand or maybe several hundreds of employees. They had machine shops and other facilities. The owners were two Jews: Schnayer and Freyer. As I mention their names, I will just mention that they were sort of assimilated Jews. One especially, Freyer, was very seldom seen in shul, maybe only *Yom Kippur*. In those days, in this small community, everybody knew everybody's business. So they would ask him, why don't you come to shul more often? He said he didn't owe anything to G-d. The other one, Schnayer, was a little bit more *frum* (observant). He would send his children to *cheder*. Both partners ran away from Transylvania when the Hungarians occupied it. They were not local people originally. They had established this big factory, but, I believe, they were originally from Vienna.

Then their factory was sort of confiscated. They were taken to concentration camp, and I recall we were standing there in line, with Schnayer and Freyer and his son, Heyne, *nebech* (unfortunately). He was selected from that line, and he was sent to extermination. We were standing in line and eating, but we had only one plate, like a metal plate they gave us for the whole line. There were ten people in the line. And he [*either Schnayer or Freyer*] said that since we knew each other and were standing together, we could eat from the same plate. This is what happened. Just going from a place where a person doesn't know anything of God, and then, I guess,

God showed us that He can do to us whatever He wants. Why He did it, we don't know. But unfortunately it happened.

Some of those employed in this factory were Jews from various parts of the country. Some were quite assimilated already, and even some of the local boys who wanted to learn the trade worked there. Some Jewish boys worked in the factory and, unfortunately, had given up observing *Shabbes.* They had to give it up because they had to work on Saturday.

We were very concerned about it because we had a situation in Borgo and in small communities, even in large communities, that we were starting to see a sort of *haskallah* (an "enlightenment" where Jews adopted the practices of their non-Jewish neighbors). We cannot really say *haskallah,* but a weakening of religious practices. Their attitude was that if somebody wanted to show he was an intellectual, the first thing he would do is cut off his *payot* (side curls) and grow long hair. And maybe he would start carrying things on *Shabbes.* [*You can't carry on the Sabbath unless there is a ceremonial wall, an eruv, around your area. Borgo had no eruv.*] They thought that this was what made you an intellectual.

So, as a result, many of the younger people were caught up in this attitude that to become an intellectual, you throw away your religion. Of course, most people went to shul on *Shabbes,* no question about it, even those who carried, because you were considered outcasts if you didn't go to shul on *Shabbes.* But we already saw a weakening of religious practices.

There were many things you could not do in Borgo, so you had to go to Bistritz by train to go shopping, for example, but it was considered quite a trip. We used to go to Bistritz very often because our dentist was there. Bistritz was about 20 kilometers from Borgo, and it took an hour at least by train. The train would stop at all these little communities. As I remember, the dentist's name was Rachmud. He would come to Borgo on Sundays. He had an office in the living room of one of the homes, and he would practice his dentistry there. It was an amazing thing, and many people used to come there. You had to sit for hours to hold your place. Naturally, whoever came first was treated first. Sometimes you had to sit for hours until he came by train. You had to sit and keep the appointment for yourself or for your parents.

What were the prospects for *shidduchim* (matchmaking for marriage)? In Borgo, *shidduchim* was a very difficult situation. If someone had a daughter, she would meet someone through a *shadchan* (matchmaker) who knew somebody in another city. Sometimes local people did marry each other. This was the case with the Marmarush family. When I was a young child, one of the sons of our landlord married Gottlieb's daughter. But in many cases, a boy would go to *yeshiva,* and someone would try to make a match for him, and he would marry in the city of the *yeshiva* or some other place. Or, in my aunt's case, my father's youngest sister, the *shadchan* was from Gross Vadein where my future uncle learned in the Vishnitz *yeshiva*.

This was not an easy matter. But in our small community, love was not practical among orthodox Jews. There was love in a marriage, but meeting a girl on the street or at a party was inconceivable. Matches were made mainly through introductions, through *shadchanim*.

Amazingly enough, *gett* (divorce) was unheard of. I cannot recall any, but there were probably some, though very few and far between. As a child, I cannot recall anybody in our community or in any other community I heard of who had a *gett*. [*In the family Appendix, he tells of an uncle who was divorced*]. I presume there were decent marriages, marriages that last. And there may have been fights, like in any marriage, but people learned to get along, and wives would work with their husbands; the wife was mainly the *hausfrau*. Though not without worries, the people were happy in a sense. There would come a *Shabbes* and a *yom tov*, and people would go to *shul*, come home, go to *kiddush* to see each other, and go visiting each other.

Already in the early 1940s, before the concentration camp, some people already had telephones. We did not. Like us, most people didn't even have radios. Of course, the radio was forbidden for Jews. After 1942, a Jew was not permitted to have a radio in the house, because Jews were looked on with the suspicion of potentially being spies. So we would get our news from a *goyish* (non-Jewish) partner, and when we wanted, a *goy* (non-Jew) would bring a short wave radio to *shul*. The *goyish* partner would listen to it and inform us of the news in *shul*. Politics actually took place at the *mikve* (ritual bath). Foreign policies and news reports were discussed in the *mikve*. People came to the *mikve*, and they brought news and interpreted the news and, of course, made news.

Chapter 5

I will describe wintertime in Borgo. Here we have a central heating system with a thermostat. But, of course, life was different in Borgo. We would have to get ready before wintertime. We needed a lot of heating lumber, heating wood. It was a special quality wood—not pine, but hardwood that would last and give more heat than just plain pine and soft wood. Since we were in the lumber business, it was easier for us. We would have a wood chopper, a wood cutter, come to the house. It took several days. He did not have a machine. In some places, like Klausenburg, they had a machine for cutting lumber, but in Borgo, men cut it by hand.

At first, they had to cut these pieces of wood into smaller pieces and then into pieces about one foot-and-a-half to two feet long, in order to fit in the stove. The stove in the kitchen could take longer pieces of wood. The one in the bedroom could take only shorter pieces of wood. The wood was stored in the shed for the winter. We called it the *klafte* house in Yiddish. The *klafte* was actually the measure of wood, so this wood went in the *klafte* house. We would have a *shiksa* (non-Jewish woman) who would come every day. She would bring in wood from the woodshed into the house and load up the house for a day or two with wood, both for the kitchen and the bedroom.

She also brought water in pails. We had no running water. We had a huge barrel especially made for water with two pails, and the water had to be replaced every day. It was acquired from across the street. We had a well, but our well water was contaminated. We couldn't use it. We had to draw water from across the street. The woman who brought the water was also the *Shabbes goy* (a non-Jew who could do chores on Shabbat that Jews could not do). She would go to a few people on *Shabbes* morning.

She knew she had to come in and make the fire in the wintertime in the stove.

We used to like wintertime, when we used to go to school, especially at *cheder* (religious school). The main street was filled with snow. You would see sleighs instead of wagons. In these sleighs was the lumber that was brought to town. In wintertime, it was easier to bring it from the forest, not far from Borgo, maybe 10 to 15 kilometers, maybe 20 kilometers. They would cut this lumber and bring it to Borgo to the lumber factories and lumber mills.

In wintertime, the *shul* `also had to be heated with wood. Very few people had ceramic stoves in Borgo. In bigger cities, they had ceramic stoves which were more efficient. They produced more heat than regular kitchen or bedroom stoves. But everything was heated mainly with wood. I cannot recall anybody heating their homes with coal. In the *cheder*, we had to put lumber in the stove constantly, and in the public school, it was the same situation. We went home from public school or from *cheder* all frozen with our socks and shoes wet from snow.

As children we used to love to slide and skid on the ice. In Borgo, like I mentioned before, there were ditches from the main square all the way to the next town, practically, on both sides of the road. These ditches would fill with water and freeze up. They were used in summertime for watering the streets, and they were drainage in the rainy season. These ditches would freeze in the winter. We would go and slide on these frozen ditches.

It was hard. My father *alav hasholem* would get up early in the morning and hire a horse and wagon. The driver would drive him 20 to 25 kilometers with the sleigh to the forest where he would go and look around and find these *goyim* (non-Jews) who sold the lumber in big quantities. During the Hungarian rule, we had people who would buy for us, because we were not permitted beyond Mureșenii where my grandparents lived. These areas were called security zones, and they always accused Jews of being traitors, so we had to stay in them. So when my father needed to buy in distant locations, he had to use buyers.

Winter was also the time when many people raised chickens in their backyard. We had a large backyard and, there, under the porch, we had like little sheds where we raised chickens or geese. In wintertime, we would also make *schmaltz*, goose *schmaltz* (fat). And this *schmaltz*, the fat, we would freeze. We had no refrigerator; we would just put it outside, and it would freeze.

I still recall the taste; they said it tasted like ham. It was very good. You would put some salt and you could eat it, practically raw. It tasted very good. This fat was used in lieu of oil and other fats for cooking.

From 1940 until about 1943—when they started really persecuting Jews and Transylvania became Hungary—the winter was a very good season for the lumber business. Business was excellent despite the war and despite the fact that we did not know what was going on in Poland and Germany. We had some reports from some *goyim* who supposedly volunteered and came back with stories that they didn't see any Jews in Poland. There were some Jewish refugees who were in hiding and came to Hungary. But we did not believe them. We did not know exactly what was going on.

Of course, one of the main events in the winter was the holiday of *Hanukkah* which we looked forward to as children. We got off early from *cheder* and rushed home to light the *Hanukkah* candles. We lit the candles outside, next to the door, as the Shulchan Aruch (law) says, opposite the *mezuzah* (a small box holding a prayer on the doorpost of Jewish homes). We were not able to get olive oil, for olive oil was not available in our area and was difficult to get, especially during the war years. But we used regular oil, and after that we used to play *dreidel* (a spinning top) and Twenty One. At *cheder* the rabbi would look away sometimes, and we played *dreidel* during intermission time, and this game Blackjack, that was actually Twenty One.

It was a very festive time. Of course, we did not have the kind of festivities there that we have in America, for in America the general public thinks that *Hanukkah* is on the same level as *Rosh Hashana* or *Yom Kippur*. But it had its significance in Europe. It was festive due to the fact that we looked forward to any holiday because it brought a little *simcha* (celebration), a little joy to a life that was very hard, a severe life living among *goyim* in an anti-Semitic atmosphere.

Purim was also an event. Many times when Purim came, it was still cold, and it snowed. That too was a great event, of course. The children would put on masks and various clothes, and sing Purim *shpills* (rhymes). We would go around from house to house. And all winter we were looking forward to spring, looking forward to *Pesach*.

Pesach was a great event. It was snowing, and quite cold, especially when we were baking the *matzos* (unleavened bread). In wintertime, we had to wear very heavy clothes, and the shoes were special shoes made in our town, in Borgo. There were no ready-made shoes. We had our shoes made every year, ordered from the shoemaker. They were called in Yiddish *vacanchen*. They were similar to ski shoes and made so that water would not get inside. A lining between the sole and the upper parts kept out the water so we could walk on the snow and water and not be afraid it would wet our feet. Sometimes we would wear these shoes all year round. Except on *Shabbes,* maybe we had other shoes, maybe not. The older you would get—like my brother *alav hasholem* who was older, he also had summer shoes that were shoes like we have today. Like half shoes, we used to call them. They were for *Shabbes.* These shoes were expensive, although labor was not expensive—the materials were very expensive.

In summertime, of course, we were naturally happier. First of all, it was not cold, and we didn't have to worry about heating constantly and getting dressed. Summertime *cheder* was easier. We would still go there early in the morning, 5:30, 5:45, sometimes 6:00. There was no public school, and that itself was a tremendous relief. We did not have to worry because from June or July until September, we had a vacation from public school. Every day in public school was full of anti-Semitism because of the anti-Semitic teachers. So, in summertime, we didn't have to go to school on *Shabbes.* We could go to *shul* on *Shabbes.*

We spent the whole day during summertime at *cheder*, with the exception of the lunch break that lasted an hour and short break period in the afternoon. When we finished *cheder*, we were happy. We would run around. One of the games we played, sometimes in the main street, used a metal rim of a wagon wheel. We would chase it with a stick; we would hit it, and run after it. We played together in somebody's backyard, and on *Shabbes* afternoons, we got to play longer. We had to go to *cheder* also, but the afternoon was longer in the summertime so we had quite a bit of time to play.

Another thing we would make in the summer was prune jelly. We would buy many pounds of prunes. Actually the peasants would sell them in what was called a hepaliter or dekaliter, which was 10 liters. Making jam was a process that lasted a day, sometimes two days. The way it was done is you would open up the prunes with spoons and remove the pits. Then you would throw the prunes into water in a big kettle on the fire and mix and mix them. And it was a whole day's process until the fruit became soft. At night, it was ready to be bottled and put away for the winter.

In summertime, we also bought cherries. The cherries and raspberries were for desserts in wintertime. We would bottle them in cans. We also put pickles in cans for wintertime. In summertime, we also made raspberry syrup. Syrups were not available in the store. You had to make all these things yourself and can them. It was quite a process to make the syrup. First, we would buy the raspberries. The peasants would bring them down from the mountains and sell them all in huge cans. We broke them into pieces, mixed and squeezed them, boiled them and canned them in large cans or large decanters. People used to make all these desserts and preservatives in case you should need it, because these preservatives were mainly used if someone got sick. Then he would get a special treat of these preservatives or syrup.

Towards the end of the summer, we bought a lot of walnuts. Farmers and peasants would come and sell those. We used to keep them in the attic, spread them out to dry. They stayed all winter long, and we would take them as needed. These walnuts were used for baking and as snacks. We sometimes used to eat two pieces of bread with a few walnuts. And also toward the end of the summer, we bought apples. Apples were stored in a kind of a shack, like a storage place. They would be stored for the winter in hay, so they shouldn't freeze. Apples were the only fruit we had in wintertime because imports from warmer climates were not available.

Vegetables practically did not exist in wintertime, because there were no imported vegetables either. So we were happy in the springtime. When spring came, we had our own garden, but we also used to buy vegetables from farmers. They would come to our door and sell them in spring and summer. The next door neighbors had their gardens, and they used to grow a lot. We used to raise some vegetables in our own garden. We had a *goy* digging up the garden. We had lots of fruits in our garden. Sometimes we would eat those fruits in the summertime and can them for wintertime.

We didn't have a vacuum cleaner, so first of all, every day, we opened the windows and sometimes hung the bedding out the windows like you see it today in Israel. We would have a beater to beat the bedding, the pillows, and covers to get dust out and to air the rooms.

Fall time, it was already getting cold. The *slichot* (special prayers around the high holidays) started as we were getting ready for *Rosh Hashana* and *Yom Kippur*. We had a kind of *kedusha*, a kind of holiness, that we felt as children. Perhaps as a result of what we've been through and also because of the secular society that we live in, life today is not as conducive to this kind of feeling.

Cheeses and such things were a luxury, a treat. We had one Jewish Bulgarian farmer, originally a Bulgarian Jew—how he came to Romania I don't know. He would come Sundays and bring butter and cottage cheese. An entrepreneur, one of the members of the *shul*, would make hard cheeses during summertime. We had difficulty with freezing it, because there was no freezing equipment in Borgo, anyway. There may have been refrigeration in some of the bigger cities.

I would just like to say that speaking of food and the sanitary conditions in Europe in our area, and most other areas, it was not very sanitary. There were many problems, such as the plumbing. There was no indoor plumbing in the smaller communities. In the larger cities, there was indoor plumbing already. But in Borgo Prund, there was no such thing in my day.

We had various methods for getting clean. To take a bath, you had to have a tub or a wash basin. You had to boil the water—since there was no hot water available immediately—and put it in a big tub. There was no special place for the tub. There were no bathrooms, so we did it in the kitchen or where we were doing the laundry. Fridays, we would go to the *mikve* (ritual bath), and there was a long waiting line to take your bath. There were a number of tubs, some made out of wood, others made out of cement. The poor *shames* (caretaker) prepared these baths, these tubs with cold and hot water. The cold water would come from the *mikve* itself, which was a well, and the hot water was heated.

In other words, it was very, very difficult to keep clean as we know it now. In those conditions, what we could do was satisfactory. Jewish people, especially, were considered much cleaner than the average non-Jewish inhabitant. Some, of course, had more amenities than others, but Jews went to the *mikve* (ritual bath) at least once a week, and had a nice bath. They kept clean, and had wash tubs and bathtubs.

In 1939, I think, the fascist government failed. I can still recall what happened early in the morning. The town rabbi's son Moishe *alav hasholem* would usually pass by in the morning and wake us up at 5:30 or 5:45 to go to *cheder*. But this time he was knocking unusually hard on the window. My parents got up and knew something must be happening. He told my parents that the fascist regime of A.C. Cuza and Octavian Goga had fallen. I don't recall exactly the name of the regime that took over. I don't remember if King Carol took over, or if it already was his son Michael. [*It was King Carol.*] This I don't recall. I was ten years old at the time. There have been lapses in my memory. In that time, from 1939 until now, 1988, almost 48 years, memories fade.

During the occupation everything was dangerous. There was tremendous anti-Semitism. The Iron Guard would march. I felt anti-Semitism more at school. By that time I was in the Hungarian school, on the elementary level, the fourth grade.

My brother Yitzhak Schmuel *alav hasholem* was already graduating from school, which was compulsory until the seventh grade.

In 1940, half of Transylvania was ceded to Hungary. I don't recall exactly what the deal was. I think Germany must have been instrumental, because Romania joined. Germany, Italy, and Hungary, who were also part of the Axis. So, there must have been some sort of compromise that Hitler arranged with the Romanians and Hungarians that included giving Hungary this part of Transylvania. Immediately when the Hungarians came in and took over Transylvania, the level of anti-Semitism rose. Many Jews were deported immediately

A number of Jews were technicians or engineers in the lumber and paper factories. Many of these Jews had come—or their parents came—from Poland. In Romania, they were considered citizens. But when the Hungarians took control of Transylvania, they immediately made these people stateless. A number of these Jews were married to local girls. One night in Borgo Prund and many other places, the Hungarians picked up these people and marched them to either the Romanian or the Polish border. Many of these people were killed, but, somehow, some were saved. I can't recall exactly how, but one distant relative who now lives in Vienna was married to one of these technicians. Her maiden name was Viezell.

Unfortunately, these technicians considered themselves very modern, and we already looked down on their religious practices. There were non-conformative, which means they were not practicing much Judaism. They may have come to *shul* on *Rosh Hashanah* or *Yom Kippur*, but they mostly desecrated *Shabbes* and *yom tov,* I believe. Wherever they came from, some of them were not brought up in a religious way. But many of them, unfortunately, had left their religious practices behind. At the time, this was happening even in our own community. As I said before, someone who considered himself modern threw away his religious practices. That was a dangerous condition in Borgo Prund at the time already. To our parents *aleihem hasholem,* it was a great worry.

By the years 1942 and 1943, it was already dangerous to travel. Nevertheless, my family sent my eldest brother who was already 15 or 16 to a *yeshiva* at Grosswardein, a big city in Transylvania which housed the Vizhnitzer Yeshiva. At that time Rav Chaim Meir was the Rebbe. Originally the

Vizhnitzer Yeshiva was in the town of Wiznitz in Bukovina. But the Romanians were anti-Semitic at the time. I don't know when the *yeshiva* stopped functioning in Wiznitz, and was transferred to Grosswardein, which was called Nagyvárad in Hungary. I will mention this later, but I visited there for a *Rosh Hashana* to visit the *Rebbi* with my brother *alav hasholem*.

However, many local boys who studied at *cheder* and grew up in *shomer Shabbes* (Sabbath observant) homes went to work in the factories due to the difficult economic conditions. For some of them, there was no other economic future, so they learned to be mechanics. Working there, they were called to work on *Shabbes*. My family and many others looked upon this as a terrible thing, of course, which it was. But it was very difficult to make a living in those days. Some learned a trade, to become shoemakers and tailors, and so on. My father took my brother *alav hasholem* into the lumber business after he went to *yeshiva*. He was very brilliant in business and in bookkeeping, purchasing, and selling, and so on.

This was a very dismal time for people who had no trade or any other way to make a living. Some people moved to larger cities, to Klausenburg, to Budapest, to Bucharest, where there were more opportunities. Young people had less opportunities locally. Even some of the girls moved away in order to get married. For example, cousin Eddie's sister Frieda *aleya hasholem*, who got killed by the Germans, had moved to Budapest. I don't remember exactly what kind of work she did, but she had more opportunities there for a job and for *shidduchim* (matchmaking).

Such were the conditions. Between 1940 and 1943, after the Hungarians came in, anti-Semitism was tremendous at all levels. The level of anti-Semitism increased among the peasants and native Hungarians and Romanians. The partnership between the Germans and the Hungarians naturally also instigated anti-Semitism. But amazingly enough, our business had some of its best years. Because not only did we have the lumber business with local people from the area within 50 miles or 100 miles of our town, we were shipping lumber to their motherland, Hungary. We would ship to Budapest in deep Hungary, shipping lumber to coal mines, and so on. Amazingly, we did very well those days.

The school system at the time was divided into two kinds of schools, the Romanian school and the Hungarian school. All Jews, to my knowledge, chose the Hungarian school because prior to the First World War, Hungary was ruled by a king, an emperor, Franz Joseph II, but he was a *melech shel hessed* (a benevolent king), and the Jews had fared very well under his rule. They were not discriminated against. Jews served in the army. My father, for example, served in Turkey, though not voluntarily. But the Jews were not generally discriminated against. The Jewish people were possibly poor, but they were not physically threatened.

In Hungary in early 1940s, after the war started, the Hungarians started drafting Jews into the labor force. When the Hungarians took over, they instituted certain German laws, for example, requiring business licenses. Many Jews had their business licenses revoked, as I mentioned previously. And without the license, you couldn't move goods; you couldn't give receipts. You couldn't give any statements, any *facturas* to certify the sale of lumber. Sometime later, my father's license was returned, and he was actually able to help a number of Jewish people continue to do their business, also, under his name. He never took money for that.

We were constantly busy with sales and purchases of lumber. My mother *aleya hasholem* was very afraid. The situation was terrible. My brother had to come home from Grosswardein He was in the *Yeshiva* for less than a year, but he learned at home. He also helped in the business. But I have mentioned that. It's so ironic—today you can calculate everything with a calculator, but in those times it took hours and hours to calculate a wagon load of lumber. Let's say a wagon's load capacity was 30 cubic meter, 40 cubic meters, or 50 cubic meters. But there were different kinds of lumber, each with different dimensions. Let's say one was eight meters, the other one was six meters by 10cm or 12cm. So if you had 10 pieces of that or 15 pieces of that, you had to figure out the amount and write it down by hand and calculate by hand, too! We had no calculator. Today, with a calculator, especially with a computer, it would probably take ten minutes. But in those days it took hours and hours, a tremendous amount of book work that had to be done.

We did business with various people; some had lumber yards in different cities. During the Hungarian time, we had a partner named Weiss. He was like a broker, and he lived in Budapest. He sold lumber to big entrepreneurs and big factories for whatever they could use it for, like furniture or building. He purchased a tremendous amount of lumber from us.

Unfortunately this got us, my father *alav hasholem* into trouble. Several businesspeople, including my father, ended up being arrested because of the anti-Semitism that existed; there was jealousy for all kinds of various things. It took the form of problems with receipts and more. I can't remember the details. They went after my father, all in an act of anti-Semitism. He ended up in jail in Hungary in a city called Békéscsaba.

I believe that was in 1943. I recall our insecurity and my mother *aleya hasholem* crying and, so on. Finally, she had to go to this city of Békéscsaba and engage a lawyer. She had to deposit bail. I don't recall whether it was 4,000 pengő, or 5,000 pengő, but it was a tremendous amount of money in those days. I would say it was probably the equivalent to $50,000 to $75,000 today. That drained our resources and reserves, but it also drained our spirits. We were so concerned about my father's future and so worried about the other Jewish people. But finally, after several weeks of incarceration, my mother *aleya hasholem* and the other people were able to help release my father. This episode left a constant worry at the back of our minds. It's there ever since. For if it came to a trial, with the anti-Semitic judges, how could my father stand a chance? Of course, it never came to trial, because, unfortunately, they deported us in 1944.

Jews were called to a military service. There was also a sort of a paramilitary service. All the boys from the age of 12 and up had to perform some sort of a paramilitary service. Non-Jews were trained in various aspects of the military. But Jews, instead, were used for menial work. We had to carve a running course so the non-Jewish military members could have a running course.

Once a week, we had to go to this paramilitary service and they singled Jews out to wear a yellow armband or a yellow star. Before it was a yellow star, we had to wear a yellow armband. The yellow was a sign that you were a Jew. We did hard, heavy work, menial work. We worked out in the open and, of course the non-Jews, the *goyim* were looking at us with a sense of revenge. Here, finally the Jews were being put in their place. So we had to do this every week. At one time, the Hungarian boy scouts had a jamboree or something in our town. They came from different parts of Transylvania. The Jewish members of this paramilitary service were called to do their work on *Shabbes*. We didn't want to desecrate the *Shabbes,* on top of all the things going on and all the problems. We had to dig latrines for them, bathrooms, and prepare running tracks. So you can see the anti-Semitism that existed. A Jew felt so insecure in those days.

This paramilitary service started at the age of 12. My brother *alav hasholem,* if he was sick or incapable of going one day, he had to bring a doctor's certificate to prove it. In order to get my older brother out of his paramilitary service, we tried to bribe someone.

A Hungarian man was in charge of it, an official at the paper factory. His landlord was a Jewish landlord, and we sort of tried to bribe him, to give him a present. It may have been some nice pillow, I can't remember exactly what it was, for his wife. I slightly recall he was very indignant about it. How dare we bribe him? We were afraid he would make a case of the whole thing and go inform the police about it. For several weeks, we had no peace. We shuddered, and we were afraid that perhaps we would end up in jail because of that. Finally, for some reason it quieted down, I don't remember the details. Although, I must say, his son was my classmate, and he would come over to our backyard and talk, and so on. He was about 12, 13 at the time. But nevertheless, it did not help very much. Because we Jews were Jews! And we were being discriminated against.

Chapter 6

My uncles on my father's side also had difficulties making a living, unfortunately. Before he was drafted, my uncle Yankal also had hardships. As a result, he had to deal with buying bread and cheeses and other foods and re-selling them. He also had a *yeshiva*, where he taught many people. My other uncles who also lived in Bistritz had major difficulties making a living when the Hungarians took over.

Then there was the paramilitary service. Non-Jews were drafted to the army, and Jews were drafted to the labor force. During that time the Hungarians provided assistance to the Germans, not only giving them passage to the Russian front through their cities, but also sending Hungarian regiments to fight together with the Germans. They sent Jews to the labor force on the Hungarian front or to different parts of Hungary, and they kept some in the local area. They worked very hard. My cousin, the Shunktofer Rav (Rabbi Yecheskal Ruttner), was drafted to the labor force, and he served as a chaplain in this labor force, in one of the regiments. But most of the Jews had to perform hard labor. They were sent to the Russian front and did dirty work for the Germans and the Hungarians. Many, many were killed; they never came back home.

Some were able to escape, like the Weismanns from Borgo Prund— who later lived in Israel. There were two brothers; one was married to the *schohet's* (ritual butcher's) daughter Goldie, my classmate in the Hungarian school. She now lives in Haifa. They were able to escape and join the partisans. The partisans were groups of people, Jewish groups, Russian groups, and Polish groups, who had escaped the army, and there were Jews had who escaped the concentration camps. Some were hiding in the forest, and they fought against the Germans. Many of them were killed.

My father helped his relatives who were forced into labor camps by buying things that they needed for supplies, even metal plates, knapsacks, blankets, and shoes, because they were not given clothes at the labor camp. But many Jews lost their lives before the concentration camps, when they were sent to the Russian front. They were practically cannon fodder— that's what they were used for.

So many men were drafted, like cousin Eddie Kahn, who was drafted to the Hungarian labor force. He served until liberation. He was also saved by his singing, for he would sing for his officers. He was liberated, I believe, in December 1944 or early in 1945.

Even before March 15, 1944, when the Germans marched in and took over, the Hungarian regime was an anti-Semitic regime, a fascist regime, but they did not touch the Jews physically. They arrested some, but generally speaking, it was quiet. At that time, Jews had already escaped from Poland and Czechoslovakia, and they were hiding under false names and false passports. They warned the people; they told the people about deportations, although nobody wanted to believe that such a thing could happen in Hungary. The Jews had so much trust in Hungary, that Hungary would not sell out the Jews. Yet, some Jews went into hiding.

For example, the Bobover Rebbi was hiding in Budapest. And, later, fortunately he was able to escape to Romania, and in Romania they hadn't sold out the Jews to the degree Hungary did. In some parts in Hungary, like in Budapest, they were trying to annihilate the Jews. They did kill many; they shot them and threw them in the Danube. Some they deported from Budapest itself. But fortunately, many more were saved in deep Hungary, in the Romanian part of Transylvania, and in the part of Czechoslovakia that was held by Hungary. This was different than in most of Czechoslovakia and Yugoslavia, where most Jews were deported to concentration camps and were killed.

We felt anti-Semitism everywhere from the Hungarian teachers and officials. The Hungarians were cruel; their policeman were cruel. We used to hide every time we saw them walking on the street patrol. We were very scared of them. Amazingly, many Jews were so patriotic they thought this was the same kind of Hungarian regime that existed before and during the First World War. So, these Jews were loyal and patriotic. But we found out very fast that these people were not the same Hungarians, and the suffering really began during this regime.

The Hungarians were replaced by the Germans who took over on March 15, 1944. Prior to that, Hungary had granted Germany passageway because Borgo Prund was on the main road to the Russian front.

We would always see, day and night, truckloads of Germans. But after March 15, we already saw Germans actually parking here and taking over the towns and the cities and the Hungarian government. Horthy was the Hungarian chancellor, or leader and dictator. Even though he had instituted many of the German laws, Jews were still safe. A few were deported, but masses were not deported. Once the Germans took over, our fate was sealed.

Unfortunately, we did not know what was going to happen to us. In May 1944, right after *Pesach,* they started sending Jews in our community to ghettos. At first, we were not told that we were going to be assembled. However, early in the morning, they knocked on the door, and there was a Hungarian assistant who told us we were to be assembled all together. Actually, the Hungarians did it themselves under German supervision. They were the ones who did it very zealously.

We had prepared some foods for an emergency, enough snacks to take along in case something would just happen, because we felt that something might happen. We didn't know what.

So, we had pre-prepared food and clothes, and we already had hidden some valuables. We dug a hole near our house which contained papers with all the names of people that we gave money to in advance; that is how we used to work. We gave them money in advance, and then a month later, two months later, they would cut this lumber and deliver it. Then we paid the rest. This amounted to many, many thousands of pengős. That was the Hungarian currency. And my brother *alav hasholem* dug a hole and hid this list together with some other documents and some jewelry. I found these things after the war. The jewelry was not much;

there was a brooch. I gave it to Mrs. Richtman. She gave it to Cousin Helen who has the brooch today.

So, one morning they came around, and they said we have an hour, or not even an hour, to get ready. And they had wagons. They took our stuff, some suitcases or backpacks. And they gathered our community in a park near the city hall. They took our jewelry. My parents had bought me a very nice Omega watch. And an Omega watch was worth a lot of money in those days. Even today it is very expensive. It was a *Bar Mitzvah* gift. And for some reason I did not remove this watch. I still had the watch, but when they gathered us in this empty lot, the Hungarian officer grabbed it off my hand and took it away.

In this vacant lot, they assembled all the people from the Borgos—like my grandmother *aleya hasholem* and my aunt who lived in Marosborgó, about six miles from us—and people from the whole county stayed there all day long. I don't believe they gave us any food at all. We did not know exactly what our fate was going to be. Incidentally the night before they gathered us, we had spoken to our neighbor across the street, the one whose well we were using to get water. He was like an alderman, and he said to us that something would happen tomorrow. I don't know why, but he warned us.

It was very late to do something, to hide. Possibly, if we had known what was going to happen, maybe we could have hidden, or done something. I don't know exactly what, but there were *goyim* (non-Jews) who possibly could have hidden us in small towns. Even the officials, the Jewish officials who knew more about what was going on in Germany and in Hungary, if they had known that the Jews were being transported to their death, they could have notified us.

It's possible that they knew.

That's why after the war they had this trial for Kastner [*Rezső Kasztner, 1906—March 15, 1957*, also known as Rudolf Israel Kastner. He was from Klausenburg, a Hungarian-Jewish journalist and lawyer, the leader of Hungarian Jewry. He became known for having helped Jews escape from occupied Europe during the Holocaust. He was assassinated in 1957 after an Israeli court accused him of having collaborated with the Nazis and having failed to inform the Jews in the Cluj Ghetto of their fate. Kastner negotiated with Adolf Eichmann, a senior SS officer, to allow 1,684 select Jews to leave instead for Switzerland on what became known as the Kastner train, in exchange for money, gold, and diamonds.]

So actually we just sort of trusted the Hungarian government that everything was going to be well. But the neighbor did tell us that something drastic was going to happen. As a matter of fact, early that morning we found that there were two men in every Jewish home—either policeman or aldermen, Romanians or Hungarians, guarding us so that nobody would escape.

So we were kept there outdoors the whole day. There was one person, his name was Ceneval. His wife was a very heavy woman. She probably weighed 350 to 400 pounds. And, *nebech,* they put her in a wagon. She had a special chair which she sat on in that wagon when they took her to city hall, then to that park, that empty lot. From there, later that afternoon, some people had to walk and some were taken by wagons on the way to the ghetto. They carved out a ghetto which was, I believe, a vineyard, a big empty space not far from Bistritz. In that ghetto, they gathered the Jews from Bistritz and the whole area, too, from all Borgos.

The only thing there with a roof was an old stable. They could only take in 200 people in there, not comfortably, back to back. The rest were left in the open field. So my father *alav hasholem* and a number of other lumber merchants had a lot of cut lumber in the lumber mills. We consented to give all this lumber and managed to build a temporary shelter. It was like a triangle, like a roof. At least, with that, the people had some sort of a roof above their head. Of course, it rained, and the rain came in, but at least we were not completely exposed. It was still cold. Let's not forget, it was the month of May. And May, in those parts of the world, is still quite cold. But it was still better than being exposed to the open air.

Whatever type of bedding we could have brought along, you can imagine it was not the most comfortable thing. So families would stay together, sort of lie down next to each other.

There were many families in this barrack-like building—not really a barrack, but a space with a roof with a triangular shape. And there was sort of a common kitchen. Some food was cooked, which, of course, was terrible. And there was not much to eat. There were no sanitary facilities, so we had to dig some sort of latrines which people used as bathrooms at the end of this open field. The Germans immediately cut off the Jews' beards and *payot* (side curls). When the Germans took over on March 15, my mother *aleya hasholem* suggested that maybe I should cut off my *payot*. She said *payot* would be dangerous when the Germans took over. I had *payot* for years and years, but I did cut them off at that time.

They brought Jews from all over to that ghetto, from the whole county, the whole area. Starvation already began at that time. Physically, we were not threatened, but we didn't know what was going to happen, what was going to be. In the ghetto, people tried to *daven* (pray) with a *minyan* (group of 10 men). I don't remember, exactly. I think we just *davened* in the open field. Some people tried to learn. At this time, there wasn't too much activity in this ghetto. We were in that ghetto about a month. But, of course, when they took us to the ghetto, everything stopped. I was 14 at the time, so the whole thing seemed funny. What is this all about? It somehow seemed like a bad adventure. Being moved, wondering what was going to happen? What would come next? We didn't know. Our parents, I could see in my father's face *alav hasholem,* my mother *aleya hasholem*— that they sensed that something dangerous was going to happen. But we didn't know what.

So we lived in the ghetto. The starvation started. My aunt, my father's younger sister Feiga, had a baby. The baby died of starvation in the ghetto. Feiga later died in the concentration camp, also.

My father's uncle, Shimon Ressler, who at that time owned a vineyard, *nebech* (pity), his wife died in the ghetto. There was no medicine, nothing. This was the beginning of the end for so many people. In this ghetto, as I said, life was miserable, very miserable. Until one day, approximately four weeks after they took us to the ghetto, there came an order that we should pack all the things we had. And they marched us down to the railroad tracks. It was a mile or two miles away. Men, women, and children, everybody, they marched us down to the railroad tracks. They were waiting for us with train cars. The windows were blocked with wire. These cattle cars were open. And there were Hungarian army soldiers and policeman and some Germans, too. The Hungarians *yimach shmam* did a very good job for the Germans. They followed their orders to the nth degree. They did even more than the Germans had told them to do and with more delight.

They marched us to these cattle cars. It took quite a few hours. We waited until all of them were full. There were two transports. One was full of people who had been taken before *Shavuous* (a spring holiday) in 1944. At that time, we didn't know anything about what happened to these people.

And then we were taken a day or two after *Shavuous*, I don't remember exactly when, to the railroad tracks and placed in cattle cars. There was a little food given, and they sealed us up. I cannot recall exactly, but there may have been more than 80 people in this cattle car. They gave each car a pail which was used for the human needs, for excretion, and so on. We were sealed in, and after several hours the train suddenly started moving. It was a special train, as I said it was a train of cattle cars, and we kept going on our unfortunate journey of death.

We had no idea, where we were going, where they were taking us, and what was going to happen to us. Families tried to stay together, but there was no room. Nevertheless everybody tried to make their best effort and control themselves as much as possible. You can imagine the heartbeat of every person. But we went through Transylvania up toward the Czechoslovakian border, then to Poland, to Auschwitz.

In the cattle car, we were so crowded; it was impossible: The stench, the smell, and no air. The windows were sealed, even those little windows some cattle cars have, were sealed with wire so nobody could escape. They opened these cars several times on the way to Auschwitz. They let us empty the waste from the cars, and they gave us a piece of bread or something, I believe. Very, very little food. I don't remember if they gave us water or not; I cannot even recall. If they did, it was very little. There were a lot of deaths in the cars themselves because people suffocated from being without air.

We tried to do the best we could to *daven* in those cars, to put on *tallis* and *tefillin* (prayer shawls and boxes holding prayers worn on the head and arm). We tried to sit together, but sitting was practically impossible because these cars were so crowded. But yet, as I said, the families tried to stick together. We were scared. We were terribly, terribly scared.

I can recall looking in the eyes of people, especially the old people. They were more scared than the younger kids. The young kids didn't know what was going to happen, either, but perhaps the older generation had more of a feeling that this was their last journey. Who knew if we would ever return or ever see each other again. After five days journey, I believe, approximately five days journey from the Bistritz ghetto, we finally arrived at our infamous destination, Auschwitz.

When they opened the train car doors, it was very early in the morning; it was dark, and it was very early. We saw the guards, the German guards *yimach shmann*. They opened the doors of these cars, these cattle cars. They made sure nobody would be able to escape. They were yelling and screaming. Of course, we were screaming—people were dying in the cars, dying from suffocation, hunger, and disease in the cars. All of a sudden, they opened the cattle car wagons, and we heard screaming: "*Raus! Raus! Raus!*" (Out! Out! Out!).

First, they yelled and screamed, "Leave all your baggage. It will be taken to you. Don't worry about your baggage, just get out everybody!" They were screaming and yelling. It was a nasty early morning in June, 1944. It was rainy and wet outside. Here we saw these people dressed very funnily. They had pajamas, like clothes with stripes; they even had hats, caps, that were made from the same kind of material. They looked very funny. We saw these people, in addition to the German soldiers, the SS, although it could have been Wehrmacht, and they were also screaming and yelling at us: "*Raus!* Leave your baggage behind!"

Naturally, families tried to stick together as they were driving us out of the cattle wagons. Again, we were scared to death. We didn't know what was happening. We lined up, thousands of people, because on one train alone there were several thousand people. The trains kept on coming in, and we saw all these inmates who were dressed in these pajama-like clothes, which we didn't know we would be wearing ourselves soon. These people were inmates in Auschwitz who were assigned to clean out these cattle cars and take away everything that we had.

Of course, they told us not to worry. To families who tried to stick together, they said that families were going to be reunited. And they were yelling. The Germans were hitting us with their truncheons and with hoses, and they were hitting, yelling, screaming to hurry up and go forward. They were yelling: Men go separate, older people separate, women with children separate, and younger people separate.

The older inmates who had been there several years already, some Polish Jews, German Jews, and Dutch Jews. and so on, from places that were occupied previously by the Germans, they already knew what would happen to us, and some of them cautioned us. They told the older people that they should try to push themselves into the line with the younger people.

They knew very well what was going to happen to the older people, that the Germans were going to gas them. But some of them also pushed older people, by force, to the line of the younger people, to perhaps give them another chance to stay alive. There were lines of thousands of people in the dark—it was still dark outside, semi-daylight.

At the head of the line, you saw these German soldiers and Doctor Mengele with his assistants. He said again: "Old people to the right." And, of course, people cried. They didn't know what was happening. They tried to hold on to their children, but the Germans said, "Don't worry, you are not going to be separated. You are just going to take a shower separately. We will clean you up, and then you'll be reunited. Don't worry about it." And that's when they separated us.

My brother *alav hasholem* and I, we went with the group of working people, the younger people. But my parents and my brother Chezki and my sister Suri, they went together, and unfortunately this was the last time I saw them.

They took them from the selection straight to the gas chambers. Of course, we were told that everybody was going to get a shower. They told us take off your clothes, and you are going to be reunited with your family. So, *nebech,* they went just like sheep to the slaughter. Not knowing. They wouldn't believe until the last moment what was going to happen to them—that they were going to be gassed.

The Germans *yimach shmann,* the cultured people—did this. And today, unfortunately, many Jews go back and live in Germany, and the Germans deny they knew anything about it. You have to remember: Never, never in this world forgive the Germans. Never forgive them because of what they did, methodically killing Jewish people, their method in fooling them. As the Torah says: "Remember what Amalek did to you." The Germans supposedly do descend from Amalek. Remember what they did to the Jewish people. Never forgive them. Even though the younger generation didn't know anything about it, never forgive them or forget what they did to us.

So that's how we were separated. They took us younger people into some sort of regular showers. They cut our hair. They disinfected us. They cut our hair all over our body, wherever we had hair. They cut the hair under the arms and everywhere else.

We were referred to as a *häftling* (German for prisoner or inmate). *Häftling* was what they called an inmate of the concentration camp. And they assigned us numbers. With our group, they did not tattoo numbers on our arms, since we were not in Auschwitz for a long time, only for several days—I cannot recall exactly how many days. Most people who were there for a longer period, they tattooed numbers on them; they gave them numbers. My number was sewn on my clothes. I believe I had 42949, and my brother *alav hasholem* had 42950. They gave us clothes—they gave us these pajama-like clothes. And we looked at each other, looking so funny and so scared. We didn't know what was happening.

Then they marched us into this huge barracks. There were several hundred people in each barrack. You had these triple-like beds. I can't remember if they were filled with straw bags, or they were not filled with anything. They were like triple bunks. It was very crowded, with several hundred people, as I said. Of course, people who came from the same town, let's say Borgo Prund, tried to sort of stick together. We looked at each other, looking very funny. How we looked with these clothes on. We were wondering what happened to the other people, to our parents and brothers and sisters.

In Auschwitz, I don't know how many hours after we arrived, they gave us a piece of bread and a piece of margarine, I believe, for supper. They would take us out several times a day and count us. And then we had to stand while it was rainy and nasty and cold outside. We stood several hundred out in front of each barrack, and these German soldiers *yimach shmann* came and counted us.

Each time, if they saw somebody short, somebody skinny, they would take him out, select him, and take him for gassing. Several times a day, they would take us outside and count us and select from us. I myself was very short at the time, but I was heavy. So even though I was short, maybe I was standing on something, and I looked older and heavier. So they didn't select me to be sent to the gas chambers on these various selections.

We heard in Auschwitz that the smell was from smoke, from burning human flesh, from open fires. And we heard the screaming, from the people they drove into the gas chambers. It was just a horrible, horrible experience, a horrible thing. And here my brother *alav hasholem* and I were standing together, cleaving, actually cleaving together, not to be separated from each other. And this was repeated every day. The selections were repeated every day for the period we were in Auschwitz.

They continued going through the same procedure—counting us, scaring us, threatening us, and taking us out in the cold weather. Then they selected a whole group of us, many from our area in Europe, and they put us on trains, and gave us some food. I believe a third of a loaf of bread with some margarine. For two or three days, we were riding on the train until one morning, we arrived at the Mauthausen concentration camp. Mauthausen was in Austria. It was one of the first concentration camps outside of Germany. We know Austria was the right

Identification card issued to Zeidy when he transferred from
Auschwitz to Mauthausen—Zeidy probably changed his birthdate
from 1929 to 1927, hoping to convince the Germans that he was
older and able to work so he would not be selected to die.

place for it. Austrians were not only great Hitler sympathizers, but they
also welcomed him after the *Anschluss* (annexation of Austria) in 1938.
More than half a million Austrians came out to greet Hitler in Vienna.
The Austrians were Jew-haters, perhaps even more than the Germans.

Mauthausen had many Jewish prisoners called *häftlings* (inmates). It
was a killing camp, and Jews were sent to their death in the gas chambers
there. It had crematoria where they burned the bodies and also other
various methods of torturing and killing Jews. The camp had some German or Austrian political prisoners and some gypsies. In Mauthausen,
we heard screams and yells, but we were placed in separate barracks.
Apparently, we were there just for transfer because we stayed about two
days only. I cannot recall whether the numbers they assigned us—the
numbers I mentioned previously—were given to us in Auschwitz or in
Mauthausen.

At any rate, it was scary there, too, and we didn't know what was going to happen to us. Again my brother *alav hasholem* and I were sticking and clinging together so we would not be separated. After about two days, they took us to the railroad station, or some railroad junction, and they placed us in cars. This time it was not cattle cars. It was regular passenger cars.

We traveled for several hours to a camp in Ebensee, a satellite concentration camp of Mauthausen, which had several satellite subcamps. When we arrived in Ebensee, it had more than 18,000 to 20,000 inmates already, mostly Jews. It was in the wilderness, in the forest. Some of the barracks had been built by previous inmates.

(* Please see the Appendix for additional background about Ebensee)

There were some Italians, Polish political prisoners, some murderers, and some German political prisoners. There were also some Spanish prisoners, in addition, who were caught in France. There were Communists who the Germans deported to Ebensee. It was a very strange phenomenon, and it was very scary to come to such a place, of course, with all the German soldiers, the SS, and Wehrmacht. They marched us into this camp. We were marched around immediately on the first day we arrived, then they placed us in barracks, gave us blankets, and supposedly deloused us. They had a delousing place, something like a bath.

At first they placed my brother *alav hasholem* and me together in the same barracks. Later on, we were separated several times. We were reunited only for the last few days prior to liberation. We were six people in one bed. The bunk had three stories of beds, so there were about 18 people to one bunk. They assigned us to barracks, and they placed my brother and I in barrack number 25. The barrack consisted of two huge rooms where approximately 600 inmates slept.

At the beginning, there was straw in the mattresses and blankets.

The first morning, they awakened us before five o'clock. They gave us what was called an ersatz *kaffee* (a replacement type of coffee). It was some kind of black mush. At noon, they would bring out special carriers. They were assigned to bring us what was called a soup for lunch. The soup consisted of potato peels and water, but sometimes it was warm. And, at least, we had something that filled our stomachs.

Everybody got what was called a *misski*, a metal plate that the Germans filled up three-quarters, maybe half, with soup for lunch times. We had to carry it all day and all night. Many times, people stole your *misski*. It was stolen from you by all kinds of thieves in the concentration camp. You had to sleep with it under your head. You had to guard everything you had, and you didn't have much. But even, let's say, if you had a leftover little piece of bread from the night before, you had to guard it with your life, because by morning it could be stolen.

They woke us up before 5:00 a.m., and we had to run to a sort of a barrack with sinks. Not individual sinks, but like running water. Everybody had to run to it and wash. It was still cold when we arrived there in June. The forest was still very cold. Every morning, we had to go and sort of wash ourselves. Regardless, if it was 20 below zero, 10 below zero, we had to run. We had to wash ourselves quickly because there were thousands of people washing themselves in one or two barracks.

At 6:00, you had to already be at this *appelplatz* (location for the daily roll calls in Nazi concentration camps). Your bed had to be made very smooth, almost like an army bed. Because during the time we were at work and out of the barracks from approximately 5:30, 5:45 a.m., until approximately 6:30 or 7:00 p.m., the SS Germans and also the barrack elders would come in and inspect the barracks.

Each barrack had an elder. We called them *Stubendienst* (the barrack orderly). If you were a *Stubendienst*, you were very lucky. You couldn't have imagined how lucky you were. I was lucky for a very short time to be a *Stubendienst*, maybe for a month or two months. That means, first of all, that you didn't have to go out to work in the regular *arbeitskommando* (labor camp), which meant doing very difficult slave labor and being beaten. The *Stubendienst's* job was to make sure the beds were straight and the rooms, the barracks, were swept, and clean. The duty of the *Stubendienst* was not as difficult as the work of people who had to go out to work in the *arbeitskommando* every day. To be a *Stubendienst* also meant that you could get some little bit extra soup sometimes during the day, which I shared with my brother *alav hasholem.*

First of all, at 6:00 a.m. sharp, the Germans *yimach shmann ve zichronam,* the SS, and Wehrmacht would come to this *appelplatz.* It was a huge empty space, like a gathering place. It was surrounded by different barracks. All inmates, regardless of whether you were sick or well, had to assemble in that *appelplatz* at 6:00 exactly, with the exception of people who worked the night shift.

Every morning and every night, we were counted by the like Germans. They went to different groups, and they commanded us: "*Mütze ab!*" and that meant you had to take off your cap. We were dressed in very light pajama-like clothes in summer and winter. In wintertime, they gave us what was supposedly a coat, but it was the thickness of pajamas. That was our coat. And the cap did not have any ear-muffs or anything. It was just a plain cap. But every time we saw a German, we had to remove our cap in order to show respect to the German. Also we had to stand up straight out of respect to the German, because, of course, we were non-beings. And they were the superhumans.

When we were counted, the SS and the German soldiers came in with their dogs. It wasn't unusual that if somebody made a wrong move—you had to stand still and wait for your group to be counted—they'd give you a *zetz*, a big hit with the rubber hose they always carried. Or with the stick. This happened for no reason whatsoever, but just for their pleasure.

So after they said "*Mütze ab!*", the Germans would count us every morning. There were 10 in each row. Let's say, I don't remember exactly, but maybe there were 200, 300 people per group. And they would count to make sure that everybody was there. If anybody ever remained, for some reason, in the barrack, and did not show up to this counting, he was considered probably dead, because they would beat him with a rubber hose, and he probably wouldn't get out of it alive.

After the counting, the Germans would scream "*arbeitskommando formieren.*" It was one of the most terrible things to hear. You had to go to your group, to get ready to go out of the camp, to line up and leave the camp in 10 to 15 minutes, and go to your assigned work. You can imagine 17,000 or 18,000 people, lining up in different groups and marching out to work through the gates of the concentration camp in Ebensee. After they gave the order *arbeitskommando formieren*, you had to run to your group, line up, and be counted again. If they made a mistake in counting, you had to stand still, sometimes for an hour, until they finished counting. They were calculating the number who had died since the previous day.

People would walk out of the camp to do different kinds of works. Some would work in the mines or quarries. These were stone mines where they made tunnels for factories that Germany stole from the whole world. They would bring in stolen machinery.

Some would build railroads. Some would build sewer cleaning facilities. Some would clear fields of wood. Some were employed just for the sake of making us weak and eventually letting us die. Some of the work had practically no value. But the final solution was to kill us all, not to leave us alive.

For our first assignment, my brother and I had to clear a field. We had to cut down these trees, and uproot their roots. Of course, we didn't have any modern machinery. We had shovels and picks, and we had to do it all with our hands. You can imagine the blisters we had because our hands were not used to that kind of labor. I don't remember how many were in that group, maybe 30, maybe 40, and one of the inmates was in charge, with at least three or four German guards watching us—not only watching us, but also making sure that we didn't stop for one moment.

So, you can imagine, we arrived there about 6:30, 7:00, and until noon we had to work with the pick and shovel with a practically empty stomach. We were lucky in the beginning, when we first came there, we got one third of a pound of bread for dinner. The lucky ones who could control their appetites—because we were always hungry—could save a piece of bread for the morning.

The first few weeks, on Saturday night, they gave us a sort of marmalade and a little bit of cheese, which was a luxury. But after the first few weeks, that stopped. So you can imagine our menu. At the beginning, we would also get a piece of margarine, which later on also stopped.

So we had to work on practically empty stomachs. If you moved, if you moved out of the area for a one slight bit, if you tried to, they were ready to shoot you.

I recall one incident specifically. It was in the beginning. One of the German guards, I don't remember whether it was Wehrmacht or an SS guard, said to me, "Go get my bag." Now, I thought it was a joke. His bag was probably a few feet away from him. The next guard was 20 feet away from him. And I, of course, obediently, naturally went to do it, and the other German saw me and immediately took out his weapon. He aimed it at me and was ready to shoot, to kill me. I started screaming and yelling, and only God saved me from being shot at that time. These are the things that they used to do to us, playing their games.

Around 12:00, or 12:30 sometimes, they would stop us and give us a break of half an hour, maybe more. A sort of rest time. And this was supposedly the lunch, the soup. They used to give us potato peel soup or some other mush for lunch. This had to keep us until 6:00. Then we marched back, all these groups marched into the camp. The camp, of course, was surrounded by wires. The wires were also attached to electricity. If somebody would run into the wires, he would be electrified and, of course, die. So as we marched into the camp, the Germans were standing there, haughtily looking down upon us. Less than slaves, less than human beings, sub-humans. Again we gathered, we had to line up again in that *appelplatz* place, and again be counted, and everybody would be accounted for.

Normally, practically every day, several dead people were brought in. As a joke, they would shoot people and bring them in dead. Sometimes they would just hang somebody in this place between two trees as a lesson about what would happen if you tried to escape—even if the person they seized didn't try to escape! These activities were going on every day, day after day. Practically, there was no hope. There was no hope of ever surviving.

First of all, nutrition-wise, there was no hope to survive. As the Germans were losing the war, there was less and less food. In the beginning, they used to even give us a few cigarettes a week. These cigarettes fortunately became very handy because those of us who did not smoke could trade them for a little bit of soup or a little piece of bread, which came in very handy. But, later on, the cigarettes were also discontinued. So it was only with the help of God and the hope of *bitachon* (faith) that a person could survive. Really, in these circumstances, it was impossible.

After dinner time, if you had friends or relatives in the same concentration camp, it was still possible to go visit them for a short time before curfew, although sometimes it was very dangerous. Because if the block elder saw you in a barrack where you didn't belong, he would take a rubber hose and beat you to death. Sometimes even the *Stubendiensten* who were assistants there, could do the same unless they were human beings. And many of them, unfortunately, were not human beings. So in the beginning, I was together with my brother. At least we had each other and could console one another. Later on, we were separated.

Now, if you were lucky, you knew somebody who worked in the night shift. During the day, you were not supposed to be in the camp because the Germans and also some of the inmates who were the elders of the barracks would check in the barracks, check in the bathrooms, check everywhere to find if anybody was hiding, to see if anybody did not go out to work. But these night shift people came in after they yelled out *arbeitskommando formieren*. So if you ran away from your group, you could mix in with the night shift people who were just walking in on the way to their barracks. So if you knew somebody, you could lie down in the same bed with him and hide there all day long. There were sometimes about 600 people in one barrack. So even the barrack elder did not know all the people in the barrack, but you couldn't get food there.

In the colder days, when it was freezing and terrible to go out to work—people froze to death because their clothes were so thin, and they had nothing to cover themselves with—if you were able to snuggle in with anybody from the night shift, it was better. I did it several times. Not too often, because it was very dangerous. If a German found you in the camp, he would beat you to death. But you could stay out of work if you were successful.

Another method was to mix in with the *Steinbruch,* people who worked in the tunnels which had pipes that heated the infirmary. Sometimes I would hide there all day long with several people in the tunnels where these pipes were. These pipes were nice and warm. This kept us out of work, sometimes for a day. But again, it was very dangerous.

There was a third method. Sometimes you had success—it depended; it was a matter of luck. Even if you were really sick, the Germans did not care about this and thought it was no reason to stay out of work. But, sometimes, when they announced *"arbeitskommando formieren"* to form the work groups, you could come forward to what was called *block shonong*, meaning you were assigned to your block and stayed that day in your block. But it wasn't that simple.

You had to go to this infirmary where there were several doctors. And the doctor would have to approve it. Or it could happen the night before. Right after they served you soup, you'd go to the infirmary. If you were lucky enough, you found a doctor who tried to help you stay out of work—and many of them tried, though it was not really under their control, and they were scared to death. Sometimes the doctor would see a young kid like me, and he would give me a note for my block elder that read that tomorrow I didn't have to go to work, that I was legally permitted to stay in camp. But, this didn't always work.

Our lives were in constant danger from being exposed to cold and hunger, every day. Even at work, you were afraid you would be shot or killed. If you survived, you'd be beaten by the *Kapos* who stood there constantly. You could not relax for one minute, not to turn around or bend down, or anything. And you were being exposed to the cold. So your chances to survive were practically nothing.

But coming back to camp during the first separation from my brother, I got some poisonous infection in my leg. They called it *crurize dextry* (right leg infection). I still have a little sign of that on my leg. It was a terrible infection, and they assigned me to the infirmary for a few days. They put on some cream; I don't know what exactly they put on. But I was there for a few days, and, of course, to be in the infirmary was like heaven. It's not like you got any better treatment, except you could stay in bed. You were not woken up in the middle of the night for who knows how many times, just like that. For no reason whatsoever, they would wake us up to line up, and they would count us. In the infirmary, you didn't have to go out to the cold world or to labor. So for a few days I was able to be in the infirmary.

But coming out of the infirmary, I was assigned to a different barrack called the *Jugendliche* block or teenagers quarters. And I was able to be assigned to barrack duty, so this, I believe, is how I came to be separated from my brother. Unfortunately, this job didn't last very long, maybe four to six weeks.

Then I was assigned to a different kind of work. I can't remember exactly. I worked at so many different things. One time I worked at the sewer cleaning project. It smelled terrible. We had to work with shovels and picks to drain it out. One time I worked in the cement factory where we made cement molds. One time I worked with the roofer. I was assigned to a roofer in the camp itself. It was very dirty work, but it seemed to me it was a little bit easier than going out of the camp and working in the quarries and mines.

I cannot even recall all the different kinds of work I did. Sometimes I ran away from a group and, if it was possible, assigned myself to work with this roofer. He was easy on me, and I helped him. And, of course, if somebody came around in camp, I was there, and I was working, so I didn't seem to be sitting idly by, and I was accounted for. Then I was assigned to a different job and had to go out to work. One of the most terrible kinds of labor was the *Steinbruch*, which literally means breaking stones.

The Germans *yimach shmann ve zichronam* robbed all the countries they occupied. They murdered, killed, and also robbed industrial goods and industrial installations. They brought back a lot of machinery into

Austria and Germany. In the *Steinbruch*, we were supposed to build warehouses and factories in the mountains. In these mountains, we were breaking stones to build tunnels or quarries. Eventually they brought machinery, just prior to liberation. Two to three months before, they installed machinery in various kind of factories. But it took us a year or so to build these tunnels.

It was terrible, horrible work. In wintertime, the coat consisted of pajama-like material, with nothing to cover our ears and feet. We had wooden shoes and no socks. We sometimes had some *shmata,* some rags on our feet. These rags wore out, of course, and it was difficult to get these rags. So you can imagine the work was a terrible thing. You had to lift these rocks by hand and put them on wagons on a tiny railroad. We were going into these various tunnels to make them deeper and higher. We had to load these huge rocks, lift them up, and put them in these cars. And we had to push them and then dump them in certain places.

We had to work with a pick and shovel. We did it by hand. It was miserable work. It actually broke us. It broke us physically; it broke us spiritually.

If your wooden shoes were torn, you had to fix them. It was very hard to find other shoes. Sometimes you did, sometimes you didn't. One time, there was some rubber around, and a fellow found a piece of rubber. He wanted to fix his shoe and was caught. He was beaten practically to death.

In the *Steinbruch,* there were all these *Kapos* watching at us, and the Germans were watching the *Kapos*. So you can imagine that at any type of work, you constantly were an object of abuse and beatings, both physical and bodily abuse. You could not relax. The only time you could relax was supposedly during lunch time that lasted half an hour, or an hour.

We worked in the cold with only a few clothes on, and as a result, many had frostbite in their bodies and faces and feet. It was so bitterly cold, but there was a fire for some reason. Every time we could, we would sneak there for a second to warm ourselves by the fire. It's hard to describe what it meant to us to have a little bit of heat or warmth.

There was a little stove in the barrack that was heated with wood. But that never lasted. They gave each of us one or two blankets to cover ourselves When we were back, we got supper. Only black coffee, sometimes little bit of soup. At the beginning, they also gave us a piece of bread, a third of a loaf of bread, and a little piece of margarine. It wasn't much; it was the whole supper. But toward the end, that disappeared, too. We got a sixth part of a loaf of bread.

As I was saying, the cold was unbearable with only these pajama-kind of clothes. Sometimes we would get an old piece of a *shmata* to put behind our back. And when you came into camp after a day's work, if the SS or German soldiers caught you with this *shmata* under your coat, it was terrible; they would beat you practically to death. Our feet were constantly cold. All winter long.

Chapter 7

The cleanliness was terrible, of course. Once every few weeks they would take us to some shower barracks. There were showers and a kind of delousing. You had to take off all your clothes, and they gave you other clothes. The delousing included disinfectant, probably DDT. You can imagine that if anybody was caught with lice, it was a problem. Later on, before liberation, lice became very prevalent.

For the last few weeks, there was no water, no showers, nothing. We were all full of lice and full of everything, every conceivable sickness and dirt, and so on. But during the last few months in 1944 until about the end of 1944 and the beginning of 1945, things were already breaking down. Very seldom did we have a shower or anything like that because, of course, there were no showers in the barracks. In the morning, there was like a community bathroom. I don't know how many toilets there were, but in one separate barrack, they had all these toilets. And at night you couldn't go to the toilet. At night they had a big barrel near the entrance to the barracks, and we would use it for a bathroom. Then, early in the morning, there was a special group of people who were in charge of emptying these barrels. These were actually privileged people because they got some additional food for doing this job. It was terrible every day; it was a sorry sight.

We were always trembling, from in the morning when they woke us up until we went to sleep. Who knew whose turn would be next? First of all, once in a while they had selections. The weak ones were sent back to Mauthausen. Or the head of the barrack or his assistant—and some of them were sadists—they would just beat and hit you.

We were bitter about all the hard work and no food, and actually practically hopeless because all that kept us alive was *bitachon* (faith in God) that somehow, some way, God would save us. Under normal circumstances, we could not see ourselves really being saved. I mean there was no way anybody really got out alive. From beatings and hard labor and seeing everybody losing weight every day. There were also the hangings. Every day as we came back into the camp, there were one or two hangings for some reason. They pretended the inmate they hung tried to run away or whatever. So there was no way out.

We had no *luach* (Jewish calendar), but some of the people were able to figure out when was *Rosh Hashana* and *Yom Kippur* and *Sukkot*. On *Yom Kippur*, we had to go out to work. My brother *alav hasholem* took a big chance and played hooky. It was really a danger to his life to do that, because it was getting very difficult to play hooky, to run into the camp after being counted. He ran in with the night shift. At this time we still received a few cigarettes a week or a month. Cigarettes were a tremendous thing, because you could trade them for soup. We gave cigarettes to the *Kapo* so he wouldn't make us work so hard on *Yom Kippur*.

On *Pesach*, it was impossible to observe not eating *chametz* (leavened bread) but my brother *alav hasholem* tried not to eat obvious *chametz*, so he would deform it and put it in a little bit of soup, in order that it not be recognizable *chametz*.

A month or so before the end, I would say sometime in early April or so, inmates from different camps were marched into our camp. They had one pair of *tefillin* (boxes worn during prayer). How they brought them was miraculous. Earlier, one boy had been able to smuggle in a *siddur* (prayer book) that he somehow brought with him. It was so precious to us. Everybody wanted to at least touch the *siddur*, or to be able to *daven* and say a prayer just from the *siddur*. Just to see it, to hold it, actually kept us alive.

Of course, very few knew about this *siddur*. And then when a person brought in the *tefillin,* I didn't even know if I was going to be able to get to put them on. I cannot remember if I was able to put on the *tefillin,* but it had to be done with great secrecy because if the Germans or even the

Kapo or the *Blockältester* had seen it and reported it, it could have put in danger the life of the person who wore the *tefillin*.

When summertime came, we were already very hungry—after just a few months—by August or September. We were hungry from the beginning, but as time marched on, we became more and more hungry. There were some string beans, like plants around the *appelplatz*, the assembly place. They looked like string beans, though I don't think they were. I was so hungry that I would stand with my back close to it and tear off and steal some string beans. They had little seeds that were like little peas. I put in my mouth, to have something in my stomach. Of course, it was very dangerous, because if I had been caught, it would have meant a terrible beating and maybe even being shot. I'm just illustrating how hungry we were at that time.

These Germans *yimach shmann* were so brutal. They already saw that the Americans were getting close to our camp. Nevertheless, they did not relent or give us a chance even to live. We still had to go out to work every day, until the last day practically. The weeks before that time, we got Sundays off, but then they made us work on Sundays, too, either inside or outside the camp. This is how brutal, terrible, these Germans were.

No one should ever forget what the Germans did to us. Of course, today's generation doesn't know anything about it. But I would say that practically every German family had somebody in the army who knew about the brutalities committed against the Jewish people.

Toward the last few months of the war, there were air raids practically every night. There was nothing we could do. It just woke us up. Sometimes the Germans lined us up in the barrack, sometimes they took us outside. There was no protection for us whatsoever.

The people were getting sicker and weaker. There was very, very little food. Then, they brought so many inmates into our camp from different camps. As the Russians and Americans came closer to liberating us, the Germans marched in many thousands of inmates from different camps to our camp, to Ebensee.

People could hardly drag themselves to work. Nevertheless, they had to go out, because if they did not, they were beaten. They had to march. Of course, many of them fell on the side along the way. Many of them had to be dragged into camp dead. We were so weak, we couldn't move, yet we had to walk to work. The infirmary was full, but there was nothing the doctors could do. The inmate doctors had no medicine, and they had no food to give to sick people. So people just died, by tens, by hundreds, people died like flies. There was practically nothing to eat, and there was nothing anyone could do about it. The Germans didn't bring in any food. Of course, they had plenty of food for themselves, but their purpose was to kill and destroy most of us. They made us work just as hard as if life was going normally, as if they were winning the war.

My brother died practically in my arms. It was April 30, 1945. It was six days prior to the liberation of the concentration camp Ebensee. Of course, it was a terrible day. The days were getting a little bit warmer at this time of the year. It was about six days before the Americans liberated us, on May 6, I believe. According to the Jewish calendar, it was on the 17th day of *Iyar*. There were hundreds and hundreds of people, thousands, falling off their feet. They were sick. They suffered from malnutrition, of course, and from beatings, and so on.

It must have been a Sunday, because I didn't go out for work. The sun was shining, and it was getting a little bit warmer. For the last few days, I had been in the same barrack as my brother *alav hasholem*.

He was so terribly, terribly weak. We tried everything. A few weeks, before I had been able somehow to get this pair of leather shoes, which was impossible because most of the *häftlings*, as we were called, most of the inmates, had to wear wood-sole shoes. And for some reason I was able to acquire these shoes from the block elder, the *lagerältester*, who was in a good mood. I met him in the *appelplatz*, and he had ordered me to go to the warehouse to get a pair of leather shoes, and it was worth a fortune.

But, unfortunately, I made a bad deal. I tried to sell them for food, so we could both have some extra soup. But this Italian cheated us. He gave us once or twice—he had access to this so-called potato peel soup, because he worked in the convalescent barrack, and he took it away from the inmates. And we got double portions of that. He was supposed to give me seven plates of that soup, one per night. But after two times, he stopped giving us soup, but he had the shoes.

My brother was so weak. We decided we had to try and get some food that would keep us alive. We ended up in the same barrack again, somehow, and I was lying down next to him. Some days before he must have realized that, *nebech*, it was toward his end.

And, of course, I cried. And he begged me to stay strong so at least one of us would survive. We had something I tried to trade for a little bit of sugar. I hoped it would revive him. But he was getting weaker and weaker, until one day he was so weak he couldn't actually move, and so I thought maybe if I took him to the infirmary, maybe they could do something for him. In the infirmary, there were hundreds of people waiting. All weak, dehydrated, hungry, sick, Typhus, who knows what else, what other sicknesses.

I could hardly walk. I had two friends, one was Yosef Schneider who is today in Israel, and the other one was Israel Rosenberg or Haim Israel Rosenberg, who was originally Czechoslovakian and was hiding for several years, the war years, and escaped to Hungary, to Klausenburg. He was hiding in our family's homes. He was also deported to Ebensee, and they helped me carry my brother. I put him down among the other hundreds of people. I was hoping, hoping, that maybe something would happen, somebody would be able to give him some help in the infirmary. Unfortunately, I believe he died the very same day. He couldn't move. Nobody gave him any help. The doctor's hands were tied; they were the inmate doctors. Most of them were good people. There was Doctor Bennet, who was a very nice person. I believe he was from Shimlo, in Hungary, but it's in Romania today.

To me, my brother's death was a terrible shock. In some way, I had hoped that something would be done. I never saw him again after that time. In a sense, I felt guilty that I should stay alive after the horrible things that happened to my brother. I tried to keep my brother *alav hasholem* with me as long as I felt there was hope, as long as I could do anything or something, to keep him alive. But as I say, at the time we had practically no food. Very little food, next to nothing. I don't believe we had bread or even some potato soup. Very little food, very little to eat.

About two days before liberation, approximately the fourth day of May, we saw a plane flying over the camp, probably an American reconnaissance plane. Some news was smuggled into the camp, and we heard Hitler was dead. So we hoped that perhaps now, Germany would surrender. We didn't know how close the Americans were. Of course, the only thing we knew was that there were more and more air raids, so we thought they were closer, but we did not know how close exactly or if we would survive.

But this plane that flew over us seemed American to me. I guess the plane was watching what was going on and trying to get information about what was happening in the camp or whatever it was. It gave us some hope again that perhaps the Americans or Russians or British were close, that somebody would come in and save us.

On the very day of liberation, these Germans *yimach shmann* tried to erase every trace of their brutality. They assembled us in the *appleplatz* and told us that the Americans or whoever it was were very close. They said that when they come, they would kill us. And that they, these Germans, want to save us. Therefore, we should assemble and march into the *steinbruch,* into the tunnels, and we would be safe there. The Americans wouldn't come in and shoot us there. Of course, the whole thing was a pretense to march us in there and blow us up. This is exactly what they tried to do, in order to erase the traces of brutality they had committed.

But, fortunately, there were still a few inmates who were strong enough to resist. Some of the leaders of the camp, some of the *blockältester* who had eaten more food than we had, they were still strong enough to say no. Also the *blockschreib,* the secretary of the camp, a French man, and other inmates resisted and said they would not go. Of course, it was very dangerous because they could have shot us. They were so brutal. They stayed there till twelve o'clock the very day the Americans came in to liberate us.

After twelve o'clock, suddenly, we saw that the military guards were substituted with civilian guards. Or were they the military guards dressed in civilian clothes in order to blend in and run away? Or were they civilians from the town of Ebensee? Nevertheless, they were there practically until the Americans came in.

I can't describe the joy we felt when the Americans came in.

I couldn't walk. I was so weak, I had to practically drag myself on all fours to get to the assembly place that was close to the gate from which we would march every day.

When the Americans came in with their tanks and their trucks, I really cannot describe the joy, the happiness. Everybody was smiling, everyone was laughing. Even though just a few days ago my brother *alav hasholem* had passed away, on April 30, the joy was so great. We couldn't overcome the fact we were liberated! That we were saved, and no longer slaves to the Germans anymore! It was a day…I can never forget that day. I can never forget.

I did not have a recorder, of course, but I am sorry that I did not record this memoir right after the liberation.

Still, these are the highlights that I remember. I remember first seeing an American soldier. They were trying to be understanding. They were shocked themselves. They couldn't realize what was happening. They looked at us, and we were as skinny as sticks. They gave some of us chocolate and candy and chewing gum. They just didn't know what to do.

The first day after liberation was a day of pandemonium, if you like to call it that. We just didn't realize we were actually free, that we did not have to go work, that we were not subjected anymore to killings and murdering and hangings and beatings and hunger.

However, after the Americans came in, on the day after liberation, they started the next day destroying some of the barracks. The barracks and the people were all full of lice and sicknesses. Typhus had broken out. Then the public kitchen began cooking a very rich meal with meat and other things, which our stomachs were unfortunately not used to. As a result many people who had suffered from dysentery, diarrhea, and many sicknesses could not stand the test of this rich meal. As a result, many hundreds died, just because of the contrast of the foods that we had before compared to this meal. There were those of us who survived after the first few days, even though we were so hungry, and our stomachs were shrunk. We could hardly crawl, really, literally, we could hardly crawl, but yet we wanted to enjoy these days of freedom.

Hundreds, perhaps thousands, of us walked out into the town of Ebensee and other towns close by. We started begging at the doors of these Austrians. Many, of course, would lock the door and not give us anything. Of course, many of these Austrians knew of our plight. They saw us marching out every day to work. They called us *Musselman.*

[This term was the German version of Musulman, meaning Muslim. This was a slang term the captives of World War II Nazi concentration camps used to refer to those suffering from a combination of starvation and exhaustion, those who were resigned to their impending death. The Musulman prisoners exhibited severe emaciation and physical weakness, as well as an apathetic listlessness about their own fate. They were unresponsive to their surroundings due to the barbaric treatment they suffered from the Nazis and the prison functionaries. Some scholars argue that the term possibly came from the Musulman's inability to stand for any length of time due to the loss of leg muscle. So they spent much of their time in a prone position, recalling the position of the Musulman during prayers.]

Many of the Austrians, of course, locked their doors. Some opened their door, and gave us some food. It took us hours and hours to literally crawl on all fours and to *shnorr,* to beg for this food.

The *Kapos* were the inmates who were also in charge of the other inmates. They were sometimes very, very brutal. There also were a number of gypsies who were horrible to us. Very few of the Jews were *Kapos* in our camp to my recollection. They weren't at the beginning, anyway, but toward the end possibly. Some of these *Kapos* who were caught were actually killed by the inmates who caught them. They caught these *Kapos,* and some beat some of them to death; some were just beaten.

During the next few days, the Americans brought in some of the

German and Austrian Nazis, or former Nazis. They were brought up to view us, to see what they did to us. The Americans made them clean the camp, clean the barracks and the big assembly yard. But it was a very little punishment. Unfortunately, there was nothing we could do; we were not permitted to touch these Nazis *yimach shmann.*

We just could not get over our liberty and freedom. After a year being subjugated in this camp, and not knowing anything different than life in camp, we didn't know how to celebrate and enjoy this freedom. It was pandemonium.

In the next few days, the Americans and the Red Cross set up a field hospital. It was amazing to us to see how fast they did it. In the empty spaces in the camp, they actually uprooted trees with their bulldozers and set up a field hospital. They put many hundreds and thousands of us in this hospital. They set up beds and stoves and so on in these tents. And doctors came in and started to try to cure us of our illnesses. Even before that, they started delousing us. They sprayed us with DDT and some other chemicals. I cannot recall the names of the chemicals they used to delouse us and shower us to clean us up. They gave us some clothes to change into because our own clothes were infected with disease and lice, and who knows what else.

I, too, was taken into this field hospital because I was very weak and could hardly move. I suffered from diseases that I cannot recall. This lasted until they nursed us back to health. We were in this tent, the field hospital, for about two or three weeks. Then they put us in some of the old barracks. We stayed in Ebensee for a while. But many of us were anxious to go home, hoping, hoping with some hopeless hope, that we would find some of our families alive.

So, one day, I believe it must have been sometime in June, but I cannot recall the day exactly, we went to the railroad station. Several hundred people. Some of my relatives were there, my cousins, the Kahanas from Bistritz. We started heading back to Romania. The trains were incredible, crowded with thousands of people going back home. Some were Romanians and Hungarians who had been recruited to work for the Germans in

Identification card after liberation from Ebensee—Ebensee was considered a subcamp of the Mauthausen Concentration Camp.

Austria. Many of the inmates, survivors from the camps around Ebensee and Mauthausen, like Gunskirchen and other camps, were also heading back to Romania.

It took us days and nights. Many people were riding on top of the trains, that's how crowded the trains were. We made various stops, but I can't recall where we got food for this trip. I really can't recall who fed us. And so we went back to Romania. It took several days. I remember that we stopped in Budapest where there was already a Jewish committee that had acquired a hospital or a hotel or something. Of course, the accommodations were not hotel accommodations.

Since thousands of people were returning after being inmates in the concentration camps, they were prepared to provide us lodging in a hospital or whatever it was. We slept on the floor. They gave us food. The city itself already had a functioning Jewish community. Let's not forget that 150,000 Jews were saved in Budapest during the war. But some Budapest Jews were shot and thrown into the Danube river, including my mother's first cousin, with the last name of Kahan, who lived in Budapest for many years. Unfortunately, they suffered a lot, but many were saved from being shipped to concentration camps.

Raoul Wallenberg, a Swedish diplomat, saved many of them. He had all kinds of tricks. He got false papers and arranged for different consulates to issue citizenship papers or transit papers to many of these Jews, so they were able to be saved.

[*Raoul Gustaf Wallenberg, born 4 August 1912, disappeared 17 January 1945, was a Swedish architect, businessman, diplomat, and humanitarian, remembered for saving tens of thousands of Jews in Nazi-occupied Hungary during the Holocaust, rescuing them from German Nazis and Hungarian Fascists during the later stages of World War II. While serving as Sweden's special envoy in Budapest between July and December 1944, Wallenberg issued protective passports and sheltered Jews in buildings designated as Swedish diplomatic territory. On 17 January 1945, during the Siege of Budapest by the Red Army, Wallenberg was detained by SMERSH, the Russian Army's Intelligence Service, on suspicion of espionage. He subsequently disappeared. He was later reported to have died on 17 July 1947 while imprisoned by the KGB secret police in the Lubyanka, the KGB headquarters and affiliated prison in Moscow. The motives behind the Soviet government's arrest and imprisonment of Wallenberg remain mysterious and are the subject of continued speculation, along with questions surrounding the circumstances of his death and his ties to US intelligence.*]

I was traveling with my cousins Hezki and Mendi Kahana, twin brothers from Bistritz. Their father's name was Btzalel Kahan, and he was my mother's first cousin. We were together in the concentration camp. Hezki Kahan got very sick. He was already sick in Ebensee, but it got worse in Budapest. So his brother Mendi said he was going to see if he could find out whether his uncle and aunt were alive in Budapest. So he went to town. He asked me to watch his brother while he was gone. That I did, but, unfortunately, his brother was so sick that, *nebech* (unfortunately) he died even before Mendi came back. This Hezki was a very bright fellow. He once wrote a poem to the King of Romania who ruled in the late 1930s. He sent it to the King and received a letter back. It was a great thing in those times. And, *nebech*, he died in Budapest.

I left Mendi in Budapest. After several days I went to Romania. It was very interesting to see the feelings of Jewish people in those days. There was such a good feeling and brotherly love. It's difficult to describe, but there was *achdus* (unity) among the Jews. At every station where we stopped while crossing the border to Romania and Hungary, refugees from the camps came to the trains. The trains were not going very often, and there was practically no schedule. They came out to the trains to see if there were returnees from concentration camps. They met us with milk and bread and whatever food they had to spare. That's how Jews felt toward one another in those days. Unfortunately, today they are so fragmented. I wish we had this feeling of unity today that we had in those days of the post-concentration camp era.

So, after several days again, first we stopped in Grosswardein and Oradia near the Hungarian border, which was already in Romania. Then we made our way to Cluj, Klausenburg.

In Klausenburg. I got off the train with a number of other people. I believe the train continued all the way to Bistritz. In Cluj, I decided to get off, since my mother's family lived there. I hoped I would find some relatives. We arrived early in the morning, and I proceeded to the *shul*. There were several *shuls* already open because Klausenburg had been liberated sometime in January or February 1945, and this was already the end of June.

In the *shul*, I asked if anybody from the Kahana family came back. I was told that my cousin Eddie, who was known as Hezki Kahana, was alive and had returned. Eddie had been in a labor camp under the Hungarians and Romanians, but it was liberated earlier, sometime in January or February or March. He had already settled down and lived in the center of the city in a nice house. One of his roommates, also named Hezki

Kahana, survived with his wife in Romania, in Bucharest, and then moved to Klausenburg. Another roommate of theirs went by the first name of Kalman, and he was a lawyer.

I came to the house that morning. I met my second or third cousin Hezki Kahana, who later on, incidentally, made *aliyah* to Israel. He was married to Elsa Davidovich, that was her maiden name. He was a tailor, a very *frum,* very fine person. He had several sons. I knew them from the pre-war era when they used to come visit my grandparents' house in Klausenburg. Elsa's father and brothers used to *daven* (pray) at our grandfather's *beit hamidrash* (study hall).

But the post war era was such a confusing time. The people's attitude was something like less *din* and *dayan* (religious Jewish practices). Many who had been religious became non-religious. It was like a free-for-all. Even those who were religious did not practice as they had in the pre-war era. People who once had beards did not have beards anymore. The attitude was confusing. People were confused, also, as a result of having been in labor camps and concentration camps. There, people could not observe the *halachas* and *dinim* (Jewish laws). Many people went away from it completely. Some strayed just partially from it. Many significantly dropped their religious practice. In a concentration camp, you could not keep *kashrut* (kosher).

So when I came into their house, they told me that Eddie had gone to Budapest or Vienna. He did business with the Russians, but so did many people. Somehow he had rented a truck and transported flour, or some other things, to Budapest or Vienna. It was the black market. Naturally, in order to survive, we all had to deal in the black market. And he had quite a business in the black market. So he was not home. I spent a short time in Eddie's house in Klausenburg, with his roommates.

Then I proceeded to Borgo. I took a train. I cannot remember how long it took us to get to Bistritz. It's about 125 to 130 kilometers from Klausenburg to Bistritz, 75 miles or so. In Bistritz, I met some people who were from Borgo, who then lived in Bistritz. There was no train going to Borgo. For some reason, it had stopped running. It was the post war era.

I stayed another day or two in Bistritz, looking for some other relatives, whom unfortunately I did not find. They did not return, *nebech*. They were killed.

I proceeded to Borgo. I remember somebody driving me on a horse and wagon. I went to see my house. I don't believe anybody lived in the house. The doors had been torn off. I met this family who were friends of ours, the Joseph family. One of them lives in New Jersey now. He was one of my best friends from *cheder*. [*I recently saw some of the brothers in Israel.*] I stayed with them. It was also a free-for-all in Borgo, with the attitude of less *din* and less *dayan*. The *shul* was not functioning, although a few Jewish families had returned. *Minyan* (a prayer group of at least 10 men) was not held and, unfortunately, there was very little practice of religion. It was strange, but sadly this was the result of concentration camps and labor camps. The Joseph family was nice to me. Their father had also returned. It was miraculous that he returned from concentration camp.

There was also the Bidermann family who took over my grand uncle's (Eddie's grandfather) house and store. They opened a general store there. They moved to Borgo from one of the little towns nearby. There were some other families, but most people were unfortunately single. Even those who survived were alone. Their wives were killed. Their husbands were killed. There were not too many people. I believe someone from the Shashtein family and Birenberd family survived and were also there, but very few survived.

A week or two after I came to Borgo, Eddie found out I was there and came running. He brought his friend Kalman, who was a lawyer. We tried to see what we could sell from the past business that we had in lumber. But, like I said, some of the lumber was donated to the ghetto so we could build something there, to keep people from sleeping in the open field. We tried to see what we could salvage and save. First of all, we dug up the papers we had buried prior to going to the ghetto. We had buried some in our backyard, some jewelry and papers, because we didn't know what was going to happen. So we dug it up, and I found a list that I incidentally have now in my house. The list had all the money we had paid in advance to lumber farmers who were supposed to deliver lumber to us once they had cut the trees. Most of it was never delivered because the Germans took us to the concentration camp, and it was not easy to collect.

But a man who operated one of the biggest lumber mills owed us a lot of money, and we had left him some of our cut lumber that was not taken to the ghetto. According to the contract he had signed, he was supposed to deliver 100 cubic meters of lumber to us. That was worth a lot of money. But, of course, we never collected the money because we left, and also because the Romanian government confiscated a lot of this lumber, and so on.

I believe I stayed in Borgo for several weeks, because I remember Eddie staying there for a while. There was really nothing to do in Borgo. We went to Bistritz to meet with some friends. There was really nothing to do there, either. All Borgo had changed. Some of the Jewish people who came back brought in electricity. And, of course, the way it was done, it was very dangerous. In some of the homes, wires were exposed, and so on. There was change, but there was no future really in staying in Borgo. So I returned to Cluj, Klausenberg, where I lived with Eddie for several months.

Kalman, the lawyer Eddie lived with, lived in a very nice house comparatively speaking. The house used to belong to a former Borgo person, Kanyoll. He was alive, but he stayed in Germany. So Eddie acquired that house. This Kalman may have belonged to the Communist Party. He came from a very religious family, but I don't think he himself was religious at all. He had a friend, a business partner, Skiribotzky, who was not Jewish. He used to stick around in the house all the time.

When I came there, Eddie had some Russian friends who were squatters in the house, some generals, and Polkovniki's (colonels). One colonel, Yossel, lived in the house. He spoke beautiful Russian Yiddish. We had another squatter there, another Russian, a lieutenant or a captain. He was a non-Jew. He was staying there. Of course, the Russians just imposed on us. We had no alternative but to let them stay.

I tried to do a little bit of business with the Russians. When the Russians came to Germany, they grabbed everything they could grab.

Rightfully so, they had it coming after all the suffering they had because of the Germans. They were entitled to something. So they grabbed watches and leather goods, coats and boots. Whatever they could lay their hands on, they took. Sometimes you would see a Russian with several watches on his arm. The Russians would sell things, trade them, keep them or take them back to Russia. They were the big shots, and they used to sell the goods.

I used to do business with the captain, and buy little things here and there from him. One time he had a very nice pair of leather boots. I agreed on a price with him, the amount of money I would pay him. I don't remember, approximately 42,000 Romanian leu, I cannot recall exactly. Later that night, he came back after I sold the boots, and he was drunk. (Many of these Russians were often drunk.) He said: "*Davai dengi!*" Meaning, give me my money. So I gave him 42,000 leu, which we had agreed on. And he said, "That's not enough." So he takes out his revolver, and he was really ready to kill me *chalilla* (heaven forbid). And he aimed it at me. Just at this second, Eddie came in, and stood between me and the Russian. I wouldn't have been surprised if the Russian had killed me. Because in those days there was less *din* and less *dayan*. There was no law. The Russians could do anything they wanted. These men used to shoot each other, to kill each other. Many times in the morning, you would see drunk Russians on the ground, killed. Anyway I gave him as much money as he wanted. This was one of my experiences with the black market during those days.

To survive at that time in Romania, everybody had to do some black market trading. There was little food. There was a shortage of everything after the war. Eddie would sometimes buy a truck full of flour and deliver it to Budapest, in Hungary, or to other parts of Romania. He also reopened his uncle's herring factory at that time. He had a number of girls working there, preparing herring, which was a pretty good business. He also dealt with a number of other things. He had many connections and was always very well dressed. He had a leather coat and leather boots. As a *matter* of fact, he supported me at that time.

Cousin Eddie with his sister Helen when she visited him in the late 1940's in Europe—Eddie was Zeidy's first cousin, but they were more like brothers. He survived the war in a Hungarian Labor Camp. Eddie, who was 13 years older than Zeidy, "adopted" him in Cluj after the war, giving him a place to stay, clothes, and money. He also saved his life from the drunk Russian captain.

I only had a few hundred leu, very little money. When I went to Borgo Prund, I found a few things that we had hidden with the *goyim* (non-Jews). Some bedding and coats and a suit. I sold some of these things to my second cousin in Bistritz, the one who is in Vienna today. (He did not give us a good reception when we visited Austria recently).

So I had a little bit of money, but, of course, it wouldn't go very far. My schedule was that every day, there was really not much to do. There was no place to learn. I would go to *daven* at *shul,* a big *shul* affiliated with Agudath Israel. I had some friends from the pre-war period who would daven there, and I went there on *Shabbes.*

Every day I would go and eat at the cafeteria which was organized by the Joint [the Joint Distribution Committee, a Jewish charity, which still takes care of Jews in need throughout the world]. There was a free lunch, or a lunch for a very small amount of money. It was quite a distance from where we lived. I would take a bicycle and ride it to this cafeteria.

So weeks passed by, and there was really very little to do in Cluj. There was no *tachless* (purpose), and no hope, nothing, because of the Communists and the Russians. I did some business on the black market. Sometimes I ran errands for Eddie.

There was this other general who came from Ukraine. He was a very nice fellow with a beautiful voice. He spoke beautiful Yiddish. He was the head of the Themata shoe factory. He tried to do a little bit of business with Eddie, but Eddie didn't get too many favors from him. Just the idea that we had these Jewish Russians for protection made us feel a little bit more secure. But there was really nothing for me to do in Cluj.

In 1945, the debate came up at the United Nations about the partition of Israel. It was around August or the beginning of September, 1945. We had a big radio, so we were listening to the news. Eddie said that it looked like, eventually, there would be a Jewish state. This was before the United Nations ordered the partition of Palestine. But our hope was up, and we were glad. Even though Klausenburg and Romania were so far from Israel, from Palestine, it was nice to hear that hopefully, someday, there would be an Israel. There would be a Jewish state.

I didn't want to stay in Klausenburg for the *yomim tovim* (High Holidays). And I had this cousin Moyshe Ruttner *alav hasholem*, who was a very fine man. He had come back from the labor camp, and he settled in Margareten, where he had lived before he was taken to the camp. This Margareten (Marghita, Romania) was a Jewish town, and some of the people returned, though not too many, unfortunately, maybe five percent, maybe ten percent. Some people who lived in the nearby small villages also moved into the town.

So I decided to go for the *yomim tovim, Rosh Hashana, Yom Kippur* and *Succoth*, to Margareten. I do have one picture from that trip where

I had a hat and a briefcase and Eddie's topcoat. Before I went to Marga-reten, I visited another cousin, Mendel Ruttner *alav hasholem.* He made *aliyah* to Israel later on. *Nebech,* he died of heart failure. He was a very fine man. Occasionally he used to come to Klausenburg for shopping trips. He reopened the store he had prior to the concentration camp. He was very fortunate because his wife, Chaya, was still alive. She lives, I believe, in Williamsburg today. And Mendel died quite a few years ago, maybe 15 or 20 years ago, maybe longer. We visited him once on our first trip to Israel, I think. He had one daughter who lives in Borough Park. She is married to a man named Paneth.

Mendel reestablished his business, and he came back to his own house. Occasionally he would come to Klausenburg to purchase textiles and various other things that he sold in his store. He would come to the wholesalers and purchase from them. I saw him in Klausenburg at least once. So I decided I would stop by his house on my way to Margareten. They were very nice. They gave me a *tallis koton* (a small tallis which had fringes, or *tzitzit*), which I didn't have, and which you couldn't buy any-where. I spent several days there. In that city, there was also this family, Heimlich, with two boys who were in concentration camp with me. I looked them up.

After several days there, I took a train or a bus to Margareten. Moyshe was already established there. He was the *Rav,* the *shochet* and the *chazan* of the city for the few people who were there. Devorah, his sister who's now married to Lippa Margolis (the head of Yeshiva Torah Temima in Brooklyn), lived with him. She also came home. But their parents were killed during the war.

So she lived with Moyshe and cooked for him, and so on. They had a very nice *shul* in Margareten. Moyshe lived in a courtyard where there were one or two other houses. There was a young fellow about my age. His name was Weinberg, and his grandfather or uncle was the previous rabbi of a *shul* in Margareten. A week or two before *Rosh Hashana,* we went to their vineyard, for they had a wine business. We went there to pick grapes for *yom tov* (the holidays) and also to make wine for *yom tov.* They had a horse and wagon, and we drove—I can't recall how many miles, maybe 10 to 15 miles. It was a whole day's trip, and we brought grapes for *yom tov,* for *Rosh Hashana,* and I guess someone was making the wine.

This young man Weinberg played nasty tricks. One time, he put a raw egg in my nice suit and then broke the egg in my pocket. You can imagine the aggravation I had. I was quite angry about these jokes. I don't know how I cleaned the jacket. I can't recall, but it was not a very pleasant experience.

But I had a good time being in this atmosphere with Moyshe, a religious atmosphere for *Rosh Hashana, Yom Kippur* and *Succoth.* I was there for four weeks, I believe. After the *yamim tovim,* I returned to Klausenburg. In Margareten, I had a spiritual uplift because Moyshe *alav hasholem* was *davening,* and he had a beautiful voice, a *hazanishe* (like a cantor) voice. I also met some other people who came for *yom tov.* All in all, after not having my parents, my brothers and sister *aleihem hasholem* for *yomim tovim,* this was a reminder of home.

There was no home atmosphere at Eddie's. At Eddie's, we couldn't cook. We had to go eat lunch in this *kosher* restaurant every day, and for supper and breakfast we had to buy stuff and improvise. The whole atmosphere was not exactly homey. But at Moyshe's home and at his brother Mendel's, there was more of a home atmosphere. Also having a woman around was an uplift after the terrible experience I had in the concentration camps.

So I returned to Klausenburg and had to go through the same routine. There was not much to do. Fall was coming. By October, it was getting cooler, and we were going into November. Eddie had somebody who came to cut wood because his heating system was not central heating. It was made up of stoves, very nice stoves, but it wasn't a central system. This house was very nice by European or Romanian standards. There was a regular bathtub, and they were able to heat the water for the bathtub. That was the luxury compared to Borgo, where we had no such facilities. There were also indoor toilets, which again was a luxury compared to Borgo.

But despite all these things, I had no future staying in Klausenberg, even though there was some sort of *kehila* (community). The Sephardic *shul* had reopened. It used to be under the leadership of the Klausenberger Rebbe, Rav. Halberstam, who is now in Netanya. But he was not there when I was in Klausenburg. Some other *shuls*, one or two, opened up. I used to daven in the Agudah minyan. But there was no *tachless* (purpose); there was no future.

So one day Eddie decided that he would go to Grosswardein to buy some fish for making the herring. We had some clothes made from suits that we found in Borgo. This included some of our clothes and some clothes that once belonged to Eddie's uncle. We gave them to a tailor. They used to take clothes from Europe and turn them inside out and make a smaller suit from a larger one. With the material turned inside out, it looked practically new. The materials were expensive, but the labor was cheap. So we had some black and gray suits made for my size. We had heavy overcoats. I think Eddie bought my coat for me secondhand. It was a very nice coat.

We rented a truck, and he drove to Grosswardein. And he gave me 2,000 leu. That was not very much, but it was enough to hold me over for emergencies. Incidentally, when I was in Klausenburg, most of my money came from him. In Grosswardein, I went that day to the *Vizhnitzer Kloise* (house)—it was like a *shul*, like a *beit hamidrash* (study hall). It was a very nice building. I don't think it was finished before they took us to concentration camp. I saw the *Vizhnitzer Rebbe,* Rav Chaim Meir, who had a small yeshiva there. The previous *Vizhnitzer Rebbe* had passed away a few years earlier.

And for some reason, I don't know why, I didn't kiss the Rebbe's hand. It was customary among the *Hasidim* to kiss the Rebbe's hand but for some reason I didn't. Maybe I didn't remember or something. I just gave a *sholem aleychem* (peace to you) to the Rebbe. There weren't too many people in the *beit hamidrash* that day, but I don't know whether the Rebbe was happy with this. I was thinking the Rebbe did not give me exactly the right kind of look after I gave him a *sholem aleychem,* but didn't kiss his hand.

Eddie told me he had some distant cousins in Grosswardein, and they could change some Romanian money to Hungarian money because I was about to cross the border which was 20 to 30 miles away from Grosswardein. I went to the small border town. I don't remember how I got there, by train or by bus. There was a small store and a small Jewish community of people who had returned from concentration camp or from work camp. I recall that night I slept on straw because they didn't have any beds. So I slept on straw. I don't know if there was a blanket on it or not. I asked there how I could cross the border.

When I went to the border, I had this money from Eddie that I traded for Hungarian money. I put it in my pants, and I pushed my pants into my socks, and this is where I put my money. When I came to the border, there were Russian and Romanian guards. Because I wanted to cross the border, I tried to change my identity card that I had received when I returned from Ebensee, from concentration camp. After concentration camp, they gave us identity cards. But I tried to change that identity card to one that said that I was born in Germany and not in Romania. But, of course, it was very stupid of me. Anybody could have seen that I erased it because I didn't do a very good job.

First of all, I paid some money to a Russian military trucker to drive me across the border. Of course, he was very gracious, and he took the money. When we came to the border, I thought the Russian would protect me and take me over the border. But the guards stopped me. They didn't care. They had a good laugh. And they took me out of the truck and made me go back to the side of the border from where I came.

In the meantime, I tried to cross. There was a sort of a ditch. I tried to cross the border again, to cross the ditch. In the meantime, my money fell out. I was scared to death, but nobody saw the money. I was a young kid, only 15 years old. Nobody saw it. So I pushed it back into my pants. And this Russian guard said, you have to go back right now or I'm going to shoot. So I had no choice, and went back to the small border town, and I stayed there overnight.

In the meantime, there was a young fellow in this Romanian town. He was about my age, maybe two or three years older. He had come there from Hungary the day before. He used to live with some relatives on the Hungarian side a few miles from the border in a town with a name I cannot recall. He had smuggled some stuff from Hungary to Romania in order to sell it. The Romanian guards caught him and took a good portion of his stuff. I don't know if he had textiles or what. The guards took it away from him and sent him to the Romanian side. So he came to the Romanian side and stayed there overnight, too. He told me he'd be glad to take me along with him, to smuggle both of us to the Hungarian side of the border. So the next day, I packed a knapsack, with some shirts, a watch, and a few other things.

When we were just in front of the border, all of a sudden we heard the words: "Halt! Stop!" in Romanian. So we got scared that these were Romanian soldiers pointing rifles at us.

The young fellow explained we were going to Hungary, that he had been born in Germany. They must have been the same guards who had been there yesterday, because they didn't bother him. He knew they were the ones who took his stuff, so they were satisfied. I started crying, saying I was an orphan. I pleaded, "Please let me cross." I figured, in Romania, unless you pay, you don't accomplish anything. So they took my watch from me. In those days, a watch was a very big deal. I gave them my watch and a few other things. And finally they let us cross the border. We arrived at a little village which had a few Jewish families. There was a big house. They were very nice people, wonderful people. Their *mitzvah* (good deed) of *hachnasat orchim* (welcoming guests) was indescribable because I stayed with these people for a while.

Chapter 8

In this village, there were probably eight to ten Jewish families. The owner of the house was named Matias. He was married to a nice woman. Young people. I was a guest in their home, and he also had his cousin who smuggled me across the border. He was an orphan. Also, there was a girl, 17 to 18 years old, who was also an orphan. And they took us into their home and gave us clothes, *bekavod gadol* (with great honor). I really just can't describe how wonderful these people were.

Matias also had a store, a general store. He would go there every day. He and his wife also had some chickens and geese. He might have received some money from the Joint to help poor people who came home and had nothing, but I am not certain of that. I will always be thankful and grateful to these people for opening up their home to me though I was a complete stranger. I had nobody in this village, unfortunately, and yet they were extremely nice to me and to the other people.

While I was in the village, there was a Jewish wedding. Of course, everybody was invited. There weren't too many Jews, but they had a *minyan.* They brought in a *rav* from Debrecen, the closest city with a Jewish community, to be *Mesader Kiddushin* (perform the marriage). I recall they had a gypsy band for music and dancing. It was customary in many places in Europe, in Romania and Hungary, anyway, that a gypsy band would play music at a wedding. In Poland, they had Jewish bands, but in our area, in Borgo, there was no Jewish band. So, when there was a wedding you had gypsies, and they played all kinds of music. It was a very happy occasion. After all the sorrow, it was a wonderful experience to see a wedding.

On *Shabbes* (Sabbath) we would walk. The weather was already nasty. It was the beginning of November. It was getting cold and rainy. There was mud, and the streets were not paved. So, we spent most of our time at the house, with a little bit of time walking on *Shabbes* afternoon. I don't recall if there was a *minyan* in this community.

I spent about three to four weeks with these people, and then one day Matias decided to go to Budapest. I can't recall if it was for business purposes, but he had relatives there. They were big *machers* (influential people) in the Communist Party. So, I told him that I would go with him, because my destination was to go to Germany. From there I would decide whether to go to Palestine or to America. It was not very clear in my mind yet.

And so, we travelled to Budapest. Traveling was not easy; trains were not dependable. Budapest was 200 miles away, and it was considered a tremendous journey, like going to the moon. Trains had no regular schedules. They would stop at cities for hours to get coal for the steam engines. So, first we went to Debrecen, the closest city. We got off there. I don't remember, but I think we waited there a day or two and walked around before there was a train to Budapest.

The trains were crowded with peasants, with their baskets of chickens and vegetables and all kinds of things. It took a very long time to get to Budapest. We finally arrived at Budapest on a Friday morning. It was already quite cool there.

I went with Matias to his relative; as mentioned, he was a very big official in the Communist Party. They had a home like a huge villa, a huge house with beautiful floors. But these people were not religious at all. Matias was a religious person, an orthodox person. His cousins used to be religious, too, but after the war I guess they shunned their religion. I saw that this was not a place for me to be for *Shabbes*. I didn't know what to do, so I decided, well, I'll go to the Jewish area.

Budapest had a large Jewish community at the time. There was great poverty. People had practically nothing to eat, but the Joint Distribution Committee supported many organizations and many people. People had to work for a living, but the Communist regime did not impose itself fully on them. However, the big *machers* in the Communist Party were Jews.

In the Jewish area, I found out that there was an Agudah [*This was an organization for very religious Jews, and it is now active as a political party in the Israeli Knesseth*]. I went to the Agudah office and said I had just come from Romania and needed a place for *Shabbes*. I asked if they could help me. So, they asked me: Are you a member of the Agudah? I told them that, presently, I was not a member of anything. The only thing I was asking was if I could stay somewhere for *Shabbes*. Can you accommodate me? Put me up somewhere? Any way they were very cold to me. I was very shocked. I was shocked that they did not really assist me.

They had already organized a *kosher* kitchen—not exactly a restaurant but somewhere refugees who came to Hungary back from Romania, or refugees in Hungary, could have something to eat. I found a place that I rented. It wasn't actually a room—it was a bed. Unfortunately, these people were very poor, but they were Jewish people, religious people. They were so poor, *nebech,* they didn't have any linen to cover the bed, but it had a fluffy cover called a *dachane* in Yiddish.

I can't recall if I had to share the bed with somebody. But at any rate, it wasn't the Ritz. Yet I paid them and stayed there for Friday night and *Shabbes*. On Friday night, I just walked into the so-called Agudah restaurant and sat down and ate with the others. And I did the same thing on *Shabbes* morning.

Sunday morning, I met some people who had the same experience that I had, who did not receive any help from the Agudah. This fellow had heard that there was something like a *hachshara* (training group), associated with a Zionist organization and located just outside of Budapest, in the suburb of Rákospalota. We took a train to this place. It was a home with a number of people living in it. All kinds—some were very religious; some were not religious. They were supported by the Joint Distribution Committee. They also had an office in Budapest itself. We went there first, but they advised us to go to Rákospalota.

There they had lectures on Zionism and Jewish history. Many of these people were previously very religious. Many of them were from the Munk-atch area of Czechoslovakia. We would hear a number of Zionist lectures that young people visiting from Budapest would attend.

Once a week, we had to go to Budapest itself, which was probably about five or six kilometers away. It was already cold and snowing. It was the beginning of December or the end of November. We took a horse and wagon, since no truck was available at the time. We would bring back food for the rest of the week. We would go to this big warehouse that was supplied by the American Joint. We brought back all kinds of foods. Flour, bread—bread was baked in this place in Rákospalota—and all kinds of foods including butter, cream cheese, and meats. Whatever was there. That sustained us for the whole week. Next week, we had to do it again.

Now these people were, of course, very poor; nobody had an overcoat. I had mine from Romania, and I lent it to whoever went to the city. In a way I was glad that I was able to do something for them. That's how the situation was.

Some of the young people who lived in this *hachshara* had parents in Budapest. I recall these brothers whose mother lived in Budapest. *Nebech*, she was so poor that she had to work on *Shabbes*. At the time, you couldn't avoid it. She tried not to work on *Shabbes* whenever she could avoid it. One time they took me to their mother's apartment, a little room, and explained to me that she did not cook on *Shabbes*. She cooked on Friday, trying to do with the little bit of food that she had so that she wouldn't have to cook on *Shabbes*. Still, she had to go to work on *Shabbes*. She had no alternative.

In Budapest, we would also go to the baths. There was a subway that went directly to these hot baths. I don't know if we had a bath in this *hachshara*, so we would go there to take a bath. They also had pools and a mineral bath. It was quite a treat for us to have a nice hot bath in the cold wintertime. The *hachshara* itself was not exactly comfortable, but it was a roof over our heads. We were hungry quite a bit because the food was insufficient. We had only what we got from the Joint.

The *hachshara* was a free for all, with all kinds of people, religious and non-religious. It was a place to wait before possibly going to Israel, which was Palestine at the time. The main idea was to prepare to go to Israel, so we had the lectures I mentioned on the history of the Jewish people and on Zionism. They tried to indoctrinate us with Zionism. There was nothing wrong with that. There wasn't much to do during the day. I can't recall if we did any special work outside, or not.

It was such a conglomeration of all kinds of people. There was one girl, her name was Pircha. She was also a guest, maybe an orphan, a young girl from Budapest proper. There was a couple who were going to get married. I understood that eventually they got married in Palestine.

The accommodations were not the best, but we had a place to wait until we were able to go to Vienna, and from Vienna to Germany, or to Italy, and then to Palestine. I would say most of these people ended up in Palestine. Some had been hidden in Budapest during the war. Some were returnees from concentration camps.

For our religious concerns, there was one pair of *tefillin* (boxes holding scripture worn while praying) because they were very difficult to get. The religious environment was not exactly what I desired, but I had no *brera* (choice), I figured. Until we got out of there, we had nowhere else to go, so I had to stay. Of course, I had no money.

I could hardly wait to leave. My final destination at the time was Feldafing, the DP camp, Displaced Persons camp in Germany where my cousin Yecheskal Ruttner *alav hasholem* was the chief rabbi. His brother Bezalel was there, too, and lived with him.

After being at the *hachshara* four weeks or so, the time came to move on, and we went to Vienna. In 1945, Hungary was a Communist country. Not only was the Russian presence strongly felt there, but Russia gave the commands. There were a lot of Jewish officials in the Communist Party at the time, yet it was difficult to go to Vienna, because Vienna was controlled by the four powers, France, the United States, England, and Russia. You needed special papers to leave Hungary and go to Austria.

A special, underground organized effort, the *Bricha* ("escape" or "flight"), helped survivors get out of Europe after the war. [*This organization, also called the Bericha Movement, helped people go to the* British Mandate for Palestine *in violation of the* White Paper of 1939, and it *ended when Israel declared independence and annulled the White Paper.*] The *Bricha* was an Israeli organization, though there was no Israel yet. It was a pre-Israel group, part of the *Haganah,* the military arm of the Zionist movement. The *Bricha* made it possible for Jews to escape from many countries, such as Czechoslovakia, Romania, and Hungary. It was partially supported by the American occupying forces in Austria. This system made it possible for us to escape from the Russian zone, from the Russian-controlled territory of Hungary into Vienna.

One day a whole group of us, including Jews from other groups, got the order to meet in the railroad station, where they had a car for us, a freight car—or several freight cars—for us to go to Vienna. The *Bricha* supplied us with false papers for the whole group. We were also accompanied in this railroad car by American or British soldiers. In other words, our new papers said that we were originally from either Germany or Austria, and we had been held captive by the Germans, who brought us to eastern Europe, and now we were returning to either Germany or Austria.

They put us on this train, and for many hours we travelled to Vienna. In Vienna, there were many refugees. Jewish groups came from Czechoslovakia, which is very close to Vienna. There were also people from Romania and Hungary. They set us up in the Rothschild hospital, though it was not functioning as a hospital. It was built by the Rothschilds prior to the Second World War. It was our headquarters for several days.

In this hospital, I met somebody who had gone back to Romania from Germany. He had lived in this Feldafing DP camp in Bavaria after the war. I told him I would like to go there to see my cousin, Yecheskal Ruttner, the Shomkuter Rav. He told me that, yes, he still was the chief rabbi of Feldafing. I asked him to send my regards, since he was going back there, and to tell my cousin that shortly, hopefully, I would be able to join him. Afterward, I checked with the Shomkuter Rav, and he told me that this fellow did send him my regards. But he was powerless then to do anything or to send anybody to come and get me.

We were in Vienna several days. Then, the time came to move through the Russian zone, in order to reach the American zone of Austria, and then go to Germany. We may have gone by train to the end of Austria's Russian zone. I can't recall exactly whether we went by train.

Then we reached Germany. They took us to a place called Iring, which was just across the border from Austria. They had like an army camp or barracks. They set us up in the barracks for several days. Impatient as I was, I thought to myself, well, I want to go see my cousin. At that time, I had decided maybe I should not go to Israel. Maybe I should go see my cousin and from there go to the United States.

But, of course, I had no money at all. My only possessions were my coat—a nice winter coat which Eddie had bought me, and he'd had it made for me by a tailor, brought down to my size and rehabilitated. And I had a knapsack with a few little things, some mementos, and two or three shirts. It wasn't very much. The leader of our group, from the Zionist organization in Budapest, was not in favor of my plan to go to Feldafing. As a result, I told him that I would leave all my possessions with him, if he could give or lend me enough money for the train to Feldafing.

To get from Iring to Feldafing, I had to go through Munich. This was at least a whole night affair. I got on a train and went to Munich. The city and its railroad station were bombed out; it was a pleasure to see that. I wish it had stayed that way forever. Practically no buildings remained whole at that time in Munich. The railroad station was full of people, not only Jewish refugees, but also many Germans *yimach shmann* (may their names be erased) coming back from where they had escaped, from Czechoslovakian and Polish territories that were regained back after the German occupation. The Germans were banished from there. At any rate, there were many former Nazis.

American soldiers, MP's, were patrolling the railroad station. There were thousands of people sleeping in the railroad station that was bombed. They checked the identification papers of these people. I was afraid, since I had no identification whatsoever. I did have that card that was given to me before I returned from Ebensee to Romania, but it wasn't really good. I had changed that card in order to be able to return from Romania to Germany. I had changed my birthplace to Germany. But, of course, that was very foolish because it was not done professionally. Anybody could have realized that this card was not an official identification. I still have it today. All night long, I was worried about what would happen to me if they identified me and thought I was a German.

But, thank God, nobody bothered me. After I waited till about 5:00 or 5:30 in the morning at the railroad station, I took the first train to Feldafing. It takes about half an hour or three-quarters of an hour to get to Feldafing from Munich by train. We passed by some of the cities, like Starnberg, and the lake, Starnberger See. *Yimach shmann,* it was a very beautiful country. All frozen and snowed in. It was already cold, since it was December.

At Feldafing, I got off the train at the station and inquired how to get to the DP camp. When I arrived at the camp, it was still dark, early in the morning. There were lights in some of the bunks. Actually, these buildings were *kasernes,* that is how they say barracks in German. They used to be former army barracks, and now Jewish survivors were quartered in these army barracks. There were a number of people, six to eight, in each room.

When I came, I met a fellow whose name was Zeidman. He had a black hat and was wearing a short coat, like a winter jacket with a fur collar. And I asked him if he knew the Shomkuter Rav and he said, yes. He pointed out to me where the Rav lived.

He had a place, a one-room apartment. He was the chief rabbi of Feldafing at the time. In this one room apartment, he lived together with Tzalel Ruttner.

When I came, Tzalel was not there. He had special papers given to him by the occupying American forces to go to Romania. At that time, he had gone back to Romania to make a *shidduch* (wedding match) between the Shomkuter Rav and his future wife Hindy. At that time, she still lived with her father, the Uyvar Rav, a big *gaon* (genius) of tremendous *godel* (greatness), a wonderful man, a very nice *frum* man. When you saw him, you saw *Eliyahu HaNavi,* with a long beard, a very majestic looking, very regal looking man. Clean and *noah labriyot* (pleasing-looking), a man you would talk to. It's hard to describe.

At any rate, the Shomkuter Rav was a *talmid* (student) of Uyvar Rav before the Second World War, before he got married. Hindy was quite a few years younger than the Shomkuter Rav, but he and Tzalel were thinking that perhaps it would be a good *shidduch.* So Tzalel went back to Romania to make the *shidduch.* It reminded me of the *shidduch* that Eliezer made for Yitchak with Rivka on behalf of Avraham.

When I first saw the Shomkuter Rav, I told him who I was because I didn't remember seeing him before the Second World War, although he was a first cousin. His name, of course, was Ruttner. He was my mother's sister's son, the brother of Devorah, Moyshe, Mendel, and Tzalel. They also had another brother Shmuel, who got killed.

He was very happy to see me, and he told me to stay and live there with him. I lived there for quite a while, although it was a small place. Then I moved to one of the barracks, one of the rooms. A number of people were there, though I can't remember their names. My cousin registered me with the camp authorities. However, I had a very big problem with registration because the camp was full, and they would not accept any newcomers. But, of course, due to the fact that my cousin was the chief rabbi, he was able to do me a great favor and register me at the camp. I don't remember exactly what excuse he used to let me be in that camp.

I arrived at the camp on January 11, 1946. This also was a big problem, because the American government had instituted a rule that stated that only those who arrived before December 1945 would be able to stay in that camp and also have special privileges to go to the United States in various ways.

Rabbi Yecheskal Ruttner—Zeidy's first cousin, the Shunktover Rav, was the Chief Rabbi of the Felderfing Displaced Persons Camp.

This was prior to 1950 when Congress passed the law to admit so many hundreds of thousands of refugees. But to be eligible to go on the special quota to the United States, one had to have arrived at the camp prior to December 1945. And I arrived January 11, 1946.

So, I would have been ineligible to go to the United States on this special quota. But, fortunately, my cousin was able to have me registered—and registered prior to my real arrival date. It was a tremendous thing, because otherwise I would probably have had to wait until 1950 to come with the big quota, which was admitted at that time; I think it was 200,000 refugees and Holocaust survivors.

In Feldafing, the daily schedule was as follows: I would wake up in the morning and go to *shul* to daven. But before davening, it was still dark, of course. I'd be there around six o'clock, generally speaking. We had *shiurim* (classes) in the morning, and people learned with *chevruta* (with study partners). The *shamash* (attendant) of the *shul* would provide hot tea with sugar. I still remember the taste; it tasted very good, though I don't remember if it was real tea or not.

But anyway, anything hot was nice. Because even though there was food, there wasn't enough of it. Even seven months after liberation, I was

Identity card issued at Felderfing—The camp's rabbi, Zeidy's cousin the Shunktover Rav, was able to officially register him at the camp even though he missed the deadline. This gave him safety, food, and accommodations, and helped him immigrate earlier to the United States.

still hungry often. The tea with sugar was something provided by the American Joint. This is how it became available to certain groups at the camp.

After davening, there were some classes, so sometimes I would go to *shiur* (class) and learn. Sometimes I saw some friends. There was this problem with rations every day. It was like a community kitchen, so every day you had to go and bring food. They would cook for the whole camp, 4,000 people approximately, to my recollection. Every day for supper or for lunch, we would have to pick up our ration, our dinner.

On *Shabbes*, it was definitely lunchtime when you picked up your ration, your food from the kitchen. There was an *eruv* (an enclosure so you could carry on *Shabbes*) made in Feldafing. If I am not mistaken, there were two kitchens. A *treyf* (non-*kosher*) kitchen and a *kosher* kitchen.

Also, for your ration you went to a warehouse, and you could receive a certain amount of, let's say, bread that was given out every day or once or twice a week, I cannot recall. And you also received some other little things, some margarine or sweets, a piece of chocolate, I don't remember what it was.

If you were a member of any service group that did things for the camp, you received additional rations. The chief rabbi had a special top ration, the same as the administrators of the camp. So, once a week, I would pick up that ration for him. For example, if you were a member of the *Chevrah Kadisha* (burial society), which was very busy at the time because many people, *nebech* (pity), died every day of sicknesses as a result of having been in the concentration camp. Also, the members of the *Chevrah Kadisha* were busy going to other places, to hospitals, and so on, to bring these people to their *kever* (burial site).

The ration of the *Chevrah Kadisha* was a little smaller than the ration of the officials of the camp, nevertheless, it came in very handy because food was scarce.

A black market started developing at the time, mostly around food and cigarettes. Cigarettes were also part of the ration, but some people sold and traded them. Incidentally we did some trading later in the black market, specifically with bread. You see, the bread that was given with the ration was very good bread. It was French-type bread. It was really delicious, very good. But the problem was that we received half a kilo, less than a pound, maybe. It was supposed to last for three days. But we were so hungry, it wasn't sufficient. It was definitely not enough bread. So, we were obliged to buy bread on the black market.

Some people attended classes. The leaders also established some form of school for secular studies, which I did not visit at the time. But I was registered officially in Feldafing and lived in Germany for many months. I arrived January 11, 1946 and left on April 10, 1947.

So Tzalel Ruttner came back from Romania and brought the good news to Yecheskal Ruttner, the Shomkuter Rav *alav hasholem* that he made the *shidduch* (found him a wife). So the Shomkuter Rav was getting

Zeidy, 16, at the Felderfing Displaced Person Camp.

ready to go to Romania and get married there, and Tzalel stayed in Germany. It was time for us to move to larger living quarters. We first tried to get larger living quarters in Feldafing so that Shomkuter Rav and his new wife, Hindy, could live there. His brother Moyshe Ruttner and his sister Devorah also came to Feldafing at the same time, so we needed to have even larger quarters.

For a short time, we thought that we would be able to get a house located by the Starnberger Lake in Feldafing. It was a beautiful house that belonged to a German racer, a Nazi, and the American authorities had taken over that home. They dispossessed him. I don't know if he returned after the war or not. At any rate, we cleaned it up. It was really a beautiful place. But unfortunately, our plan was very short lived because some American officer—I can't remember if he was a colonel—came with his German girlfriend and dispossessed us, and said this home was off limits for us, for refugees.

At that time, every American soldier, whether a private first class or a plain private, had many privileges compared to us. As Holocaust survivors, we did not have anything. Every American soldier, even with just a piece of chewing gum, was a big *macher* (an important guy). Of course, we could not do anything about it. We never moved into that house. We just cleaned it up, and they took it away from us.

So we moved to a town named Weilheim, about a half an hour or so by train from Feldafing, further to the east near Garmisch-Partenkirchen, a big resort town in Germany. A number of Jews, survivors, moved there. They lived in the confiscated German homes where they would get a room or sometimes two rooms. The Germans were immaculate, very clean people, *yimach shmann ve zichronam* (may their names and memory be erased).

When we moved to Weilheim, I was still registered as living in Feldafing, so for almost a whole year, I was registered as living in both places. We came to Weilheim a little before the Shomkuter Rav and the Uyvar Rav (his father-in-law) returned from Romania. I lived with Tzalel on the second floor. We shared one room, very nice and clean.

There was already a Jewish community in Weilheim. There were also two hotels sequestered there by the UNRRA, the United Nation Relief and Rehabilitation Administration. Many Jews lived in these hotels, where we had something like a restaurant. One was a *kosher* hotel, and one was not a *kosher* hotel. They had a community kitchen.

In Bavaria, we drank a lot of beer, like the Germans, because that's where we were living. The beer was very cheap. It wasn't very strong beer, and we drank quite a bit. We had beer with practically every meal. We ate dinner in a sort of community restaurant. For the other meals, we were able to get a special ration as Holocaust survivors. Everything was rationed at the time; things were rationed for the Germans, too.

This room where we lived was in a house owned by an old lady. She had a lot of jewelry. Later on, I bought a gold watch from her—I believe I paid with some coffee. I bought about $5 worth of jewelry from her, a gold watch and a gold chain. We still have the gold chain, and Mommy is still wearing it. We still have the gold watch somewhere. It was a very cheap price, but we gave her American coffee, which was at a premium at the time. You couldn't buy it. Either we were able to get it on the black market or we got some rations of coffee. We also got some chocolate, and so on. These products were not available to the general public. Later on, I also bought a diamond ring for Tzalel, which he gave as an engagement ring to his *kallah* (bride), to Shifra *aleya hasholem.*

I was partially a *shadchan* (matchmaker) there. In Feldafing, Tzalel lived in a barrack. At the time, his future wife Shifra was living with her father, sister, and two brothers in another barrack where I also lived. She was a young girl at the time. She was, I don't know, 16 or 17, and she was a very beautiful girl. They were *frum* people, Hungarian Jews, and I would see her very often.

They would all make *cholent* (a stew that cooks overnight) for *Shabbes*, besides what we had from the canteen, the common kitchen. They would send some of this *cholent* to the Shomkuter Rav, and I would bring it. As a result, somehow, I brought them together, as Tzalel had not met her before. Anyway, it became a *shidduch* (match), and I bought the engagement ring from the lady who owned our home. They got married later on in 1946.

When the Shomkuter Rav came, and the Uyvar Rav came, and Moyshe came, we all lived happily—happily, a joke!—in Weilheim. And Moyshe *alav hasholem* was called the Weilheim Rav because he was the rabbi of the refugees and Holocaust survivors in that city. He was also the *hazzan* (singer) and for *Rosh Hashana* and *Yom Kippur*, he would sing in a big hall in one of the hotels, where all the Jews would come to *daven* (pray). Otherwise, we had a sort of a *shul* in a smaller space in another hotel.

At that time I had a railroad ticket. I would

The Weilheim Rav—Rabbi Moshe Ruttner, Zeidy's cousin, lost his first family during the war. He became the official rabbi for the refuges in the town of Weilhem. He had a beautiful voice and led the high holiday services.

Zeidy applied for an orphan visa to obtain early entry to the USA.

commute four or five days a week to Feldafing. The reason was that, first of all, I could cash in my rations in Feldafing and, second, I heard there was a special visa quota being issued for children, orphans, and survivors younger than 18, to get into the United States. They gave the quota that had not been used during the war years to underage survivors—anyone below the age of 18. I was 16 at that time. I turned 17 in November 1946. And so I registered to go to the United States.

It wasn't that simple to register. You had to have many papers. You had to have a birth certificate, and a police report that your conduct was good, you had never been in trouble, and you had not been arrested. I had lots of trouble getting all this. I could not get a birth certificate. Of course, I explained that to the authorities. Romania was a Communist country, and there was no correspondence. But, ironically enough, I did get the birth certificate, because I wrote right away to somebody in Borgo to go and get it for me, and it came just a few days before I left for the United States. But I did not have to use it. I still have this birth certificate from Borgo.

Official certificate of good behavior—Zeidy needed this document to be
admitted to the United States. Considering the amount of Black Market
activity he was involved in, it is remarkable he never was arrested.

The other reason I had to commute every day, except on *Shabbes* and
Sunday, was because I had given my address as living in Feldafing. I was
constantly waiting for months and months to hear from the immigration
authorities in Munich. All the big offices were in Munich—the Joint Distribution Office, the UNRRA, and the Vad Hatzola, which I will explain
it later and which was organized by rabbis in the United States.

So I would commute to Munich several times a week, and go to these
immigration offices. It was not really an immigration office, it was either
UNRRA or the American Red Cross—and I would go bother them about
what would become of me, of my immigration. Meantime, I was also
going to Feldafing to see if I got any mail, to see if I had been called in to
present myself to the immigration officials.

By 1946, some people had already gone to America. This Mr. Teich-man, who lives now in the Valley, also went to the United States as an orphan child. As a matter of fact, I didn't know for a long time, till I found out, that there was such a thing as the quota. I was afraid if I didn't go every day to both Feldafing and Munich, I would miss my call up. Later on, before I left for the United States, Rav Moyshe Ruttner *alav hasholem*, the Weilheim Rav, was able to get us a telephone. To have a telephone was practically impossible. Until then, we had no other way to communicate with anybody. So I had to commute from Weilheim to Feldafing and Munich.

This was my schedule. I would leave Weilheim by train and go to Feldafing to go to *shul*, learn for an hour or so, have some hot tea, and then go to my room where I was registered, eat something, and wait for the mail to see if any mail had come. I would spend the day there with one thing or another. Later on, I was also able to get a little bit of business through Moyshe Ruttner. It was a bread business.

The Shomkuter Rav and his wife Hindy, and the Uyver Rav, lived at 14 Schmiderweg in Weilheim. That was the house owned by the old German lady. She was unmarried, and her name was Olga. She lived there with her niece, a young girl. Where they lived was very interesting. They had two rooms. One was like a kitchen, and they also had a sort of basement. It was very neat and clean. There was a huge bathtub made of cement. The Uyvar Rav used it as sort of a *mikve* (ritual bath) to *tovel* (immerse) himself. It was very big. For a man's *mikve*, it was alright. For a woman's *mikve*, you had to go to Feldafing, which had a *mikveh* that the Agudah had organized

I'm coming back a little bit to describe Feldafing. In Feldafing, you had these various organizations. You had an Agudah. In the barrack where I lived, there was Rabbi Ziembah *alav hasholem* and his brother, who were nephews of the great Rav Ziembah from Warsaw, a tremendous scholar. [*With the outbreak of World War II and the German invasion of Poland, Rabbi Ziembah became the single most important force in the War-saw Ghetto. In the darkest days of despair, he was a source of hope, optimism, and inspiration. He set up secret locations for the study of Torah and, at great personal risk, constantly visited these clandestine places to strengthen those who studied there. He was killed by the Germans in the ghetto.*]

They also issued a Yiddish paper that carried some Jewish news. And, of course, there was a *shul*, and a sort of a school, but I never attended it.

People lived in these barracks. This little German town of Feldafing also had a lot of villas that were sequestered by the camps' administration because, previously, German Nazis and Germans lived in them. Now some survivors were quartered there because the barracks did not have enough room. There were two or four people, or maybe more, in each room.

There were *levayas* (funerals) practically every day. *Nebech*, people who were weakened in the concentration camps later died of various illnesses and sicknesses. Tzalel was a member of *Chevrah Kadisha* (Jewish burial society). When he left for Romania, I took over his job and his ration. Even when he came back, I would go many times to the hospital in the town of Gauting. It was a sort of tuberculosis hospital, and there were some other hospitals. I would go out with the *Chevrah Kadisha* any time it was needed. We had sort of a van, and we would take the body for the *tahara* (purification bathing) and get the person ready for the burial. I cannot recall off hand where the Jewish cemetery in Feldafing was. It was organized after the war.

Also for a time in Feldafing, the Shomkuter Rav was given a car with a German chauffeur. For some reason, that didn't last very long. Either the car didn't last long, or this provision didn't last very long. And, of course, after he returned to Germany, the Shomkuter Rav and the rest of his family settled in Weilheim. So this provision of a German car with a German chauffeur was only short-lived.

I was sort of envious. This fellow came from Romania from the city of Barshahay or Targu Mures, the city where the Shomkuter lived before the war. He considered himself a friend. He lived in some other camp, but he worked for the Americans. Many survivors worked for the Americans as cooks and in other functions. They had access to canned food, which was a tremendous thing. They had apricots and other things in cans. It was a big *yehuss*, (a big deal) to have it. He would come to visit from time to time. He was also given a sort of an American army uniform, but, instead of being green, it was blue. I was sort of envious that he had access to these things, and that he was wearing this uniform. These are just some of the little things that occurred in the camp.

The Agudah was also organized in the camp, I still have my membership card. The name of the head of the Agudah was Ruttner—he was a distant relative of Tzalel. I don't know what they did, what function they served, or whether it had something to do with learning or not. There were some other organizations, such as Zionist organizations, which I also did not have very much to do with.

Agudah Membership Card

My main occupation at the time, as I said, was commuting. Every *Shabbes* I would go to Weilheim and sometimes during the week, too. I went every day to Feldafing. But *Shabbes* I would spend mainly with the Shomkuter Rav. If we had any meat, I would bring it from Feldafing for *Shabbes* and make a *cholent* and bread. Fortunately we had access to bread through the courtesy of the Weilheim Rav, Moyshe *alav hasholem* who was able to get sufficient black bread.

Food was in very short supply, but we had sufficient black bread at the time. I was able to bring some of it to Feldafing to sell or trade for money or some other food. People would also sell their cigarettes to get money. There was a ration of American cigarettes. People were doing black market business with these American cigarettes. There was a very big business with cases smuggled into Czechoslovakia, and a lot of people made a lot of money on the black market.

In Germany, there was a special *platz* (town square) in Munich where the black marketers would gather to deal in foreign currency, meaning dollars. We had American dollars and also the occupation money that the German occupation authorities issued. This money had greater value than German marks. I still have some of this occupation money. From time to time, the American official authorities would raid this place, and arrest many people for dealing in dollars or in gold and various other articles you were forbidden to trade in. Sometimes when they came to raid this *platz*, people would tear up dollars, and you would see pieces of them on the floor.

The first wife of the Shomkuter Ra*v* was the daughter of the old Shomkuter Rav, her name was Tzipi *aleya hasholem,* and she had a brother called Yitzchak. He served on the front line as a laborer with the Jewish labor brigade. He was captured by the Russians after the war. He was liberated and somehow came through Munich. The Shomkuter Rav registered him and set him up. He also had a brother who lived in Czechoslovakia, and he was a big black marketeer. (The only way to live really was to do something on the black market because the rations really were not sufficient to live on.)

The authorities caught him and some other fella at the border as they tried to smuggle cigarettes to Czechoslovakia, and they were jailed. So

I was dispatched to the border. It took the whole night to get to the border by train, because you had to go from Feldafing to Munich and from Munich to the border town. We took Yitzchak some clothes and money—whatever it was. I think eventually they were freed, but I don't remember how long they had to stay there.

In Feldafing, there was a Jewish photographer, a survivor, previously from Shomkut, who became very handy. He made us a lot of pictures, because we needed all kinds of pictures. Eddie also had given me a picture of my mother *aleya hasholem,* and he enlarged it. From that picture, we had the painting made that is now hanging in the living room.

There was another Rav, but he was not the official rabbi. His name was Gottlieb, and he was from Miskolc, a Hungarian city. He lived with his son in one of the rooms in the barrack where I lived. He was a big *talmid hacham* (scholar).

There was also a great Rav in Feldafing at the time. Before he was in concentration camp, he was the Rav of Mátészalka, a town in Hungary. He was a tremendous *talmid hacham.* He eventually came to the United States, and I saw him once or twice. He lived in Williamsburg. He was also a *mechaber* of a *sefer* (the author of a book).

Another person who was close to us in Feldafing was a man by the name of Binder. He was a *frum* fella, but he also had a secular education. Of course, at the time we were very naïve, and we thought very highly of him because he had a high school education, which only a few *frum* people had. Maybe he had some college education, too. We thought when he went to the United States, the whole country would be open for him. Who knows, maybe he would be received there with open arms. But when he came to the United States, he became a *shamash* (a lowly sexton in a synagogue).

The Shomkuter Rav passed away several years ago, on a Friday afternoon I believe. As he was going up to the subway station, he suddenly fell back and died of a heart attack. He really was a wonderful man, very nice, always very nice to me and to everybody else. He always had a smile on his face, and was a very big *talmid hacham.*

Later, we had another apartment in Weilheim. The landlord's name was Picha. He was a very big anti-Semite, *yimach shmo*. In our home in Weilheim, there was a bakery downstairs whose managers were Germans, quite decent people, who gave us bread. We were able to purchase bread from them above the ration that we were entitled to. Our cousin Moyshe Ruttner arranged that deal because he was friendly with this German. Sometimes, I would take some of these breads to Feldafing, since I was still traveling to Feldafing or to Munich practically every day to see if I had received any papers regarding my trip to the United States. I would take 10 to 15 loaves of bread and sell them in Feldafing. It gave me some additional money to be able to buy certain things I needed for myself.

Finally, the authorities caught up with me, that I had a double registration. I don't know exactly how, because it was pre-computer age, pre-pre-computer age! How were they able to catch me with this double registration? I don't know how it happened. But I had to give up one residence, so I kept my residence in Feldafing.

Usually the whole family would spend *Shabbes* together—Tzalel, the Shomkuter Rav and his wife Hindy; the Weilheim Rav, Moyshe Ruttner, my cousin; and the Uyvar Rav. So we had a family reunion at least every *Shabbes*. During the week, we lived separately. But many *Shabbesim* we spent together.

Then in Weilheim, the Shomkuter Rav arranged a place for the *tefilas* (prayer) for the *Yamim Noraim* (high holidays). It was in the big assembly hall of the non-*kosher* hotel. Moyshe Ruttner *alav hasholem* led the *tefilas*. It was a beautiful davening; I still remember it. There was a *minyan* (prayer group of at least 10 men) every day in the *kosher* hotel in Weilheim.

Then *Sukkes* (Succoth, the festival of booths) came, and the Shomkuter Rav went with the leader of the Jewish community in Weilheim, in his car, looking for *hadasim* (a specific twig used for a *Sukkes* ritual). Finally they found some sort of *hadasim,* in a hothouse, maybe. It was quite a tedious task to find *hadasim* for the *lulav* (unopened palm frond that is part of a ceremonial plant holder used on *Sukkes*). I can't recall where they got the *lulav,* maybe from friends.

Weilheim was about 15 to 25 kilometers from Feldafing. And as I said, I would take the train almost every day into Weilheim and into Munich. The train would leave about 6:05 or 6:10 and it would usually be very packed. It was a beautiful trip, the area there…the Germans *yimach shmann* had a very beautiful area. Feldafing was near a beautiful lake. Of course, we were not on the lake, but the original villa that we had acquired and once thought we'd live in was on the lake. It even had a boathouse with access to the lake.

Chapter 9

Near Weilheim, there was a city called Garmisch Partenkirchen, a renowned winter resort. People come from all over the world to ski there. We had some friends who lived there, but I don't believe I was there too many times, maybe once or twice.

I was travelling often to Munich to bother the immigration authorities again and again about my papers. Two young ladies, Miss Amie and Miss Ballanger, were in charge of immigration for children under the age of 18, for orphans. The United States gave orphaned children entry preference using quotas which it assigned to different nationalities based on their pre-war populations. The Romanian quota was naturally very low. Nevertheless, I tried.

So one day I came to Munich to the immigration office. Finally after I had bothered these young ladies for all these months, they said, "We filed your papers. Take whatever you have and move to Prien am Chiemsee."

Prien was approximately 120 to 150 kilometers from Munich. It is on a lake called Chiemsee. It took quite a few hours to get there, four to five hours by train. In Prien, two hotels were reserved for orphan children who were about to be processed to go to the United States.

Prien was a resort with beautiful hotels. Of course, it snowed there. I still remember the area, which was surrounded by mountains and especially beautiful in the wintertime. I was there for several months in the winter. In Prien, one of the old German rulers had a castle called Prien am Chiemsee.

Our hotel was not the most luxurious, but, nevertheless, it was livable. There were several people in a room, and we had a *kosher* kitchen. We had our own *minyan* (prayer group of at least 10 males) and our own *shul*. We were about 40 to 50 orthodox kids. And we would *daven* (pray) with the *minyan* on *Shabbes*. I can't recall if we had a *minyan* on weekdays.

We had a kosher cook. The Joint or the American authorities gave us food, and we were also subsidized with money from the Klausenberger Rebbe, who went to the United States in 1946. He was one of the first refugees to come to America and to alert people about the plight of the refugees and survivors of the German camps. He raised a lot of money. He had a *yeshiva* (Jewish school) in Föhrenwald, another DP camp. It had been a German barracks during the war. Quite a few boys learned at that *yeshiva*. He also brought money to the Orthodox institutions that were organized right after the war, including another *yeshiva* in Landsberg. He also gave some money to our group.

On *Shabbes,* we had a special treat. On *Shabbes* morning after *davening* in the early *minyan* we had breakfast and a chocolate cake as a treat. Believe me, there weren't too many chocolate cakes in Germany. That was a very good treat. Even today, I still like chocolate cake!

I don't know how we wasted the time actually, but we wasted a lot of time. During the week we played ping-pong or other games. We would travel around the area. When I was there, it was winter so we didn't spend much time outdoors, although the area was so beautiful, with the snow, the mountains, and the lake, like a picture on a postcard.

Lake Chiemsee is a mile or two miles long, and in the middle is an island with a castle on it. One of the German rulers used it as a summer home. The lake would freeze over in the winter, so we would walk on the ice to this castle. I walked it once or twice.

Once an American soldier was walking there with his German girl-friend. He asked me directions, how to get to the castle? We looked up to the American soldiers. Of course, they had liberated us, and they had chewing gum and cigarettes and chocolate. To us, the Americans symbolized wealth and freedom, and who knows what else. So this soldier gave me a piece of chewing gum. We did not have much access to chewing gum. We had some access to chocolate through the black market. There was some chewing gum, too, but it was a big *yehuss* (a big deal). At any rate, this castle really was a sight to see.

I was in Prien for several months. From there, I would sometimes travel to Munich or to Weilheim. In Prien, we had a religious group and a non-religious group. We had a group of boys and girls all waiting to hear from the offices in Munich about when they would go to the United States. I recall that one fellow was about to go to Mexico City.

Every few weeks or so, an order came that some of the boys and girls were being transferred to Munich to a place called Funkkaserne, a former German soldiers' barracks being used as an assembly point for people who had papers. Being transferred to Funkkaserne meant they were almost ready to immigrate to the United States. People usually spent one or two months there. One day, I got notice from this office that we were going to leave for Funkkaserne right after *Pesach*.

Before we left for Munich to go to Funkkaserne, I went back to Weilheim to say goodbye to my cousin, to the Shomkuter Rav *alav hasholem* and the Uyvar Rav and Tzalel, Moyshe, and Devorah. When I left, I was 17 years old. I remember standing on the steps where the Shomkuter a Rav and the Uyvar Rav lived with their wives at 14 Schmiteneweg Hertzen, a very small street. I remember standing on the step there, and the Shomkuter Rav *alav hasholem* gave me a *musar* (lesson) that I should remember to conduct myself religiously and so on and so on: it was a *tzeida la-derech* (literally provisions for the trip).

So I said goodbye, and then we left. We boarded this train that looked like it would take forever. First, we went to the port of Bremerhaven. We had boarded the train before *Pesach*, so we were worried about what would happen on *Pesach* when we would need *matzos* and wine, and so on. To our pleasant surprise, we arrived at Bremerhaven a day or so before *Pesach*. And, fortunately, the Joint Distribution Committee had arranged for us to have some *matzos* and other *Pesach* food.

I think we had a community *Seder* in Bremerhaven. We had *matzos* and wine. They had like a kind of a carnival or an amusement park. A problem arose about leaving Bremerhaven and boarding the ship on *aharit shel Pesach* (the eighth day of the Passover holiday). We asked a *sheila* (question to a rabbinic authority) and the *psak* (answer or religious ruling) was that we could board the ship because of *pikuach nefesh* (impending danger).

So, we boarded. The ship was an American army transport boat that held at least 1,200 people. It was divided into two or three rooms. Each room held about 600 people. We boarded in April, and they had plenty of food. I hadn't seen so much food since before the deporta-tion, before concentra-

S.S. *Marine Perch*—This US Army transport ship brought Zeidy to the United States.

tion camp. They had oranges and grapefruits, many things we still didn't have in Germany. We had plenty of food, so we were very happy once we boarded the ship. I still have one of the pictures of this event.

Zeidy on the ship (second from right).

It was April, and the seas were very stormy on the first day. I woke up the next morning, and I was so sick. Terribly seasick. I kept throwing up until the last day before we arrived in the United States. We traveled for ten days and, you can imagine, it was shaking and rocking. It

Proof of smallpox vaccination given aboard the ship.

wasn't the *Queen Elizabeth*, believe me. I remember all the other people were also very sick.

For nine nights, I did not go down into the ship. I went down only for using the toilet facilities. But, otherwise, day and night, I was on deck, on top of the ship. I was so sick, throwing up. I ate very little food.

However, the food was very good. They had *kosher* food. I don't know if we had meat, but we had many fruits and vegetables, bread and margarine. But I was terribly seasick. Like many others who just couldn't take it, I spent the days and nights on deck. There was not much to do there for ten days except watch the ocean and talk to each other.

One morning, there was an announcement on the loudspeaker that we should watch the shores for the United States. Of course, the anticipation was so great, I can't describe the *simcha,* the joy we felt arriving off the coast of the United States. From a distance, we saw the shores of New Jersey. Then we saw the Statue of Liberty. Then, we saw some skyscrapers from a distance, so we knew we were about to disembark.

I was worried about how I was going to communicate. What was I going to tell people? I couldn't speak any English. My vocabulary was 20 to 50 words. So I made up my mind, somehow, to learn some words.

I had my uncle's address, and I learned how to ask for the way there. But surprisingly, someone, possibly HIAS [the Hebrew Immigrant Aid Society] had already notified my relatives that I was arriving. I guess the Munich office asked if we had any relatives in the United States and notified my uncle Yitzhak Ayzik Kahana. He was always a nice man, a very charitable man, a very good man. And Rabbi Richtman also was there. I think he was with Mrs. Richtman, and they came to the port although they did not really have access, so they had to wait in a different area.

Uncle Yitzhak Aizik Kahana—Mrs. Richtman's father, Fetter Ayzik, dancing the mitzvah dance at his granddaughter's Eva's wedding.

The *Agudah* was represented by Rabbi Schonfeld, who tried to bring boys and girls to Beit Yaakov (girls school) and to Yeshiva Torah Vodaas. Then, to my pleasant surprise, I saw my uncle, and the family was so happy to see me. Rabbi Richtman gave me five dollars. It was equivalent to, let's say, $20 or so. I didn't have a penny to my name, but it was enough for car fare or whatever I needed. They took us to the Bronx. This organization for orphans who came to America—I can't remember its

Rabbi and Mrs. Richtman at their Haifa home, 1975—They opened their house to Zeidy and treated him like a member of their immediate family. They were instrumental in his going to Yeshiva Torah Vodaas.

The Richtman family at son Chezki's Bar Mitzvah—(from the left, standing) Lizzie, Herby, Chesky, Zeidy, and Eva. (sitting) Auntie (Yitchak Ayzik's third wife), Yitzchak Ayzik, Rabbi and Mrs Richtman, and Rivka

name—had rented this facility for young people below the age of 18. We were there for several days.

Then Helen Baum (Zeidy's first cousin and Eddie's sister) came to visit me. She took me down to Brooklyn to the Richtmans' house. The first time, it was a weeknight. I remember Eva was there, with her brothers and sisters, my cousins, who were young at the time, Herbie, Hezki, and Suri *aleya hasholem.* At that time, Rivka was a baby. She was about six months old or so. I was under the impression that Eva was the maid, and she was feeding the baby.

The Richtmans lived on Hart Street at the time. Then it was a very nice area in Williamsburg, and the street had brownstone houses. There were many shuls in the area. From Yeshiva Torah Vodaas, it was less than a mile.

Then I went back to Coval Avenue in the Bronx, until finally they had to arrange my release to a family member. Actually, I was released under the auspices of the Jewish Family Service, because some organization had to guarantee that it would take care of me. They had an arrangement with the Richtmans, who would vouch for me.

After I left this Bronx establishment, I spent two or three days with the Richtmans. Then Rabbi Richtman *alav hasholem* took me to Yeshiva Torah Vodaas, and I enrolled there. Quite a few boys were there already. They had come maybe six or eight months before me. Some refugee children also were there—some of them may have come from France and, later on, some came from Sweden. We already had a whole group of European boys in Torah Vodaas.

The *yeshiva* was located in Williamsburg at 41 South Third Street. There was the main branch, the *beit hamidrash* (library and study hall), and the high school. The junior high school was on Bedford Avenue, and the elementary division was located at 204 Wilson Street. All these locations are in Williamsburg, within about half a mile of each other. I would spend weekdays in the yeshiva. Sometimes, I would go to the Richtmans who lived not too far away, about a mile or so. I would take the trolley car on Tompkins Avenue and get off at Willoughby Avenue or Hart Street.

At that time, the Richtmans lived in a remodeled brownstone house. They had a huge kitchen downstairs because they were in the catering business. The kitchen was on the bottom floor, along with a huge room where they dished out and prepared the meals—the food they prepared for weddings, *Bar Mitzvahs,* and such occasions.

On the next floor, there was the wedding hall. It wasn't very large, but it could accommodate 120 to 150 people, maybe. On the next floor, there was the *beit hamidrash.* The Richtmans had a *shul* where they held *davening* with a *minyan* (prayers with at least 10 men) morning and night. It was getting difficult to make the weekday *minyanim.* Of course, *yamim noraim*, they had a big *minyan,* with quite a few people. They lived on the next floor, the fourth floor after the basement, where they had a living room and their bedrooms.

They would spend most of the day downstairs, since they used the preparation room as sort of a dining room. Sometimes, we ate in the hall on *Shabbes,* if no event was being held there. Downstairs, they also had the laundry room.

In those days, they were quite well to do. There were soldiers in a hurry to get married and, of course, there were *Bar Mitzvahs.* Since there weren't many locations or fancy places where people could have weddings or *Bar Mitzvahs,* the Richtmans did very well financially during the war years. But they worked very hard, and everybody in the family had a job to do. At that time the girls, Suri *aleya sholem* and Eva, both already attended college. And, of course, I was the greener (greenhorn or newcomer). I was a refugee, I hardly spoke any English, and I had a very limited vocabulary. It felt strange, but, of course, they were really nice to me.

I spent almost every *Shabbes* and *yom-tov* with them until they moved to Israel. I was a *ben bayit* (like a member of the family). And at that time Hezki and Herbie were going to Yeshiva Torah Vodaas, so, of course, it was logical for me to go there as well.

However, I must say that at the time, the Klausenberger Rebbe had already started a *yeshiva* in Williamsburg. This *yeshiva* was small, with only a few *bachrim* (students). It was also in a brownstone building, and

I went there a few times. My uncle *alav hasholem* was a *Satmar Chassid* (a member of the Satmar Hassidic Jewish community), so he went to the Klausenberger Rebbe. He took me there to listen to his *Torah* (lessons), and so on.

My uncle very much wanted me to go to the Klausenberger yeshiva. But it was a *Hassidic yeshiva* and Torah Vodaas was more *Litvishe*, a more modern type of Orthodox boys school. Of course, today we have a lot of *Hassidic* boys in Torah Vodaas; it changed over the course of these 43 years. Then Torah Vodaas was more modern, so I chose to stay there at the time. Incidentally, today it's entirely different. In those days, you hardly saw anyone wearing *tzitzit* (fringes) outside, which is the custom in all *yeshivas* today, even *Litvishe* yeshivas. We had a more modern climate in those days, compared to today.

Coming back to the Richtmans, I would spend *Shabbes* and *yom-tov* with them. Sometimes, I visited them during the week and ate with them. That lasted until they moved to Israel. First Rabbi Richtman went in 1951, and then Mrs. Richtman followed him. They bought an apartment there. Unfortunately, they had a bad experience with their business partner. They were trying to establish a mattress factory, and they had difficulties and lost a lot of money.

The Joint guaranteed support for every Jewish refugee so that we would not fall on the state for support. I received at that time, I think, $50 a month. Out of that money, I paid $20 a month to Torah Vodaas where I had a room and board. The food was *yeshiva* food, of course, but the breakfast and lunch were not too bad. For someone coming from Europe who was constantly hungry, it was really very good.

With the rest of the money, I had to buy clothes, trolley fare, and other things. I was also under the auspices of Jewish Family Service, which was located somewhere in midtown Manhattan, I believe on the Upper East Side. About once a month, I had to meet with a social worker who would question me about how I was being treated, what I was doing, and how things were going. This continued for about three years.

Chapter 10

My cousin Joe Kahana *alav hasholem* lived in New Rochelle, which is near New York City, and I would spend *Shabbes* with him every so often. He was a very prominent member of his shul, where Rabbi Froelich was the rabbi and Joe was its president. He had a big house with a number of bedrooms and a huge yard. It was a very green area, so it felt like country living. People who lived in Brooklyn were actually envious of people who lived that way. Of course, there were nice areas in Brooklyn, too, but not with such big yards.

Once, a few weeks after I arrived in the United States, cousin Joe took me out. He gave me a spring coat. The bottom part was little detached, but he meant well. He also took me to his brother-in-law's store, I must say, and he outfitted me with a beautiful suit and some other clothes. I can't remember the details. He was very nice to me. *Nebech* (pity), he went bankrupt later on.

He was in the watch sales and repair business, and he made a very nice living. During the war, it was very difficult to get new watches. He had a company, Kane Watches, on Canal Street on the east side; I believe it was Two or Four Canal Street. They would buy old watches, or people would send them old watches, and he would renovate them, and sometimes restyle them during the war years. My uncle Rav Yitzchak Ayzik Kahana worked for him as a salesman. He traveled to various cities for the purpose of selling these watches.

Later, when Sam and Helen got married, the wedding was in cousin Joe's yard. This is why we appreciated him in later years when, unfortunately, he was bankrupt and sick. Eddie gave him some money then. Until this present day, when I think of him, I still feel sort of hurt. He was such a prominent member of the community and in his last years, he was sick. He lived in a sort of old age hotel, not far from Long Beach, where Helen lived. He was *yored*, that is, he came down in the world. He was sick, and didn't have money. It still hurts me.

Many times I would meet Joe when I went to *yeshiva* in New York. We would go out for lunch. He took a train every day, five days a week, from New Rochelle to Grand Central Station. From there he would take the subway or elevated train to Canal Street. He gave me watches once or twice. He always had a car, and he always let me use it without any question. You see, the Richtmans didn't have a car until 1949 or 1950. In those days, a car cost a lot of money. They did buy a very fancy car, a DeSoto. It was a Chrysler product, but it doesn't exist anymore.

I'm coming back now to my early days at the *yeshiva*. Our first task was to learn Torah. Then, we had to get on the road to start learning and speaking English. As I said, there was a group of boys in the *yeshiva* who had come about six or nine months earlier than me. They already spoke some English and were partially integrated into the Torah Vodaas high school, in the Secular Studies department. To me, it seemed that they had made a lot progress. I was envious in a way that I had not yet reached that *madrega*—that level

Those who arrived in my time were assigned to a building on Bedford Avenue that they called the junior high school. One of the *rabbanim* who also had come recently from Europe gave us the *Gemarrah shir* (Talmud class). We had a special class for catching up with English language, history, literature, and so on. We had an English review course, and we studied English grammar and, partially, the history of the United States. We got the basics of English. I don't remember if we had math or not.

The conditions during that period of two or three months while we had classes on Bedford Avenue were not too bad. We were under control, but the hours and so on weren't too strict. We had many things to do and to arrange. We had to go to the Joint Distribution Committee, or whatever committee it was. I had to go to the dentist, because I had trouble with my teeth.

Zeidy as a student at Torah Vodaas.

I made a lot of new friends there. I haven't seen many of those people for many years—some I haven't seen for 40 years. The three Katz brothers were there. This Joe Leibovitz, who is a professor somewhere, was a very bright fellow. I taught him how to drive. Incidentally, at that time, Yossi Tzuker arrived in the United States. We became best friends, and he was also my roommate.

We were sort of a happy group. But the problem was that we were always concerned about how to make a living and make money, even enough for the basic things. We had some subsidies from the Joint Distribution Committee, or some other group that was sponsored by them. But we still didn't know what would come in the future. I was only seventeen at the time, but my concern was always how to make a living. I mean, of course, I was also interested in my learning that had been interrupted for so many years, at least three years in the concentration camp and Germany. But I still didn't know what my future would be.

Friday afternoons we would take the train for about an hour to go play soccer in the Bronx for our recreation. The whole group came, and we were all in the same boat. Most of them were older than me. Some stayed at the *yeshiva* for only few months. Some stayed for several years and got *smicha* (rabbinic ordination). Some transferred a few years later to Yeshiva University. Some are businessmen today, some are professionals, and so on.

This lasted for several months. As I said, I would go to the Richtmans sometimes for *Shabbes* or during the week. I lived in the dormitory of Torah Vodaas at the time that Rav Mendelovich *alav hasholem* was the principal. Rav Mendelovich, who was the founder of Torah Vodaas, would give a *shir* (class) in *nach* (Prophets), which was beautiful. He was a tremendous man, very compassionate. He helped out other *yeshivas*. He was very loved.

Rabbi Shraga Feivel Mendelovich—He was the Head of Yeshiva Torah Vodaas and one of the pioneers of the American Orthodox Movement.

As a matter of fact, I just went to Israel this year, and Rabbi Hamlik gave me a letter, a copy of the speech that Rav Mendelovich gave when the United Nations voted for the partition of Israel in 1947. Rav Mendelovich's attitude toward the state was that we would rebuild *Eretz Israel*, so we could go back to *Eretz Israel*. Even though many people there were not religious, our task was to help them spiritually and revive them spiritually and revive them physically in every way we could to build the land of Israel.

He loved *Eretz Israel*. As a matter of fact, in one of the books I have read, it says that the voting for the partition [Palestine in 1947] was on a *Shabbes*. At that time, the United Nations headquarters was in Flushing, New York, a suburb of New York City. Rav Mendelovich left the radio on for 24 hours so he could hear the news about what was going to happen with the partition on *Shabbes* because he loved Israel that much. At any rate, he was a tremendous *baal midot* (an ethical person) and a man who understood problems.

I remember one time the *mashgiach* (boys' supervisor) came. It must have been 1947. He didn't come very often, and I think he died in 1948. He lived in Spring Valley. He would come in periodically, so it must have been in 1947. The *mashgiach's* name was Rav Wolfson, and he unfortunately was not the wisest of all men.

You have to understand that boys like me, unfortunately, could not always concentrate. We had problems. We had no immediate family. We had to do everything by ourselves. We were constantly worried. We came from a concentration camp and could not exactly concentrate all the time. We felt that we were entitled to a little bit more leniency, although we did not take advantage of it. But, yet, we had problems.

Instead of discussing our problems with us, Rav Wolfson, the *mashgiach*, decided to send me to Rav Mendelovich. He told him that my learning was not up to where it should be. But, Rav Mendelovich was a man who understood people with problems. Instead of giving me a *mussar schmooze* (critical rebuke) or anything, he started discussing where I was from, my history, and some people we had in common. He let me go with that. He understood people of our kind who came from a concentration camp had problems and could not exactly adjust to the situation like other boys who were brought up in the United States. But Rav Mendelovich was a great man, like I said.

I was in this preparatory sort of English and Hebrew course until the end of June when the classes ended. Then Torah Vodaas had a summer camp in the Catskill Mountains. Torah Vodaas was the first *yeshiva* to have a summer camp. Today most yeshivas do. Chaim Berlin Yeshiva also had a summer came, but maybe it started only later.

Boys would come to the camp in the summer. The camp had two sessions of three weeks each, starting at the end of June. Boys from various *yeshivas* would come spend three to six weeks. This camp did not have the most modern facilities, but it was very nice. It was in the Catskill Mountains in a cool area, in Ferndale, New York, not far from Liberty. It had a big *beit hamidrash* (study hall) on top of the hill.

Usually the program consisted of learning in the morning and in the afternoon for approximately an hour or an hour and a half each time. We spent the rest of the time in recreation, playing softball, handball, basketball, and baseball. And eating, naturally. There was plenty of food, and they served bread and butter.

There was a retired couple at the camp, a man and a woman. I can't recall their names, but they were wonderful people. They devoted their lives to the children, to the boys and the camp. Every summer they would come out and work very hard from morning till night. They were not paid for it, they did it *leshem mitzvah* (as a good deed). I think even in the city they also volunteered for the *yeshiva*. I hope they will have a lot of *schar* (rewards from God), and that they lived until the age of 120 years. But I don't believe they are alive anymore—don't forget it was 1947 or 1948.

It was pleasant there. We had a ping-pong table, and I still have pictures of me playing ping-pong with Yossi Tzuker and a fellow named Fishoff who was a nephew of the owners of Barton's Candy. They were the first *shomer Shabbes* industrialists. They manufactured candy. They came here before the war. Their name was Klein, and they were very helpful to Rabbi Kotler in establishing Lakewood Yeshiva in New Jersey.

Zeidy at Camp Mesivta in the Catskills during the summer.

At one time, they had 39 or even more stores throughout the city. There may have been some other *shomer Shabbes* stores (businesses that keep the laws of the Sabbath), but not of this caliber. They were closed on *Shabbes,* and so many *shomer Shabbes* people tried to get a job at this company, with Barton's Candy. Yet, they had a problem because they would close very near to the time *Shabbes* came in, and the people working had to rush home and get dressed and ready for *Shabbes.* Yet, it was a way for *shomer Shabbes* people to get a job. Let's not forget that it was not easy for a *shomer Shabbes* person to get a job at that time. It was 1947, 1948. Today a person can walk in and say, well, I don't work on Friday night, I have to leave early. I don't work on Jewish holidays. But then it was not that easy. Of course, many people did it, but it was difficult because many people did not sympathize with our religion.

Back to camp. Our *seder* in camp was that we woke up, at 7 o'clock or so, and *davened* (prayed) in the *beit hamidrash*. Then we had a very hearty breakfast. We returned to the bunks to make the beds and clean up. Then we had a learning *seder*. Then we had a recreation schedule, and then it was lunch time. After that it was rest time. Then we had a swimming time. In those days, the camp did not exactly have a pool. It was actually a big hole in the ground, and the water was very cold. It was natural water, like a well. The boys loved it. The following year, I served as a lifeguard at that pond.

I received my lifeguard certificate from a fellow whose name was Roy Shafken. He was, I believe, the only *shomer Shabbes* person who had an instructor's license from the Red Cross to give the examination to certify a lifeguard. Not too many boys were able to swim in those days. Most of them were brought up in a city [without access to swimming pools] except some of the boys from smaller communities who had access to city swimming pools. There was a large swimming pool in Brooklyn, in the Greenpoint section not far from Williamsburg, so some of the boys would swim there.

I had to learn swimming when I was a child and went to *cheder*. On Friday afternoon, our *rebbi* would sometimes take us to the local river, and he would teach us to swim. I acted as a lifeguard, and I still have the certificate somewhere.

I spent one summer learning in Torah Vodaas's camp before I received *smicha* (rabbinic ordination). I learned *Yordea Deah* (the part of the *Shulchan Aruch*, code of laws, having to do with *kashrus*—the laws of keeping *kosher*), and reviewed it prior to my examination. It must have been the summer of 1951, and I got my *smicha* in 1952. I learned with my friend

Rabbi Ruben, *hazzan* (cantor) Ruben. He has a very pleasant voice and has been a *hazzan* for many, many years. He is my friend until this day. We learned with a contemporary friend who was a class ahead of me, Yaakov Pollak. I believe he is now rabbi of a Sefardic shul in Borough Park in Brooklyn.

The time I spent in camp was very pleasant. Of course, the camp was restricted. We could not leave camp unless we had permission, even though we were already considered older boys. I was 19 the first time I went to camp. We would leave the camp with several boys. We would hitchhike. It was not dangerous those days. Everybody, all the boys and girls, would hitchhike.

We would go visiting some *kosher* hotels. They were called *kosher,* but I don't know to what degree they watched their *kashrus* (kosher observance). One hotel was called Gross's and another one was called The King David Hotel, and later on there was the Pioneer Hotel.

The Gross Hotel was on Route 17. It was built before they built the special freeway coming from New York to the Catskill Mountains. The hotel was owned by a family named Gross. Incidentally, when cousin Sam Baum came back from the Second World War, he had some money, and he invested it with the Gross family. He became like a silent partner, but I believe he lost a lot of money with these people. Later on in the 1950s, I understand this hotel burned down completely.

The King David Hotel was owned by partners Mr. Ziegler and Rabbi Bronstein. Rabbi Bronstein became very famous, and he is still well known because he was one of the first *mohalim* (a *moel,* the person who performs circumcisions) who went to Russia and Poland in the early 1950s. In those days, going to Poland for any purpose, even religious purposes, was prohibited—any American who went to those countries was accused of being a spy. It was very dangerous. He was arrested a few times in Romania and in Russia, but he secretly went there and trained the Russian Jews how to circumcise. He also circumcised a number of Russian Jews, and he took messages from the Lubavitcher Rebbi and the Skeulener Rebbi.

Rabbi Bronstein was a partner in those days in this hotel. I don't know exactly what happened to that hotel. But for a few years, around 1950, I worked as a lifeguard in that hotel. I also worked as a waiter in this Gross hotel for about four weeks or more in the summertime. I was making a little bit of money. I was also a lifeguard in camp *Agudah* in Iman, New York. It was a very nice camp, and incidentally it was among the first camps to have an outreach program.

As I said, camp was pleasant. Sometimes we went to New York because the European boys had to be in touch with their supervisors at the Joint Distribution Committee. We would hitchhike to New York. The city was about 120 miles from the camp. It was safe then to hitchhike. I did not have a car those days, but I always said to myself that when I got a car, I would pick up every hitchhiker. But, unfortunately, it turned out that giving rides to anybody became very, very dangerous.

There were also bungalow colonies where people came during the summertime. The Ruttners—the Shomkuter Rav *alav hasholem* would rent a cabin with his wife Hindi and her father, the Uvyar Rav. When they came from Germany, they settled in Williamsburg, but the streets were congested and space was so tight in Brooklyn at the time. And, summertime in Brooklyn and Manhattan is not exactly a dream of recreation.

Today renting a bungalow is not as popular as it used to be. Some bungalows had a little kitchen plus a number of rooms. One would fit eight or ten people. There was space outside, so you could sit and enjoy the fresh air. There was very clean, fresh air, and it was cool. This is the way that people would get away from the city.

People whose economic situation was better would go to hotels. They would go to the Gross American House or later the King David, which was a fancier hotel. Later on, the Pioneer opened and was even fancier. People would come to Pioneer, young people would meet there to make *shidduchim* (to meet for marriage). I went there as a guest later on, and I went there many times as a visitor while I was at camp.

The camp administrators did not exactly want us to visit these hotels because they were afraid some of the boys would miss their *shiurim*. They were also afraid that there would be problems. Sometimes these hotels had shows, but the *yeshiva* administration did not exactly consent to letting boys watch some of these shows. Although the shows themselves were not what I would call adult shows, not at all, they felt this wasn't befitting for *yeshiva* boys.

Later I worked in the Gross American hotel. It was not the most luxurious *kosher* hotel, but they paid me some funds, and I was able to save some money. As a matter of fact, by that time I already had a car that I had bought in 1950 or 1951. I was working with a friend called Gross who now lives in Los Angeles. We were very close friends.

He worked as a busboy, while I worked only as a waiter, because I had experience as a waiter from working *motzaei Shabbes* (Saturday evening) and Sunday afternoon and Sunday nights at

One of Zeidy's many old cars—He is seen here with his friend Baruch Gross while working one summer in the Catskills.

the Richtmans's catering hall. So I was a big shot. I was already a waiter.

The guests would leave tips for the waiters. If someone was there for a *Shabbes* and Sunday, or for a week, they would generally leave a known amount of money for the waiter and the busboy. So I saved a few hundred dollars during the summer. And when we worked at the hotel, we got room and board there.

In those days, incidentally, they had fancier kosher hotels. You had the Grossinger. It had its own town named after it, a small village named

Grossingers, New York. It was a very fancy hotel. There was also the Concorde Hotel, but the Grossinger hotel was known more as being reliable in its *kashrut* and *Shabbes* observance, because you couldn't smoke in the dining room. Still, those who were better off went to Grossinger's, which was more expensive. I once visited Grossinger's and stayed there. I believe I once visited the Concorde, too, but I never stayed there.

Some of these hotels, like Grossinger's, the Pioneer and the Concorde, were open all year round. There were two partners at the Pioneer, Mr. Gottenberg and Mr. Shechter. Shechter later passed away, but his son still manages some hotels during *Pesach*. This Gottenberg had adopted two children and later on they managed the hotel. One of them became a partner in the Central hotel, together with Rabbi Porosh in Israel, in Yerushalayim.

When I first came to the United States and registered at Yeshivat Torah Vodaas, it had an old building at 141 South Third Street. The dormitories were in three different buildings. There was the central building where the *beit hamidrash* and classrooms were. That was for the older groups, the high school level and *beit hamidrash* level. The top one or two floors were dormitories. Then, they had another two old buildings that also served as dormitories.

During that time when we came from Europe after the war, there were a number of kids who came from China. These people had been in China for generations. Their grandparents had come from Iraq, and the Sassoon family probably brought them over. The Sassoon family was one of the wealthiest families in China.

My first roommate in the dormitory was a very heavy-set Los Angeles fellow, but I don't remember his name. Moyshe Luish was also one of my roommates. His family lived near Niagara Falls. He was older than me, about one or two classes above me. At that time, there were also three Zaharish brothers. One is a rabbi today in Detroit, one is a rabbi in Staten Island, and one is a *rosh yeshiva* (head of a school) in Bnei Brak. Of course, to us it was a revelation that they all came from Los Angeles. We had heard something about California and started asking question about it. It seemed far away in those days. Very few people were able to afford to take an airplane to California. So when boys went home to California or even to Detroit, they had to take a train or a bus. It took them four or five days to get there.

In about 1948, I believe, Torah Vodaas got a new dormitory building. The two old buildings where most of the boys lived were demolished because they were dilapidated. All of the boys moved into the new building. It was very nice there. Every Friday, we had new linens, which we had to change ourselves, of course. A person came in once a week to do the cleaning and wash the floors.

There were strict rules. At that time, Rabbi Rivlan, who now lives in Toronto, was the dormitory supervisor and the liaison with the administration. He also taught *halacha* (Jewish law). He would wake us up every morning at 6:30 or 6:45, and he would make sure that everybody attended the *minyan* (daily prayers). Since I worked *Shabbes* night, sometimes getting back at four o'clock in the morning, it was very difficult for me to go to *minyan* on Sunday morning, and he was not too happy with me if I overslept once in a while. He may have reported me to the administration of the *yeshiva*.

Rabbi Rivlan was also in charge of seeing that the boys didn't waste time. Radios were not permitted. In those days, he would come check all the rooms to see if anybody had a radio. And if anybody had a radio, he would confiscate it. However, I was able to learn English through the radio, I was always interested in the news, and I liked classical music. So I did have a radio, and in those days the radios all had antennas. It was very easy to trace if somebody had a radio because they had an antenna wire stretching up on the wall or on the side of the wall behind the bed.

I had an Arvin radio that had an antenna. The radio was confiscated a number of times, and many times I had problems getting it back. Rabbi Rivlin would be very strict about it, and he would enforce these rules. In those days, in 1948, there was some television, but nobody in the dormitory would even dream of having a television because the administration would have confiscated it right away.

In 1949, not too many people in apartments and homes had televisions yet, because they were very expensive. But some stores, like a corner cafeteria or a corner candy store—as they call them in New York—had a television. There was a candy store right across from the *yeshiva* on South Third Street where sometimes, if you were hungry, you could go buy a sandwich or a chocolate bar or something like that. Already in 1949, I would say, it had a television. But, we didn't have time to watch television. The only time off we had was between 1 p.m. and 2 p.m. for lunch. One o'clock was lunchtime and two o'clock was already *mincha* (afternoon prayers) time and after that, we would go back to the *beit hamidrash*.

But anyway, at night I would go to college, and late at night, I would sometimes be very hungry, so I would go to the candy store, since it was open until about 11 o'clock or later. Sometimes, I would take a peek at the television, but otherwise I did not watch any television at all. Even the Richtmanns didn't have a television and went without for quite a few years. They probably didn't get a television until 1950 or 1951. Of course, our children wondered how people were able to survive without a television. It's a very, very good question, but I guess people did survive without television in those days.

Breakfast was in the cafeteria in the main yeshiva building. Surprisingly enough, it was a very very good breakfast. We used to get as many rolls as we wanted and two eggs and cereal and milk, and there may have been coffee. And we got a cooked lunch, which was not exactly the best, but it was edible, and it was the same for dinner.

Now how did I support myself? In the beginning, when I first arrived in the United States, I was under the auspices of the Joint Distribution Committee. Then it turned me over to the Jewish Family Service. I had to see a social worker about once a month.

For the first two years, I received a subsidy of about $50 a month, plus $120 a year for clothing. From this money, I paid $20 a month to the *yeshiva* for the dormitory and food, which was quite reasonable. Don't forget that in those days $50 was more than $50 today, but still it was not enough for me to live on, and I had to buy books for college.

Brooklyn College could be free for the first year if you passed a test, but you needed good English skills. My English was still weak, since I had been in the US for just one and a half years. So, I was not able to get in on that basis. But, I believe, if you made a B average for the year, then you were admitted as a free matriculated student. So I was able to do that. I arrived in the United States on April 22, 1947, and I was admitted as a free student in September, 1949.

So that's why I came in late at night from college, and most of the time I was hungry and bought a sandwich. I was able to subsidize my income by working sometimes three times on the weekend, like on *Shabbes* night, at the Richtmann's as a busboy or waiter. Depending on how many hours I was able to work, sometimes, over a weekend, I would earn about $60 to $70, which was quite a lot of money in those days. This was the money that actually saw me through *yeshiva*, high school and college. I also used it for entertainment when we went to the movies once in a while, and I had money whenever I needed some clothes, and so on.

I must say, it was very hard work, because being a waiter you had to carry the food, and you were responsible for serving the people and taking the dirty dishes downstairs. The way the wedding hall was, the kitchen was downstairs and the wedding hall was on the next floor. And you had to *schlep* up and downstairs, taking the food to the second floor. The job had a lot of pressure, but, of course, I welcomed it in the sense that I was able to go and do some work and have extra income, because after those first two years, I would longer receive any subsidies from the Joint Distribution Committee.

After that, I was strictly on my own. At that time, also, I told the administration at Torah Vodaas that I could no longer continue to pay because I just did not have the money. So I was on a complete scholarship after that. That is why I usually make a nice contribution every year because I am grateful to them for giving me a place to stay and, of course, for the learning. Life in the dormitory was nice. Boys would get together, sometimes they would *schmooze*. And it was nice that between one and two, after eating, I would have half an hour to rest or do some homework in the dormitory room. It was right across from the *yeshiva*. There was ample heat in the dormitory, and we had showers and a sort of community bathroom, one or two bathrooms on each floor. I have a picture of the dormitory building somewhere.

Publicity photograph—One of Zeidy's sources of income was to go to small towns and act as the rabbi and chazan for the High Holidays. This may be a publicity photo for one of those synagogues.

I felt sorry for some of the boys who came from various other countries, such as the South American boys. Of course, their parents made an effort to send them away to *yeshivas* because they had no *yeshivas* in South America at the time. The pity was that these were little kids, some only eight or nine years old, and the parents would send them away to *yeshiva* to make sure they remained Jews. But it was sad when they got sick, and they had nobody, because their parents were so far away. At least, I was older at that time; I was about 17 or 18.

A doctor used to come in once or twice a week. I can't recall his name, but his son is today a principal of a *Beis Yaakov* (school for girls). The doctor was from Germany, and he came here just prior to the Second World War. Sometimes, some boys would try to bring you some food if you were sick, but it was not a pleasant situation being sick.

I was at the *beit hamidrash* level for most of my years there, with the exception of two months immediately after my arrival in the United States in 1947. The schedule was that from 9:00 a.m. to 11:30 a.m., you would prepare for the *shiur* (class) and go over the *shiur* of the previous day. By 11:30 a.m., six times a week, you would go to the *shiur*. I cannot remember whether we had a *shiur* on Sunday, but we probably did. And the *shiur* went until 1:00.

On Tuesdays, we would have the *Rosh Yeshiva* (head of school) Rav Grozovsky, who was a great *godel* (scholar). He was the son-in-law of Rav Baruch Ber Lebowitz. He would come and give the special *shiur*. Anyway, he gave a *shiur* on Tuesdays, tremendously *beyun* (in depth). You usually had to take notes to remember the references.

I also had Rav Chazan as a *rebbe*. [Rav Chazan was one of the greatest teachers of his time.] He was a tremendous *godel, alav hasholem*. I have his *sfarim* (books) here. Then we had a special *shiur* sometimes, with Rav Kaminetsky and Rav Shisgal, the son-in-law of Rav Moshe Feinstein. He was a very fine person who passed away at a very young age. They were all very nice people, and they would come to *beit hamidrash*. During the morning seder of the preparation, if you had anything to discuss regarding the *shiur*, you would discuss with your *Rosh Yeshiva*.

I learned with a number of different *chevruta* (study partners). I studied with three main ones for a long time. One was Abe Grossman, who was also a *hazzan*. He lives in Israel today. He made *aliyah* with most of his children; he has a very big family. I studied *Gemara* with him. I can't remember if I studied for *smicha* (rabbinic ordination) with him. Today he has his own *kollel* and learns in the *kollel*. I spoke to his brother, the rabbi with the largest membership Orthodox congregation in the United States, the Baron Hirsch Synagogue in Memphis. I happened to meet him in Los Angeles.

Another *chevruta* was Chaim Sovchevsky, and we remain friends to the present day. When he comes to Los Angeles, he always looks me up here. Sometimes when I'm in New York, I don't have too much time to look him up, unfortunately, because I have such short visits, but we remain friends to the present day. He was very nice. His family was originally from Israel. His father was an agent of one of the institutions of Israel, one of the yeshivas or one of the other institutions. And I used to go to their home once in a while. Then another *chevruta* of mine was Pinchas Reuben, who also was a *chazzan*. I think he's still a *chazzan* in Borough Park in the shul with Rabbi Yaakov Pollack, who was also a contemporary and friend of mine. He was one or two classes ahead of me in the *yeshiva*.

I went to high school for secular studies in the afternoon. I think there were some classes that began at 2:30. But, anyway, right after *davening* there was another short *seder* for the boys who went to high school. The high school English department taught us starting at 2:30, each class was 45 minutes and the last class ended at 6:05.

In the beginning, of course, my English was very poor. When I first came to the US, we had a class that studied preliminary English and some history. Then in September, 1947, I entered the regular high school and, at first, I had difficulties because of my poor English. When it came to mid-terms, especially in English class, it was very difficult, with the poetry and other things that we had to learn. But at the end of the semester, the teacher gave me a passing grade. Unfortunately, my grades in history were poor, not because I didn't understand the subject, but because of my English.

But I did manage to pass that semester. It just goes to show you what effect a person can have on another person. My average came out to 60, but I actually needed 65 in English the first semester. So I walked over to this teacher, Mr. Lieberman, and I told him, "Look, it's up to you, but if you can give me a passing grade by stretching the grade that would be great." There were a lot of essay questions, and some short true or false questions, but the grade on the essay questions depended on the teacher's interpretation.

So I told him that if he could stretch the grade to make it a 65, I would be able to continue in high school, and he did. He was a very fine person. Incidentally, he was a public school teacher in the mornings. Most of these teachers would teach in the public school system in the mornings. It was really an anomaly for us, because we were not used to Orthodox people or Orthodox teachers in high schools. In Europe, we didn't see that, but here in the United States, we had already met professional Orthodox teachers in New York. Mr. Lieberman was very understanding, and he was very nice, and he gave me a 65, which really motivated me to continue with high school.

I practically could have finished in a year and a half. But I had another obstacle. In those days, you needed two languages besides English to pass the high school finals, tests you had to take in New York state. You also had to take the state's additional Regents examinations, which covered some of the main subjects like math, English, history, and so on. I decided to take the examinations instead of attending courses. You needed three years of one language and two years of another foreign language.

So I took a course in what was called Hebrew 6 in the last semester of the third year of Hebrew. I just took the examination, which I passed just fine. If you didn't take the course, then you needed a 75 in the final in the Regents instead of the 65. So, that was no problem.

I didn't take any classes at all in German, because I felt my German was good enough since I had been in Germany for a little over a year.

But you also needed a 75 for that, I believe, and I took the Regents exam without taking any classes, and I was short by about 5 points.

Apparently I originally passed, but Rabbi Lannard, the Principal or Assistant Principal at that time, was the one who marked the German Regents. When they re-examined the Regents exam in Albany, and they found that the grade was stretched a little bit too much, they sent them back. Then, I had to take a night class at Washington Irving High School on South Fortieth Street on the East Side of Manhattan. Many *yeshiva* boys would take night classes there. I passed the examination for the two-year German class, but all of this held me up for another half a year.

Chapter 11

In 1949, I graduated from the high school secular studies department. I still have the yearbook somewhere around the house. Of course, I continued learning at the *yeshiva* as I made the transition from high school to college.

Zeidy's Torah Vodaas high school graduation picture (top, center).

Attending college was not that simple or easy. We learned all day long in the morning session and the afternoon session at the *yeshiva*. The first semester in September, 1949, I was taking six college credits in the evening after a day's study. And it was a ride of about 45 minutes to an hour to get to the college. If you took your first class, let's say, at 6:35 p.m., you were able to take nine credits or fewer credits if it was a science class. If you started at 6:35, then your last class ended at 10:45 p.m.. Anyway, it was quite a ride, 45 minutes to an hour to get to Brooklyn College, where you got off the trolley and then had a long walk to the college itself.

At the beginning, I would attend college twice a week. Each class was an hour and a half. At that time, in my first semester, I took six credits. Then next semester, I started taking nine credits. And so, I fulfilled the 15-credit requirement for being admitted as an accredited student without having to pay tuition or, anyway, with paying a very small amount of tuition. Of course, you had to pay registration and books, and so on.

At the time, quite a few boys attended the College from Yeshivas Torah Vodaas, and from other *yeshivas*, including Chaim Berlin, Tiferet Yerushalaim, and so on. It was nice. Very few boys wore *yarmulkes* in those days. Even the *yeshiva* boys didn't in those days. I mean they wore them on campus, but not in the classroom. It is not like today when you see professionals in government offices wearing *yarmulkes*. It was not that way those days. Only one or two boys in my class wore *yarmulkes* in the classrooms.

I took various courses. I also took a non-accredited course that was given for foreign-born students, a course to help eliminate your accent. It did help quite a bit. One time I had a professor who was a conservative rabbi. I used to argue with him all the time. There were quite a few Jewish professors in Brooklyn College at that time. One was a history professor who apparently was a communist, and we used to argue about communism. I told him I had lived with communism, and I know what it is. As a result, he gave me a B grade instead of an A, whatever. Then we had to do papers. It was quite a bit of work. Even at night, I had work when I came home and, of course, I was very tired attending *yeshiva* and college at the same time.

We would go at night at around 11 o'clock to this candy store across the street from the *yeshiva*, and have a sandwich, and relax for a while. Remember, I was not too prosperous in those days, so I tried to buy the cheapest sandwich available. The cheapest sandwich was a cream cheese on toast with lettuce. As a matter of fact, the taste remains with me until the present day! I still like cream cheese with lettuce on toast.

It was nice to have Orthodox boys at my college, and there were also some *Beit Yaakov* (girls' religious school) girls and other Orthodox girls with us in classes. It was not all easy. For example, the psychology course was difficult because of the language. But I overcame that course, though, incidentally I got a D, because of my difficulty with the English language. This was the only D I got in all my college courses. Remember that it was 1949, and I had been in the United States for only two years. Naturally, I was making headway in English, no question about it, but some vocabulary words and expressions were still new to me.

We instituted a *minyan* for *maariv* (prayer group of at least 10 men for the evening prayer) every night at college. It was something unheard of because the American Jewish Congress at that time was very strong against mixing religion and state. But we were able to secure a room for *maariv,* for the *yeshiva* boys and some others who wanted to daven with the *minyan*, so we were able to meet Jewish boys from different classes. We also had a nice lounge. At that time, the campus was not very large. There were several buildings: the Royce building, the Inglewood building, the Roosevelt building, and maybe some others.

Gym was one of the courses. It was a requirement, though I don't know if it still is today. I recall I took it during the summer with a number of *yeshiva* boys. It was the *Ninth of Av* (a fast day), and our gym instructor was also a Latin teacher. We asked him to let us take the day off or to make it easy. But he was very nasty. He would not do it, and we had to attend gym class. It was very difficult, a very strenuous class. However, I also had some very fine instructors too. A fellow named Horovitz, an Orthodox person, taught night classes at the college. I took a number of courses in statistics and economics from him.

I attended the Brooklyn College in the evening for a number of years until I got my *smicha* (ordination) in 1952. At that time, I started attending Brooklyn College during the day, for one last semester. I took about 16 credits. It was quite a load, but I accumulated 74 credits.

I also started teaching Hebrew School in the afternoon in East Jamaica or Canarsie, I don't know what the area is called today. I taught in an Orthodox *shul* where the rabbi was Rabbi Frankl, a nice person.

מזל טוב
לחברנו היקר, המושלם במעלות ומדות טובות, ה"ה
הרב צבי אלימלך רעסלער
לרגל סמיכת הרבנים
מהמתיבתא תורה ודעת
י"ר שתזכה להיות מנהיג ומורה דרך בתוך עם ד' בדרכי ד'.
יוסף צוקער, משה בלוי, כהן גדול...

Yiddish newspaper—After Zeidy's ordination, this announcement was published along with congratulations from his friends.

I was new to teaching, but I did a fairly good job. Most of the children came from families where the parents belonged to the Orthodox shul, but some were *shomer Shabbes* and some were not. So, of course, I tried to do my best to impart a little *yiddishkeit* (Jewish consciousness) to these children.

The pay was not much in those days, and I taught in the afternoon for four hours. I had to take a bus from Brooklyn College for about 45 minutes to get to this *shul*. I finished teaching at about 6:45 or 7:00 and went back to Flatbush, where I rented a room.

I can't recall if it was $25 or $35 a month. I had no kitchen privileges. I used to keep some food in my room. There was only one little *kosher* delicatessen restaurant in all of Brooklyn that was open at night; actually, there was another one in Williamsburg. Flatbush was not what it is today.

Rabbi Sharfman, a very fine man and a good speaker, had a large congregation of modern Orthodox Jews. There was also the *shul* on Cornell

Avenue, where Rabbi Mintz was the rabbi. I can't recall the name of the *shul*. And there was one *shtiebel* (small *shul* often in someone's house) at the time. I believe the first *shtiebel* belonged to our cousin, the Shomkuter Rav, Yecheskal Ruttner *alav hasholem*. It grew with time and has a nice *minyan* now. He passed away a few years ago. I used to *daven* there at the *shtiebel,* and many *Shabbesim* I would daven at Young Israel. Once in a while, I would go on Friday night to the Richtmanns, and we would walk to a lecture or to a *shiur* (class).

There was also Rabbi Halpern's big Conservative Temple around the corner, but we would never *daven* there. Once we went to *daven* in the morning, sometimes we would go there for a lecture, but, of course, Conservatism was foreign to us, and so we had nothing to do with it.

Sometimes, on *Shabbes*, we would *daven* with Rabbi Appelbaum who also had a private *shtiebel* about half a mile away. He was the father of an English teacher I had in *Torah Vodaas* high school. He had a son named Carl and a son named Louis and some other children. Carl was a chaplain in the army during the Second World War. Later on, he became a rabbi and took over this *shtiebel.* I think now his grandson is a rabbi there, in this *shtiebel* on Avenue M or 13ᵗʰ Avenue in Flatbush.

Teaching was alright. Every weekday night, I would eat dinner in this delicatessen. I paid $2 for dinner, but since I had no cooking facilities, I was forced to eat out. For breakfast, I had cereal and milk, and I would eat lunch in the room I rented. It was on the second story of a private family home. This room was not, let's say, a palace, not the greatest of rooms, but it served the purpose. I was about a block away from the Shomkuter Rav's *shul* between Avenue J and K.

Eddie came to visit me many times in my room. He lived in Washington Heights and used to travel around throughout the country selling jewelry. He struggled. At the time, he had a partner. He borrowed some money from his brother-in-law, Sam Baum. They went into the jewelry manufacturing business. For a while, it was going alright, but, unfortunately, it eventually went bad, and they lost a lot of money. Then he was travelling and selling jewelry. He sold or tried to sell jewelry in practically every city in the United States. He made a living, and he would spend a lot of time with me when he had a chance. He would come to the room, and later on, when I was a rabbi in Hornell, New York, he would also come there to spend many *Shabbesim* of the year with me.

He was very lonesome, at the time. Of course, I was also lonesome, even though the Richtmanns were nice. Still, it was not like the family from home in Europe, because I did not grow up being like brothers and sisters with the Richtmanns. But Eddie was somebody from home, someone I knew from Europe.

Interestingly enough, during the time I was in *yeshiva*, we had sort of a club of newly arrived European boys and girls who were more mature. Even Rabbi Brissman came to this club once in a while. At first, the club was in Williamsburg; then we had a club in Borough Park. We used to go from time to time, but it didn't last very long.

I was quite lonely by myself, not having any parents. *Shabbes* I would stay at the Richtmanns, which was very nice. Still, it wasn't the happiest time of my life. Once the Shomkuter Rav tried to fix me up with some nice girl who was born here, who lived in the Bronx. She was a nice girl, but nothing happened. We just went out once in a while, but my first and constant concern was how to make a living. It was not very easy those days, unless you had a good profession.

Chapter 12

Just at the time Rabbi Chaim Lifshitz was in charge of the offices of Yeshiva Torah Vodaas. He lives in Israel today. He had a proposition for me. He told me that they were looking for a rabbi in Hornell, New York. That's upstate New York, western New York actually, about 60 miles southeast of Rochester.

At any rate, I went there just for an interview. They had some other candidates. Some didn't want the job, and some were not wanted by the *shul*. At any rate I had a successful interview and stayed there for *Shabbes*.

"In spite of it's infrequent use, it is very much treasured by the citizens of Hornell, by the children, grandchildren, and great-grandchildren of its original founders, by the Jewish families who have settled or passed through the area, and by generations of Jewish students at...Alfred University and Alfred State College."

From the NRHP application

Beth EL—This is the synagogue in Hornell, NY, where Zeidy was the rabbi for four years. It was built in 1947 and is still in use. It is now listed in the Registry of Historic Places.

Anyway, I was hired to be the Rabbi there. Some things had to be changed. It was an Orthodox congregation to some degree, but many things did not please me, so as soon as I came, I started a little revolution and changed a lot of things. I stayed at this position for four years. I came there to become the rabbi in January or February, 1953, so I was 24 years old. For the first three years, I was still single, and then in 1956, I got married. We left Hornell at the end of 1956. It was very lonesome to be a single rabbi there for three years. The only thing was that I was able to get away quite often and go into New York.

Rabbi H. Roszler Named Hornell Spiritual Leader

Mr. Landman, President of Congregation Beth El of Hornell, N. Y., takes pleasure in announcing that Rabbi Herman Roszler has accepted the call to serve as spiritual leader of the Jewish Community of Hornell.

Rabbi Herman Roszler comes to Hornell Jewish Community with years of experience in the Rabbinate, administrative and educational field.

He was ordained as Rabbi in Israel, wtih great honor by the Theological Seminary, Mesivta Torah Vodath. He attended Brooklyn College and the School of Higher Research in Monsey, N. Y.

Rabbi Roszler served as associate Rabbi in Congregation Machzikey Torah Bnei David, in Brooklyn. He had experiences in organizing youth activities for two years as district director for the Committee for Furtherance of Jewish Education. He also served as assistant principal of the New Hyde Park Jewish Center.

The Jewish Community of Hornell feels honored to have acquired the services of such an outstanding Rabbinic personality.

Announcement of a new rabbi for the shul in Hornell

In New York, I visited family and friends. I was able to go every week to either Rochester or Buffalo—usually on Wednesday afternoon, sometimes on Sunday. I used to drive there myself. I had a good friend in Buffalo, *Hazzan* Markovitz, whom I knew from New York. He and his wife and children always welcomed me. And in Rochester, I also had a good friend, Rabbi Pearl, who was a *shochet* (ritual slaughterer). He was always happy to see me because he was also lonesome in a way. He lives in Los Angeles now.

I would buy some *kosher* products in these cities. Many times, I also would go to visit Ben Bier, a congregant who was also a friend. He had no children, but he lived in a very big house with many rooms. He was in the furniture business. His *yiddishkeit* unfortunately was lacking. I did not know his father, but Bier told me he had very good Jewish education and even may have learned in a yeshiva in Europe. Many people who came to communities like Hornell tended to cast away their tradition.

Ben Bier must have been in his sixties, but he was a close friend. He didn't have a Jewish education, but he supported the *shul*, and it gave him a good feeling that he was friends with the rabbi. I don't know if he had a religious feeling, but I also don't know if I really could judge.

I mean, these people didn't keep *kosher*. Of course, I could never eat anything in their house. I tried and had success with helping some people grow further in their *Yiddishkeit*. It gave me a good feeling. I used to go with Bier for rides in the countryside. He loved nature. He was a very wealthy man, and his whole pleasure was, unfortunately, to buy a new Cadillac every year. He lived his whole life in Hornell and visited New York for only several days in his sixty years, but otherwise he was toiling day and night.

He had truck drivers delivering furniture, and sometimes he would do deliveries himself. People came from the countryside and little villages and purchased furniture from him there. It was a very close-knit community. Most of the Jewish people in the community were professionals or in business.

Max Leinmann was one of the wealthiest Jews in Hornell. He always covered the deficit of the *shul*. He was retired and happily lived in Florida. In the springtime, he would come back for *Pesach* and spend the summer, the *Yamim Noraim* and *Sukkes* in Hornell. Then he would go back to Florida. He had two sons. He was married to a non-Jew, though she probably converted. Where and when I don't know, but there was a Rabbi Solomon at the time in Rochester. Maybe he had been married before this Rabbi Solomon was there, but they were good friends.

She probably did convert because one son, Nate Leinmann, was very Jewish. He married a girl from Trenton, New Jersey who kept *kosher* and was very interested in Jewish things. I'm not saying they were *tzadikim* (very righteous religious people), but at that time and situation in this small community, he was president at the *shul*.

The other brother, his name I think was Max, married a non-Jewish woman. Unfortunately, the intermarriage rate was great in those days. It was 1953, that was 37 years ago, and the intermarriage rate was very bad in those small communities. Some doctors and businessman were intermarried.

Fortunately, some of my students, my *talmidim,* became very *frum*. I had great success with the Jacobson family. I'm still in touch with them. One lives in Staten Island, Jerry Jacobson, and the other lives in Monsey, Larry Jacobson. He's a pharmacist, and the other one is a businessman, a salesman. Their father had a drugstore. They were very nice people. They kept *kosher*. Their mother had relatives in a town called Elmira, New York about 60 miles from Hornell. Many times, when they went to Elmira, I would join them. They had family there, and they also kept *kosher*. It was a big deal, keeping *kosher,* let alone *Shabbes*.

Jacobson was a pharmacist and had a very big, good business in Hornell. He kept *Shabbes*. He was very dedicated to the *shul*, the *minyanim,* and so on. He was also president of the *shul* for a while. I befriended this family. I would eat with them a good many Friday nights. And when Eddie came, he would also eat with them. They offered great hospitality. As a result, I was able to influence them so that the youngest boy went one summer to camp *Agudah*.

Then, the *Baal Tshuva* (Jews who become Orthodox) movement was practically unheard of. And he was among the first *Baal Tshuva* who started the movement. The *Agudah* magazine, a *Yiddish* magazine, even wrote twice about the boy who came to camp *Agudah,* the boy who was sent by me, and today he is *frum.*

His brother married an Orthodox girl, too, and their children are *frum.* His sons went a few years ago to Israel. Sometimes I talk with the father on the telephone and, of course, he wrote me a very nice letter that he is still very grateful for helping him becoming very *frum,* very religious.

They also had one daughter who was already a few years older, and I did not succeed there. She went away to Syracuse University. She married a Jewish fellow, they got divorced, and—after we left Hornell—another sister was born. She visited us here in Los Angeles, but, unfortunately, she is not religious. But at least I was successful to some degree with this family.

The *shul* in Hornell was very nice, not very large. People would come from all around. There were small towns, small villages of 3,000 to 5,000 people. There was Canisteo, Bath, Alfred University, there were many others. Dansville, New York, around 17 miles from Hornell, had a hotel that was built when people were not aware of special aerobics exercises and special diets and special foods. It was run by a very famous man, Bernard Feddan. I even have a picture with him. I was the rabbi in that hotel, too.

It was not a *kosher* hotel, but it was vegetarian. People would come from all over the United States and Canada, sometimes from South America, for weight reduction and health reasons. A lot of Jews would come there. They would come visit the *shul.* How they got to *shul* was not by *Kfitzat Haderech* (literally, this translates as jumping over the road, but it means miraculous travel); they had to drive.

A Jewish family named Gladner lived in Dansville, and I would come every week and give their son private lessons. I would teach him Hebrew and some *Chumash* (bible) and stories. I also prepared him for his *Bar Mitzvah.* The Gladner family kept *kosher.* It was amazing to find a family that kept *kosher* in the little town of Dansville, New York.

After two years in Hornell, I was contacted by a large veteran's administration hospital in Bath, New York. It functioned also as an old age home. There were perhaps 2,000 veterans of the First World War and some of the Spanish-American War. This facility had a significant Jewish population. When I came, there were at least 70 to 80, maybe 100, Jewish retirees.

A rabbi in Elmira, New York, was the chaplain for that facility. After he left, they contacted me because they needed someone to replace him. For two years, I was a quarter of a chaplain, which means I'd spend a day there each week, approximately eight to ten hours a week. I would go have services and *davening* for them and give them a little lecture. During the holidays we would have special parties. At that time the Jewish Welfare Board was also sending special products and literature that we gave out. I would visit all the sick people, including those in the mental ward.

A number of staff members were Jewish doctors. Unfortunately, I don't know how *frum* they were, although one doctor came from Czechoslovakia in the 1950s. It took time for refugee doctors to get licensed to practice in the states, but some were able to work here before getting their license. This doctor was quite a *frum* fellow. He spent a *Shabbes* with us before he left; he was there for just a short time.

Announcements in the Yiddish and English press of a new Chaplain at the Bath, NY, Veteran's Administration hospital.

The hospital was outside the town of Bath, New York. Some Jewish families lived in Bath. Some doctors would occasionally come to the shul in Hornell for *Rosh Hashanah* or *Yom Kippur*.

I travelled around to a lot of little communities just for the sake of observing nature. The area was beautiful, really very pretty. Once a week, on Mondays or Tuesdays, I would go to Bath to do my duty as a chaplain for the veteran's administration. On the way back, I would go back another way through Dansville and stop by at the Gladners. I would give the boy a lesson. Many times, I would eat with them at the house and then return to Hornell.

Being a chaplain was an interesting thing. The men at the Veteran's Administration facility were all elderly people, and they were all happy to see me because I was quite young. This was from 1954 to 1956, so I was about 26. I gave them literature and taught them and *davened* with them. I would visit them and discuss their problems with their families. Unfortunately, many of them felt discarded, abandoned. Many of them were from New York City and only seldom had visits from their families. So, they felt very lonesome and abandoned. I tried to cheer them up as much as possible. Before *Pesach,* we would conduct a model *Seder* and invite the Catholic chaplain and the Protestant chaplain.

Seder ceremony at the Bath, NY, VA Hospital

In Hornell on *Shabbes* night or sometimes on Sunday, I had a *Talmud Torah* class. The first year I was there, we had three *Bar Mitzvahs* consecutively. It was my job to teach *Talmud Torah* about three times a week.

Chapter 13

The community of Hornell had 16,000 to 20,000 inhabitants at the time. It is in the western part of New York state, about 60 miles from Rochester and about 96 miles from Buffalo, near the Canadian border.

In Hornell, I had a very nice apartment. You can just imagine how the cost of living has jumped. The apartment had two bedrooms, a living room, a dining room, and a kitchen. It was fully furnished. I rented that apartment from a couple for the first three years I was there. The husband went to the army, and I paid $45 a month including linen.

Cousin Eddie would come there very often and spend *Shabbes* and sometimes a few days of the week with me. He was also single then, and he was also lonesome. He would travel around the country to try to sell jewelry. It was a very tiresome job. He was happy when he came to see me. Usually, we were invited out on Friday night and *Shabbes*. We would spend a few days together. One time he came, and I was not home. He didn't know where I was. He left a note on the door: You're a *fleefoidel*, a flying bird! You are never home! It happened that I had bronchitis at the time. In those days if you had bronchitis, they would put you in the hospital. I was in the hospital for 10 days.

The community was very happy when Eddie visited. He used to do more singing than he does these days. He used to sing and entertain people. He was very well liked, very well received. Everybody would say: "The Rabbi's cousin is here! The Rabbi's cousin is here!"

When the army couple came back, I had to find another furnished apartment. I found one upstairs on the second story of a home. I had a separate entrance and a kitchen, but it was not as nice as my previous apartment.

I stayed there until we got married, and then we found a different apartment and bought our own furniture from Beir, a very loyal *hassid* (follower) of mine.

The community had a number of different families who treated me very nicely; they were very good to me. I had the *Talmud Torah* (elementary school) and tried to establish a nursery school. I tried to teach the adults how to extend their religious observance. Some kept *kosher,* like the Lanmann family, and some unfortunately didn't. Some of their children became somewhat religious. I don't know to what extent.

I used to eat with another family on *Shabbes* morning, the Spultunicks. One time I got sick, because I had an ulcer. I had a special diet, but my own cooking was one of the worst things I could eat. Even to the present day, I hate cooking. So, I had an arrangement with the Spultunick family. The parents were elderly, and there were several brothers. They always gave *tzedakah* (charity). Before *Rosh Hashana* and *Pesach,* Mr. Spultunick would give me money to send away to different institutions as donations from him. He came from Europe and had a big junk yard, selling metals. He used to fabricate some metals, and the whole family was involved in that business.

On *Shabbes* morning, we would go to the Spultunicks for *Kiddush* after *davening* (praying) and eat breakfast, because the davening started at 8 a.m. Usually the younger kids would come to my house after that, and we would have a discussion—a 'rap' session—and I tried to teach them a little bit of religion and discuss the *Parsha* (Torah portion) of the week with them. I tried to influence them and give them something to do on *Shabbes* morning.

Usually on Friday nights, I would go to the Weinberg family. Weinberg owned a store with a *goyish* (non-Jewish) partner. He was very much beloved by the whole Jewish and non-Jewish community. He used to go around speaking with people. I would go to them on Friday nights. The wife came from a very religious family. She lived in Hornell quite a few years. They had a daughter and a son, Elliot, who was in medical school.

Their son fell in love with a non-Jewish girl in Switzerland, and they got married. At that time, it was difficult for Jews to get into medical school in the United States, so even though he was a very bright boy, he had to go out of the country for medical school. Supposedly this non-Jewish girl converted before Rav Doctor Herman married them. He was a very Orthodox Rabbi who was originally from Hungary or Romania. So Mrs. Weinberg, the mother, was very distraught; she was upset about this marriage and didn't know what to do. She begged me to correspond with her son's rabbi in Switzerland and to get him to try to talk Elliot out of this marriage. But I guess it didn't help much.

Doctor Herman said that he converted their son's bride because she was very sincere. He reminded me that when someone wants to give themselves to religion sincerely, you have to accept them. I never met Elliot's wife. I left Hornell before he came home, so I don't know what happened.

His sister was attending Cornell University in New York state. I visited there a few times. The Young Israel Movement established a *kosher* kitchen there. They also had Orthodox dorms with *kosher* facilities, which was very good. The Weinbergs were really nice people, but Mrs. Weinberg never felt at home in Hornell even though she lived there for 25 or 30 years. She was not part of the community, because she was a refined person, and she was more religious. She could not socially connect with people who were less religious. I could see that. So, the Weinbergs were very happy to have me there on Friday night for a cup of tea and some socializing.

In Hornell, I was in demand as a speaker to talk to various clubs: The Elks, the Rotary Club and the Masons. I spoke on various topics about Judaism and what Judaism is like. People were not aware of what it is to be a Jew. I also talked about the Holocaust. I was in demand not only in Hornell, but also in Canisteo, Bath, Dansville, and other places.

Once I spoke to the Masons, and they asked me to become a member. They said I should knock on the door to be admitted. They were shocked by what I told them about myself, what I went through in the Holocaust, and what it was like, and they asked me to become a member.

I never became a member, although Rav Gadalya Shor who was the *Rosh Yeshiva* (head of school) at Torah Vodaas said there was nothing wrong in becoming a member of the Masons, as long as you didn't join the Catholic branch of the Masonic movement. But, for some reason, I never did join.

I spoke to different organizations in different communities in different towns. It brought good will to the Jewish community, living among non-Jews. Hornell, one of the larger communities in the area, was sort of a central shopping city. People came from small communities, farmers and professionals. Hornell was also a railroad town. For some period of time, the meat that came from Nebraska had to go through Hornell. It was shipped by the Erie railroad. When the meat came, they would ask me to inspect the meat and wash it, because it had to be washed within 24 hours. So, they would contact me from the railroad, and I would come inspect the meat and hose it off so that it would be *kosher*.

The Jewish community also included the Miller family, the Shapiro family, and the Nabosak family whose son went to Princeton. The mother came from a very religious home, and the father was a famous surgeon who lived in North Hornell, a suburb of Hornell, a newer area. A number of Jews were managers at company stores.

I liked the idea of being a rabbi, but it was very lonesome living by myself, not married, and not having a large Jewish community, not a community of people I would have liked to associate with religiously.

I don't know if I mentioned how I met Mommy. One summer, I decided to visit California during summer vacation. I drove all the way there. First, I went to Detroit and spent a *Shabbes* there. From Detroit, I drove to Cleveland. I was supposed to meet Eddie in Cleveland. I think I was supposed to spend *Tisha b'Av* there, and then go with him to Los Angeles and San Francisco. But Eddie got tied down in Cleveland, so after *Tisha b'Av*, I went to Chicago. Then I drove myself across the country and stopped in few places.

I arrived an hour or so before *Shabbes* in Los Angeles. The only person I knew in Los Angeles was a friend of mine named Moyshe Gross, who lives not far from us on Sixth Street. He was my friend from *yeshiva*. He

Rabbi Reports Religious Revival Found in Midwest, West Coast

A religious revival movement, encompassing not only the Jewish religion but others as well, is now taking place in the Midwest and on the West Coast in the opinion of Rabbi Herman Roszler of Temple Beth-El in Hornell.

Rabbi Roszler recently returned from a six-week tour of these sections of the country where he made a survey of the religious needs of 64 Jewish communities. His tour was sponsored by the Rabbinical Alliance of America.

As a result of talks he had with church officials of all denominations in the cities he visited, Rabbi Roszler feels that the past five years have seen a tremendous rise in religious development.

While he feels that the same trend is prevailing in the East, Rabbi Roszler thinks that the revival is taking place on a larger scale in the areas he toured. He believes that the main reason for the general "movement back to God" is that people have lost faith in the scientific approach to the problems of humanity.

Rabbi Roszler stated, "People are beginning to discover that only through religious faith can they solve their problems adequately."

"To met the needs of the people today," the Rabbi said, "a religious instructor has become a combined psychologist, social worker and psychiatrist."

Another reason Rabbi Roszler gave for the revival movement was that people are getting more and more to feel the need of "belonging" to a religious group. They are finding that it is almost impossible to go without religion.

Concerning the purpose of his tour, Rabbi Roszler said that development problems facing the expansion of the Jewish religion were different in almost every community he visited. He did note, however, that a lack of qualified personnel and a lack of proper organization are two of the biggest factors preventing a more rapid development program.

Rabbi Roszler believes that the

BACK FROM RELIGIOUS SURVEY—Rabbi Herman Roszler of Temple Beth-El in Hornell, is going over one of the survey reports he made while touring the western section of the United States for the Rabbinical Alliance of America. Rabbi Roszler visited 64 cities during his six-week travels and returned to Hornell last week.

Rabbinical Alliance of America will be able to solve many of the problems of the Jewish communities by distributing literature explaining procedures and methods which have proved successful in other places.

He is presently working on in-

dividual reports for each of the 64 communities which he must submit to the Rabbinical Alliance in the near future. Rabbi Roszler will also go to Brooklyn early in October to give an oral report to the Alliance which has its headquarters there.

During a summer vacation road trip, Zeidy surveyed the religious needs in multiple Jewish communities.

Zeidy took many summer
road trips from Hornell.

had come to Los Angeles in
1949 or 1950 and worked
in construction. Later, he
became very successful
in real estate. Now he is
retired, and he has real estate
and some other investments,
I believe. He was also in the
insurance business, and he
was my life insurance man. I
stayed with him for *Shabbes.*

The next week, I stayed
one *Shabbes* in the Stetler
Hotel. It was a problem. It
was a very high hotel, 12
to 14 stories, and I had to
walk up and down, because
I would not use the elevator
on *Shabbes.* In Detroit, I
had met somebody from Transylvania, and I talked to him. He told me
to look for his friend Joe Pasternak in Los Angeles. Pasternak was a very
famous producer of musicals.

[Pasternak was one of eleven children of a Jewish family in Szilágysom-
lyó, Austria-Hungary His father was a town clerk. In 1920, Pasternak
immigrated to the United States as a teenager and stayed with an uncle
in Philadelphia. He worked in a factory, punching holes in leather belts,
and he did a variety of other jobs. Pasternak spent the "Golden Age"
of musicals in Hollywood at MGM Studios, producing many successful
musicals with singing stars like Deanna Durbin, Kathryn Grayson, and

Jane Powell, as well as swimmer and bathing beauty Esther Williams. His career as a film producer spanned 40 years and earned him two Oscar nominations and three Golden Globe Award nominations.]

I was supposed to give him a call and tell him that this man from Transylvania sent me. So I did. He invited me to come visit the studios. But I never went. I don't know why. I just didn't.

Anyway, I met Eddie in Los Angeles, and after a few days we went to San Francisco. In San Francisco, Eddie called on a woman who was called The Duchess. She was a very well-to-do woman whose daughter married a Jewish man in San Francisco. It was in 1955. And this Jewish husband sort of mistreated her and their daughter, and they got divorced. The ex-husband was supposedly the owner of Harris Tweed from Scotland.

I don't know how Eddie met The Duchess, but she was staying at the Hirsch's, who turned out to be Mommy's aunt and uncle. When we got to town, Eddie called the Duchess and told her we were there. She made arrangements for us to come to the Hirsch's, whose daughter Rozie showed us around the town (she now lives in Bangor, Maine). Uncle Sam and Bela *aleya hasholem* were there. And the Hirsch's called their niece Maureen to come meet some boys. So, this is how we met.

Just before I left Hornell, I had purchased a brand-new car, a Pontiac. While Eddie and I were driving Route 99, I drove into a ditch off the road. I must have been tired, but I damaged the car very badly. It cost $600 to fix, I think. That was the equivalent of several thousand dollars today. Anyway, we ended up in this town, Los Bonos, 100 to 150 miles south of San Francisco. We spent several days in the motel there. We couldn't leave because we had to repair the car and have the insurance company approve the money for the parts. We decided to go back to San Francisco for *Shabbes*. We called the Hirsch's, and spent *Shabbes* with them. They invited Mommy to spend that *Shabbes* with them, too.

So, we got acquainted with Mommy. We played chess during *Shabbes*. Mommy said that she let me win on purpose. She said she played better than I did. That's a good possibility. Mommy was home on vacation at the time. She was living in New York and going to Brooklyn College and to the Mizrahi School, a predecessor of the Stern School—a school for Hebrew teachers. She worked as a nursery-school teacher in the Jewish Center, which was not far from where the Richtmans lived at the time.

Anyway, I left her my address, and when I got back to Hornell, I made contact with her. She wrote me a postcard from the airport when she was leaving San Francisco. That's how we kept in touch. After *Rosh Hashana* and *Yom Kippur,* during *chol hamoed Succoth* (the middle days of the Succoth holiday), I went to New York and took Mommy out on a date. After three dates, I proposed. Mommy wasn't so certain. She said we shouldn't jump in so fast because of all kinds of details. But, I said I think the *shidduch* (match) was made in heaven, and we should go ahead.

Zeidy and Grandma Maureen's engagement picture from 1955.

Mommy said we should wait until after *Yom tov* to announce it, but I do everything fast. When I came to daven on the morning of *Hoshana Rabba* at the Shomkuter Rav's, Rav Yecheskal Ruttner *alav hasholem,* who was already living in Flatbush, I announced it. I told him that I was engaged, although the night before, incidentally, we had said we would wait and not tell anybody, to make sure of everything. But, Mommy had already called Grandpa and Grandma, and they told her they were happy. At that time, it was already past midnight in San Francisco. I also told my uncle Rav Yitzhak Ayzik Kahana *alav hasholem.*

I came back to Hornell on the night of *Shmini Atzeret,* and I told the people there. They were elated. They were anxious to meet Mommy. Then she came to visit one *Shabbes.* She stayed at the Jacobsons, and I stayed in my apartment. The Jacobsons were very nice to her and were always nice to me, too.

She came once or twice more, and also at Thanksgiving. At Thanksgiving, I was in New York and drove Mommy out to Hornell. She stayed for the holiday, again at the Jacobsons, where we had Thanksgiving dinner. Then she went back to New York and back to San Francisco. I was very anxious to get married, even though she was going to Brooklyn College, and the wedding would interrupt her studies right in the middle of the term. She went back and had a

Zeidy and Grandma Maureen's wedding
Picture from January 1, 1956.

wedding shower in San Francisco. And I went there, and on January 1, 1956, we got married *besha'a tova u matzlahat* (at a good and auspicious time).

This is the story of Hornell. We stayed there for another year after we got married. We got married in January, and we left the next year in February, 1957. In the meantime, Raizel was born. She was three months old when we moved to Duluth, Minnesota. Mommy and Raizel took a flight to San Francisco from Rochester, New York. And I drove for several days to Duluth, Minnesota. It was quite a distance, about 1,200 miles from Hornell. Before we left Hornell, the community arranged a big send-off dinner and gave us a wallet of money. They were very sorry to see us go.

They had some other rabbis afterward. I don't remember who they had. A number of

Wedding Bells

RABBI AND MRS. Herman Roszler (Maureen Joyce Bloomberg) are ready to cut their wedding cake at the reception that followed their recent nuptials at Congregation Chevra Thilim. The bride is the daughter of the George E. Bloombergs.

—Fireside Studios

Wedding announcement

years ago, we flew to Buffalo, New York, and went to Niagara Falls and rented a car. From Niagara Falls, we went to Rochester and Buffalo, and then to visit Hornell. They had a big party for us. The Jacobsons arranged it, and so many people were there. It must have been about 20 some odd years ago when we went back there from Los Angeles. Everybody was happy to see us, but I haven't been in Hornell since that time.

Rabbi H. Roszler Accepts New Position in Duluth

Rabbi Herman Roszler of Temple Beth-El will leave Hornell Dec. 24 for Duluth, Minn., where he has accepted a position at Congregation Adas-Israel.

Since coming to Hornell in February, 1953, he has reorganized a Hebrew School and organized many activities in the Jewish community.

For the past three years he has served as Jewish chaplain at the Veterans Administration Center in Bath.

As a member of the executive council of the Rabbinical Alliance of America, he has traveled extensively as a "trouble shooter." He made a religious survey in 64 cities throughout the country in 1955.

Rabbi Roszler has been active in Scouting and other civic activities and has spoken to service clubs in Hornell and surrounding communities.

He is a graduate of Brooklyn College and Torah Vodath Seminary in Brooklyn and received his doctor of divinity degree from McKinley Roosevelt College in Chicago, Ill.

Rabbi and Mrs. Roszler and their infant daughter now reside at 64½ Maple St.

Prior to coming to Hornell, he served at a synagogue in Brooklyn.

He said that a successor at Temple Beth-El will be chosen in the future.

RABBI HERMAN ROSZLER

Announcement issued when Zeidy took
a rabbinical position in Duluth, Minnesota.

Chapter 14

When we left, we moved to Duluth, I had a much bigger congregation with a big balcony and a big *shul*. The *shul* in Hornell was nice, but not very big. In Duluth, there was a *baal batish* (impressive) shul with Jews who were learned. There were some who were *shomer Shabbes*, unfortunately not that many, but a number of them. They knew more about *Yiddishkeit*, and there were many *sfarim* (books) in a large library in the big *shul*.

My new synagogue in Duluth, the Third Street Shul, was a beautiful old shul with a big balcony with attractive old-fashioned shul benches. Downstairs was an office, a kitchen and a small *beit hamidrash* for learning that served also as a social hall. We remodeled the downstairs to make classrooms.

The previous rabbis in Duluth were *gadolim* (great rabbis); one was a *mehaber of sfarim* (an author of books). And you could see from the *sfarim* (books) on the shelves that the congregation included Jews who could learn. When we went back to visit in 1990, I saw that somebody had donated a six-by-six foot picture taken about 1910 to 1915 that showed members of the shul wearing black hats and beards. However, many of their children joined the Conservative and Reform temples.

When I arrived, Orthodoxy was very weak. The *shul* was called the Third Street Shul because it was at Third Avenue East and Third Street. A block above that, on Fourth Street and Third Avenue East, was the Conservative *shul*, which once upon a time was an Orthodox *shul*. Not too many years before I came, it was called the Russian *shul*. I was rabbi at Adas Israel, which was referred to as the *Litvishe shul*, because most of our members came from Lithuania.

The Synagogue in Duluth—Adas Israel, The Third street Shul
or Litvishe Shul, was a beautiful 117-year-old synagogue that,
unfortunately, burned down in 2019 due to arson.

There was a smaller Orthodox *shul*, called the Ninth Street Shul because it was on Ninth Street. It had a number of members. They did not have a rabbi, so I served as the rabbi there on various occasions. I would officiate for them for weddings or funerals. But their spiritual *manhig* (leader) was a man named Covel. He was a big *talmid hacham* (scholar), and he was a *shochet* (*kosher* butcher). When I came there, he *shechted* (slaughtered) only a little bit, just enough for one *kosher* butcher. Just to show that there was some order in that community, it had at least four *kosher* butchers, perhaps more. There was one in the area of the Ninth Street Shul, but we didn't eat the meat from this specific butcher's store. I think that fellow married a woman who converted. The other butcher's name was Meyer. There also was a butcher by the name of Goldberg and one by the name of Sher.

I will speak of Sher. The Sher brothers were partners, and their store also had a separate section for *treyf* (non-*kosher*) meat. Their father was in the meat business and was one of the founders of the Orthodox community in Duluth. The founders were Lithuanian Jews, Orthodox people. They weren't necessarily *talmidei hachamim* (great scholars), but they kept the *Shulchan Aruch, Shabbes, yom tov* and *kashrut* (the book of laws, Shabbat, the holy days, and *kosher*). Just the mere fact that this small community had four *kosher* butchers indicates that very few of the Jews there did not keep *kosher*. Later on, as the Reform movement came in, and its temple became more popular even among former members of our shul and their children, the community's *kashrut* (*kosher* observance) was weakened.

The shul in Duluth had a few main families who would actually inter-marry with each other. There were the Kerens, the Kanes, the Kanners, and Goldishes. They were all related and intermarried, so many members of the *shul* were actually members of several great families whose members married one another.

For example, Shabsi Keren was the elder of the *shul*. He was already 98 or 99 years old, and he would come to *shul* every once in a while on *Shabbes*. He lived half a mile away from *shul*. We will always remember him because when Myer was two and three years old, I used to take him to visit Mr. Keren. He would give Myer 50 cents to buy candies, and he would say that Myer has a friend who is 100 years older than him.

The people in Duluth incidentally lived very long lives. Even today, when we went back, we saw people in their 80s and 90s, going strong. Possibly the cold weather preserved them.

As I said, when I arrived, Orthodoxy was very poor, very weak there. I had to rebuild the name of Orthodoxy so a Jew wouldn't be embarrassed to say that he belongs to the Third Street Orthodox *shul*. I immediately got to work. First, I had to separate the downstairs story to make class-rooms for a community *talmid Torah* (school), which the Conservative and the Orthodox shared.

The Reform had their own Sunday school. The Reform rabbi had an Orthodox background, too, and he was learned. He was, perhaps to some degree, *shomer Shabbes* (Sabbath observant), but I cannot recall.

The Conservative Sunday school attracted children of the nursery-school age once a week. For the Orthodox to bring people back into the fold, I had to do the same thing and build a Sunday school. Somebody said it was a *shadma* school. *Shadma* means embarrassment in Yiddish— and sometimes these Sunday schools were.

In addition to the Sunday school, we had Hebrew School four or five times a week. I was instrumental in helping with that. One of the teachers in the Hebrew school was named Wiesel. He was a *hazzan* (cantor) at the Conservative shul, and his wife was a teacher. They both had an Orthodox background, and they were both friendly to us. But, naturally, being the *hazzan* in the Conservative shul, he was influenced by them. So we had to try to instill a little bit of Orthodoxy into the community. And, we had to give a supplement for teaching. I also taught a class at the Sunday school.

Once we attracted the little children, members no longer left the *shul* to go to the Conservative and Reform *shuls*. In addition I taught *Shabbes* adult classes on the weekly *parsha* (Torah portion), *Pirkey Avot* ("Ethics of the Fathers"), and *Ein Yaakov* (legends of the rabbis).

We were instrumental in bringing back a few members. We started putting out a monthly bulletin and inviting speakers for various occasions. On Friday night, we had *oneg Shabbes* with singing and refreshments and the spirit of *Shabbes*.

We were there almost six years, in Duluth. Little by little, the *shul* became stronger under the influence of Orthodoxy. That happened as people heard of us, and the members felt more secure saying that they were members of the Third Street Shul.

One problem was that people kept *kashrut* (kosher) only to some degree. As far as supervision, it was a very difficult thing with these people. I, myself, was very careful to make sure we had the right meat. We would buy meat in Superior, Wisconsin, the sister city across from Duluth. The town had Rabbi Chait, a *schohet* (kosher slaughterer) who had *smicha* (rabbinic ordination) from Yeshiva University. He was a very *frum* fellow. His father was a *shochet* before him, going back

Donation of three
Torahs to Israel

RABBI HERMAN ROSZLER, right, receives a Torah or scroll from Judge Sidney Kaner, left, and Samuel M. Karon, president of Adas Israel congregation.—(Herald photo.)

For New Israel Settlements

Presentation of Torahs Slated

Three Torahs, or scrolls of law, which will go to new settlements in the state of Israel, will be presented at the annual Chanukah festival of Adas Israel congregation Sunday night.

The presentation ceremony will be held at 7:30 p. m. following a 6:15 p. m. dinner.

The presentation will be made by Judge Sidney E. Kaner whose father, the late Ben Kaner, was the original donator of one of the scrolls. Also taking part in the presentation will be Samuel M. Karon, congregation president, in behalf of the synagogue, and B. H. Edelstein, Superior, formerly of Hibbing.

Rabbi Herman Roszler, spiritual leader of the congregation, will accept the Torahs in behalf of the new settlements and forward them through the courtesy of Alex J. Lurye.

Presentation of the scrolls is made in response to requests from settlements of recent immigrants to Israel. Approximate cost of each hand-written scroll is from $1,200 to $1,500.

Also part of the program will be devoted to installation of newly-elected officers and trustees of the congregation. They are: President, Sam Karon; vice president, Maurice Krovitz; secretary, Alex J. Lurye; treasurer, Ben S. Karon, and trustees, M. J. Widdes, Charles Bruzonsky, Harry V. Cohen, Lawrence Cowan, Abe Friedman, Sam Ginsberg, Abe Golden, Ben Goldish, Max Gordon, Abe Markus, Morris Markus, Ralph Munic, Nathan Schneider, Louis Shapiro and Ted Widdes.

A new memorial tablet will be dedicated in memory of the late Barney Karon, Virginia.

Dinner chairmen are Mrs. Jennie Cohen and Mrs. Sam Klatzky. Toastmaster will be Abe Golden. Vocal numbers will be rendered by Mrs. Sidney Laskin, and a chanukah narration will be presented by the following teenagers of the congregation: Sanford Baddin, Danny Cohen, Charlotte Garon, Mark Berger and Janet Widdes. Isidore Zien will give the benediction.

probably to 1910 or 1912. [*Incidentally, Rabbi Chait is the uncle of Rosalie Zellas; her mother was his sister.*]

The *shamash* (sexton) of the shul, Mr. Rosenberg, was a big *talmid hacham*. He had a tremendous memory. He was also a *shochet*. He used to show me the *halavim* (the slaughtering knife), so I could be sure it was an excellent *halav* and had no indentations, which of course would make the beef *treyf* (not kosher). Usually, I would take meat from the *schita* of this Rabbi Chait. Sometimes, I also bought from Rosenberg, who would *shecht* for the Shers.

But it was a difficult thing, the supervision. I would go to the butcher shops. I would say they kept *kosher,* so there was no fear of *treyf* meat. But Goldberg and Meyer were from the Fourth Street *shul,* the Conservative *shul.* I understood that after we left, there were only two kosher butchers left, the Shers and Goldberg. There was no *schita* (slaughtering) at all. Rosenberg, the *shamash,* became sick and died before we left. He was a very smart fellow. He had arrived in Duluth in 1936. Of course, he had his enemies, like the Witteses family. They had *machlokot* (arguments) from time to time. They argued also with the previous rabbi, who was very humiliated by this. He was a very fine man, but he left for Minneapolis.

So the meat was *kosher* and reliable, but there was little I could do, walking into butcher shops, and so on. There was a bakery that used *kosher* ingredients, but the baker himself was not *shomer Shabbes.* However, the ingredients were no problem; I would go there and check myself.

The community in Duluth was much larger than in Hornell. Some *kosher* products were brought in. Incidentally, today there is no *kosher*

Riding in the snow—Esther, Myer, and Raizel riding bikes in the winter.

butcher in Duluth. There is only the Sher family, who were originally
from Lithuania, and their great grandchildren, and he brings in meat in a
freezer from the east and from Minneapolis.

We came to Duluth in February, 1957. It was a very cold winter. All
winters are cold in Duluth. We had an apartment a block away from the
shul. The address was 213 Second Avenue East. After a year, we moved
to 1226 East Third Street. Incidentally, Myer was there about a year ago.
He had a conference in Minneapolis. He drove to Duluth and went back
to see the house where he was born. He couldn't get in. There was no
answer. He saw it from the outside. The *shul*, too, was closed.

When we went back we were, of course, able to get in because I called
some people. Myer didn't know anyone. I had to give him some names,
but he called the office that used to be the Jewish center. They told him
to contact someone, but he just couldn't get in. But we were able to get
in. We saw the *shul* on the inside when we went there last summer. It
was remodeled very nicely, but unfortunately there were very few young
people.

When we visited Duluth, the *shul* had a *minyan* for *mincha* and *maariv*
(afternoon and evening prayer groups). It was summertime. I *davened*
mincha there for the *Amud* (led afternoon services). There were about 12
to 15 people. I wanted to learn with them for a little while, but they were
not disposed to learn.

Not many young Jewish people are left in Duluth, not many who are
Orthodox, and no one who is Conservative. The Conservative combined
with the Reform. Maybe a few came over to the Orthodox. The *shul* itself
remained strictly Orthodox, but a number of years ago they unfortunately
removed the *mechitza* (barrier separating the men's and women's sections)
and put in a microphone in hope of attracting new members and avoiding
the loss of existing members. Regrettably, they lost in one way and didn't
attract many members. They told me that all year round, there is no big
problem, because no Orthodox women come to *daven*. But I presume on
the *yamim noraim* (high holidays), men and women probably sit together.
[Unfortunately the beautiful, historic 117-year-old synagogue was burned

down by arson in 2019, a tremendous loss to the city and the Jewish Community in Duluth.]

In recent years, most communities in the United States experience just the reverse. *Shuls* that were not Orthodox, that had no *mechitza*, are turning more Orthodox. In Duluth, it was the reverse. It happened a number of years ago, about 10 or 15 years ago.

There were interesting people there in Duluth. I remember Louis Cohen, who had several brothers and was *shomer Shabbes* (Sabbath observant). He was a very nice man, not a wealthy man by any means, but nice. He was a candy man, too. When the children—Myer, Raizel, and Esther Sue—came to shul, he always had candy for them.

In the wintertime, we used to *daven* (pray) downstairs, because it was very cold upstairs. With the exception of a *Bar Mitzvah* or a special occasion, we *davened* downstairs because it took a lot of gas to heat that *shul* upstairs. It was very big. It could seat quite a few hundred people, and we had 60 to 70 people. So we *davened* downstairs where it was warm.

Let's not forget, the temperatures in Duluth could reach as low as 32 to 35 degrees below zero in wintertime. The winter started at the beginning of October, if not earlier sometimes, and maybe lasted until the middle of May. So when it got warm after *Pesach,* we started *davening* upstairs every *Shabbes*. Sometimes on Friday nights, if we had a special speaker or something like that, we would heat the upstairs *shul* and *daven* there.

Otherwise, downstairs we set up a *mechitza* made of boards, so the women were behind a separation. Actually there was a *mechitza* behind the *bimah* (podium) itself, which was in the middle of the floor. There were not too many women, maybe three or four unless there was a special occasion. So we had a *mechitza* downstairs.

Speaking of women in Duluth, I would lecture many times in front of women on *Chumash* (Torah) and other Jewish subjects.

One woman was very nice to us. We have a picture of her. Her name was Mrs. Fogel. Let's not forget that we were strangers in Duluth. There were not many young Orthodox people. I mean, real Orthodox, in the sense that we knew it. We were very friendly with the people there, but religiously we were not very close. Still, they didn't want us to leave. They wanted us to stay and gave us all kinds of things we didn't want to accept. [We nonetheless had to leave because there was no day school for our children].

Mrs. Fogel was originally from Germany. She told us that she, her son, and her husband came on the last boat that left Germany in 1939, so their lives were saved. She, too, was a stranger in Duluth, though she had a son, Bernie, and a daughter-in-law, but they incidentally moved to Los Angeles. Mrs. Fogel died in the old age home in Minneapolis.

Many of the people were elderly people, but Duluth had no *kosher* nursing home, so many of them went to the old age home in Minneapolis, one of the finest *kosher* nursing homes in the nation.

Mrs. Fogel would come sometimes when Mommy would leave. She was like a friend of the family, and she would babysit if me or Mommy left for a day or so. She would take care of the children and visit on *Shabbes*. She was a *bat bayit*, a member of the household, and a very nice lady. She became very useful to us because she was *shomer Shabbes*, and she would come every *Shabbes* to *shul* to *daven*. I don't believe her son was much of a *shomer Shabbes* person, but he would come to *shul*, though.

It was a trend in those times in Orthodoxy that many people came to *daven* on *Shabbes* and Friday night, but they also had business to do. It was not that easy. I cannot accuse them, perhaps they were like a *tinok shenishva* (like a baby, they didn't know any better). But that was the trend in the United States. It's a miracle that today, thank God, we have strong Orthodoxy; it's really miraculous. A lot of this is due to Holocaust survivors who came from the beginning of 1945 to 1946. They brought in a lot of the community's *yiddishkeit* (Jewish life). Some of the *rosh yeshivas* (heads of yeshivas) were survivors from Shanghai and Japan. People from Europe escaped through Japan at the beginning of the war and came here to the United States. They had some influence. Many of the Hungarian and Polish Jews who survived brought *yiddishkeit* to many cities.

Some Holocaust survivors lived in Duluth. I used to visit a *shomer Shabbes* family who moved to Minneapolis. There were several families whose older generation was *shomer Shabbes*, but very few of the younger generation were *shomer Shabbes*. There was a family named Jacobovitz who moved to Los Angeles. I see Mr. Jacobovitz from time to time. He had a store on Superior Street, the main street. He is *shomer Shabbes,* I get together with him every once in a while. The Conservative rabbi and his wife were also *shomer Shabbes.*

But socially, there was not very much for us. I would say it was lonesome. I was busy going every day to the office, going to visit the hospital. In the morning and at night, I would go to *daven,* but the weather—of course, that is something to remember. It was very cold. It was very, very cold. I didn't feel like going outside, though I had to every day. When the children were small and it was cold outside, they would sit by the radiator and look out, seeing how everything became white with snow. They would look at the passing cars for about a year while they widened the street, and this was the entertainment for our children.

But we had a big house, a very warm house. We moved there after a year, just when Myer was born. Raizel was born in Hornell, as I said, she was three months old when we came to Duluth, and Myer was born in Duluth. And when Mommy and Myer came from the hospital, they came to the new house on Eastern Street.

Comparatively speaking, it was a big house. There was a living room, dining room, and a huge kitchen with a breakfast area and a pantry. And the second story had three or four bedrooms. Some were small, and one was big. There was plenty of space. Then we had a basement with a laundry room. It was quite adequate. The children played a lot inside. Later on, the Jewish center opened a nursery school, and Myer and Raizel were very happy to go there the first year. The center director picked them up in a station wagon. In the second year, they had a bus.

But Raizel decided at the start of the second year that enough was enough, and that she would not go to nursery school. So Myer would go by himself, and sometimes he would wait outside. Esther Sue was too young to go to nursery school. Just getting the children dressed in winter clothes was a full time job by itself.

When I first came to Duluth, before the furniture arrived, I stayed with a lady named Miss Wine. They had a big house, and that's where the *shamash* (sexton) lived. He had his own room. It was about a block from the *shul*, I think on East Fourth, on Third Avenue East. I stayed there for a few weeks until the furniture arrived and Mommy came with Raizel. Then we lived in another apartment, the first apartment we had in Duluth.

It was on Second Avenue East and Third Street, and there was a funeral parlor as part of the house. It's still a funeral parlor; we saw it when we visited the apartment. It had a huge, long hall walking in, and it was very hot; there was a lot of heat. But when Raizel was small, we would take her outside even when it was zero degrees. We covered her up in a carriage. We believed in those days that everybody has to have fresh air. So every day, cold or not, we would take her outside. Of course, she was very well dressed and covered up. There was also a small porch in the back where we could take her out.

In the beginning in Duluth, we were very happy. The congregation was much larger than the one in Hornell. But as the children started getting older, we started thinking about getting out of Duluth. The problem was, naturally, needing a day school, a *yeshiva ktana* where the children could go. We saw that the results of the *Talmud Torah* were very poor. Compared to some of the *Talmud Torahs* I saw in New York, this one was pretty good, but it was still poor.

The environment itself was not good for bringing up children. Children would go to public school, and as they grew up some became paper boys, delivering papers. And in their homes, the environment on *Shabbes* and *yom tov* was not optimal.

We had instituted junior services at the *shul*. I sent some of the children to NCSY, which was then a small organization. Children who come from non-religious homes become religious under the influence of NCSY and go to *yeshiva*. Yet the environment in Duluth was not really suitable for bringing up Orthodox children. In the beginning years, things went well. As far as happiness, we were very happy there, but Mommy was lonesome. I was at least busy with the people. Mommy would give lectures

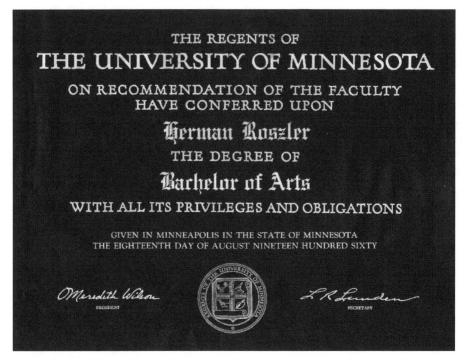

THE REGENTS OF
THE UNIVERSITY OF MINNESOTA
ON RECOMMENDATION OF THE FACULTY
HAVE CONFERRED UPON
𝕳𝖊𝖗𝖒𝖆𝖓 𝕽𝖔𝖘𝖟𝖑𝖊𝖗
THE DEGREE OF
𝕭𝖆𝖈𝖍𝖊𝖑𝖔𝖗 𝖔𝖋 𝕬𝖗𝖙𝖘
WITH ALL ITS PRIVILEGES AND OBLIGATIONS

GIVEN IN MINNEAPOLIS IN THE STATE OF MINNESOTA
THE EIGHTEENTH DAY OF AUGUST NINETEEN HUNDRED SIXTY

PRESIDENT   SECRETARY

Diploma from University of Minnesota.

sometimes and speak about the Hadassah Hospital Chagall windows and other things. I also continued going to school and got a Bachelor of Arts in business and economics.

I went there at night and during the day, since I had left Brooklyn College in the middle of my studies when I went to Hornell. In Hornell, I was supposed to start school, but I got sick so I stopped. But in Duluth, I went to the University of Minnesota and graduated with honors and got a bachelor's degree in 1960. I have the diploma here [with all the works and the ring]. Unfortunately I never did anything with that degree, but I figured maybe it would come in handy if I had to stop working in the *rabbanut*.

So in the later years—after we were there five years—we were thinking about the future.

Raizel was already in kindergarten, but there was only one Jewish boy in her class. The interesting thing is we used to send Raizel with her own snacks, because the kindergarten gave the children cookies, and Raizel never ate them. We could not know if they were *kosher* or not. The children would all say a prayer, "God is great, God is good," and so on. And Raizel would say *the bracha* of *borei minei mezenos.* The funny joke is that many of the children really learned the *bracha* that Raizel would say. So one time Raizel was absent, and the teacher told us that one of the non-Jews, a neighbor, made the *bracha* because Raizel was not there and somebody had to.

Anyway, I am just trying to point out the problems that we had. We felt although it was a pretty good position, a prestigious one, from the *yiddishkeit* point of view, there was no future for us because of the children. So we tried many ways to get out.

In Duluth, I was naturally trying to inculcate and influence the children to join Orthodoxy. We tried as much as possible with both the boys and the girls. I succeeded with some of them to some degree, because I heard some of them became *frum* (observant). They no longer live in Duluth. One is in Minneapolis now. Now this is hearsay that I heard from other people, but what these people consider as *frum,* I don't know. I'm not sure what that means.

As far as the members of the *shul* at the time, I believe I was successful to quite a degree in restoring the name of Orthodoxy, as far as learning and so on. Though it is not now a *kehila* (community) that one can be proud of or say that they have *hazra atarah leyoshna,* (that the crown is returned to the way it was). When I visited there, I saw unfortunately more or less the *churban* (destruction) of Orthodoxy. But, of course, we can never be *meyoash* (without hope), since we never know what the future will bring.

I have been corresponding with this fellow, the president of the *shul,* to suggest that he invite an Orthodox rabbi at least once a month, twice a month, to lecture for them. But I don't believe this is going to happen in the near future. Unfortunately, there is no *Chabad* there. That's really sad, because the *Chabad* movement goes all over the world.

I'm coming back to describing a little bit more of Duluth when we were there. The city was built on hills. Friday nights I would walk to *daven,* or we would have an *oneg Shabbes* (Shabbos party). I would bundle up with a very heavy wool overcoat and a fur hat and cover my face with a scarf. I wore long heavy underwear because the temperatures could be 30 to 35 below zero, and it would stay that cold for weeks! As a matter of fact, when Mommy and Raizel arrived in Duluth, it was 22 below zero, and I went to meet her with a fellow named Keren who drove us from the airport. It was quite a cold reception, as we call it.

The summer was nice. It was not too hot. In the summertime, we would go to Lake Superior. We lived a few blocks from there. We went there for swimming a few times. It was very cold for swimming. As a matter of fact one time Myer, *chas ve shalom* (it should never happen), almost drowned there. The wife of the Conservative Rabbi saw it and screamed and yelled and ran fast and grabbed him.

We would also go to Superior, Wisconsin. There was a nice lake that was much warmer. We would go there in the summertime. But most summers, for about four weeks or so—I believe every summer we were in Duluth—we would go to San Francisco and spend time there with the grandparents.

The daily schedule in Duluth was that I would go to *minyan* every morning. We *davened* at 7 o'clock. We *davened* and discussed some things with people. Then I would come home during the day after *davening.* Later on, I would go to the hospital to visit some of the sick people, and sometimes I would learn and then go to the office at *shul* again in the afternoon. I had a secretary who came for two or three hours in the afternoon. We had bulletins and special notices, and I prepared for learning and giving speeches. I would speak on various topics, on Judaism and the Holocaust, and so on.

Then I would come home about 5:30. In the wintertime, the days were very short. It would get dark at around 4:30 or 4:45, so we had the *maariv minyan* (evening prayers) every night at 7 o'clock. In the summer as the days would get longer, we would daven both mincha and maariv at 7 pm.

Letters to the Editor

Duluth Rabbi Disagrees With Some Colleagues

Editor, The American Jewish World

I read, with great interest, the comments by the eighteen Twin City rabbis regarding the death penalty to be given Eichmann for the crimes committed against the Jewish people and against humanity.

I fully agree with my learned colleagues that the crimes committed by this Nazi butcher are so enormous that no penalty is commensurate with the crime. May I, however, point out that in our society the ultimate penalty is still capital punishment.

I do wish to disagree with a number of my colleagues who are against capital punishment in this case for the reason that man is a creature of God, therefore must not be destroyed by human hands. May I refer them to the Bible, where it is explicitly pointed out that when dealing with these types of renegades and social outcasts, "Thou shalt have no mercy on them."

According to Jewish tradition, man is born with "Behirah" (free choice). Therefore it is man's duty to choose the right path. "Uveharto Bahaim" (thou shalt choose life).

Eichmann, too, was born with free choice. It was he who voluntarily chose to become a murderer, therefore we must not have pity on his body and soul, and we must fulfill another Biblical command, "Uviarto Horo Mikirbeho" (thou shalt cleanse the evil from amidst you).

I concur with Rabbi Levin who states that the death penalty for Eichman would not be against Jewish law. Although the Israeli courts of today do not have the power of the Sanhedrin of old to mete out the death penalty, they nevertheless would have the power to sentence Eichmann to death, not as a Sanhedrin but as the Goali Hadom (Biblical passage referring to the revenge taken by a person whose next of kin was murdered).

The Israeli court is the next of kin to six million Jews who were murdered by the hand of Eichmann and his accomplices.

We have confidence in the Israeli court that whatever penalty will be given Eichmann, even death, will be consonant with the Jewish spirit of justice and law.

Rabbi Herman Roszler
Adas Israel, Duluth

Letter to the Minneapolis Jewish Newspaper—*The American Jewish World* was still being published in 2021.

As I said, I used to be friendly with Rabbi Chait from Superior. I used to see him from time to time. There was also a Conservative temple in Superior, Wisconsin, and I recall that the rabbi there was also an Orthodox man. I would see him, too, from time to time. Sometimes I would go visit the people at home. Most Jews in Duluth were merchants; they were in business. Some of the families, like the Kerens, were in the scrap iron business. Some were in the building metals businesses, some had small stores, and some were professionals.

Mommy had some help from a neighbor whose name was Mary. She was about 12 years old. She was like a mother's helper who came every day for about two or three hours. This girl was so reliable, more reliable than any adult person. She used to help Mommy give the children a bath, and she would help around the house. She was there with us for about two years. Her sister took over from her. We also had a cleaning woman. She would come in once every two weeks to do the heavy work.

Mommy was very skinny at the time. First of all, she had three children already. Esther Sue was born, and we had Raizel and Myer. In those days, you did not have any paper diapers like we have today. We had to change linen diapers, and we did not have a bathroom downstairs, though it was a nice house. We had only one bathroom upstairs, and she had to go upstairs to change the baby's diaper. Just from running all the way upstairs to change diapers and so on, one could become skinny going up and down.

The butcher did not *kasher* the meat, so we had to make the chicken and meat *kosher* downstairs in the basement. So even with all the help we had, Mommy still had quite a hard job. I tried to help as much as I could, because I was home quite a bit. Yet Mommy was still very skinny those days. I think one time we were very scared. We wondered why she was so skinny. We had tests, but thank God, everything was alright.

I was also instrumental in bringing in the Talmud Torah principal. His name was Halperin. His father was a *Hassidishe rav*. He was from Poland originally, and had learned in *Kfar Haroe* in Israel. He and his wife Julie were *frum*. They had a child just before they left Duluth. We were friendly with them. He tried to teach as much as possible and imbue the children with an Orthodox outlook as much as he could as principal. That wasn't easy because the board of the *Talmid Torah*, which used to meet once or twice a month, had many Conservative members. They were trying to fight us; they didn't have too much.

OPPOSITE:
Announcement from
the Duluth Jewish
newspaper of the Zeidy's
move to Los Angeles

BULK RATE
U. S. POSTAGE
P A I D
Permit No. 966
Duluth, Minn.

JEWISH
FELLOWSHIP NEWS

THE ORIGINAL JEWISH NEWSPAPER IN DULUTH PUBLISHED SINCE 1936

VOL. 25 — NO. 9	DULUTH, MINNESOTA	MAY, 1962

Rabbi Herman Roszler Accepts New Position In Los Angeles

Rabbi Herman Roszler of Adas Israel Congregation will leave Duluth in June for Los Angeles where he has accepted the position of Director of the Pacific Coast Region of the Union of

RABBI H. ROSZLER

Orthodox Jewish Congregations of America. The Union of Orthodox Jewish Congregations of America is the parent body, representing 3,000 Orthodox congregations throughout the United States.

Since coming to Duluth in January, 1957 he has doubled the membership of the congregation and organized many activities in the Congregation. He was a member of many organizations in the city.

As a member of the Executive Council of the Rabbinical Al-

liance of America, he has traveled extensively throughout the United States on behalf of Orthodox Judaism.

Prior to his coming to Duluth, he served as spiritual leader of Bethel Congregation, Hornell, New York, for four years. and for three years, he also served as the Jewish chaplain at the Veterans' Administration Center in Bath,

New York. In 1960, Rabbi Roszler was honored by his Alma Mater, Yeshiva Torah Vodaath, for his outstanding devotion as a spiritual leader.

Rabbi Roszler is a graduate of Brooklyn College and the University of Minnesota, Duluth, and was ordained at Torah Vodaath Theological Seminary in Brooklyn, N. Y.

Fellowship Clubs Spring Festival Fine Success

The 27th annual Jewish Fellowship Club festival again was a success in all respects. The event, one of the highlites of clubs varied program was enjoyed by all. Members of the Fellowship Club had worked for months making preparations for the festival which attracted many hundreds to the Hotel Duluth on May 6. Co-chairmen Ben R. Greene, Abe Golden and Alex J. Lurye were ably assisted by the following hard workers: Burton Shapiro, Benjamin Shapiro, Henry Goldfine, Harry Levenson, Louis Fishman, Barney Rich, Jack Karsner, Fred Danelko, Gordon Bruzonsky, Charles

Bruzonsky, Nathan Bruzonsky, Harry V. Cohen, Edward Greene, Morrie Segal, Sam Galburt, Al Davidson, Ben Litman, Maurice Krovitz, Saul Sander, and Sam Breitbord.

Don't forget to attend Fellowship Club meetings on May 17, June 7 and 21.

New Talmud Torah Board Members Elected

The annual meeting of the Ida Cook Hebrew School took place Sunday afternoon, April were elected: Mrs. Sam Klatzky, George Stewart and Alfred Zyroff. Charles Bruzonsky was re-elected to serve a second term.

Adas Israel Sisterhood To Install Officials May 22

The Annual Chapter Meeting

Chapter 15

When we left Duluth, we stopped in a number of places including Salt Lake City, where we toured the city and the tabernacle. Then we drove on to San Francisco, where we arrived Friday afternoon and spent *Shabbes*. That was sometime in June, and I left the family in San Francisco for about two weeks.

Then I went to Los Angeles to set up shop. I was coming to Los Angeles to become the director of the Orthodox Union (OU), the field representative for the West Coast. I went to meet with the board and set up the office. Mommy, Myer, Raizel, and Esther Sue arrived by plane on July 4, and I picked them up at the Burbank airport. They came by PSA Airline, a discount airline which no longer exists.

Some of my duties with the Orthodox Union included organizing the Orthodox congregations to strengthen Orthodoxy on the West Coast. In addition, I had to deal with the Orthodox congregations in setting up various functions. For example, we had meetings of all the presidents of the Orthodox organizations and congregations, and monthly meetings of the presidents of the Orthodox men's clubs and the presidents of the sisterhoods. We also had training sessions, and so on.

The Roszlers in the early 1960s.

The main support and the big mover of this position was actually Rabbi Dolgin, rabbi of the Beth Jacob congregation, along with some of his members. Some other *shul* rabbis—Rabbi Spiegelman, Rabbi Shoham, and Rabbi Brenner—also gave somewhat weak support to this goal, but the Beth Jacob congregation was the main mover.

Rabbi Spring, who was originally from Chicago, held this position, which was about a year old, prior to my arrival. He left for some reason. In the beginning, most things were going well, although I still did not have a contract, and I never did get a written contract. However, this was supposed to be a steady position, and the New York office was supposed to pay expenses until we became self-sufficient here and raised enough funds to support our office and pay me and the secretary. My position was also supposed to include furthering and continuing the Torah University.

Now let me just give you a little bit of background about what happened in Los Angeles just 29 years ago, when we first arrived. Unfortunately, Orthodoxy was quite weak. There were a few Orthodox *shuls*, but they had very few members, and some Jewish day schools, but they also were very few in number.

The Conservative and Reform movements were very strong. The Conservative movement already had an institution called the University of Judaism, located in a huge building on Sunset Boulevard. And the Reform had their own school, which was created with the Hebrew Union College of the Reform Movement. Orthodoxy had just begun to come into its own here. For instance, a few *bilabiate* (community members), rabbis, and Rabbi Spring established a night school called Torah University. It did not function very well, but it was the beginning of something. The Orthodox felt that they also had to establish a teacher training college to further Orthodoxy and to create a reservoir of teachers, because many of the teachers were imported from the East coast. They also needed an adult education school where people who were Orthodox could advance their education.

Today, most of the teachers still come from the East, but now we have, thank God, some local people who went away to *yeshivas*, came back, and went into *chinuch* (teaching). The Torah University was supposed to balance the gains of the Conservative and the Reform movements, and this was also part of my position.

At that time, however, a number of people, such as Rabbi Dolgin, Rabbi Spiegelman, and some lay leaders, felt that perhaps the answer was to affiliate our school with Yeshiva University. So after discussions with Rabbi Belkin *alav hasholem,* the president of Yeshiva University, it consented to establish a branch here. It was supposed to be a teacher's college in the evening and offer adult education. The faculty was assembled from local rabbis and additional lecturers from New York. One of the local rabbis who lectured at that time was Rabbi Uri, now Rabbi Emeritus of the Young Israel of Beverly Hills.

The faculty included Rabbi Shimonovitz, Rabbi Gruman, Rabbi Chamenitsky, and some other local rabbis who were also teaching in the day schools. I was the registrar. It was my position to organize the staff, work on the curriculum, and recruit a student body. That was very difficult because membership in Orthodox institutions was not very large. Lining up young people for teacher training, for the teacher's seminary, was very difficult because not that many were interested. Nevertheless, we tried to enroll as many young people as possible in our various courses.

We didn't have many courses to start, but we had classes four nights a week. I continued with this YU teacher's college at night for approximately a year to a year and a half. And, for about six months after my arrival, I also continued with the OU.

Unfortunately, the OU did not have much cooperation from the congregations. Most of them did not pay the dues they were supposed to pay, dues that would go toward the maintenance of the office and staff, that is, the secretary and me. We had an office at that time at 590 North Vermont Avenue, known as the 590 building. It housed most of the Jewish organizations, like the Mizrachi, and even the Reform had their office there. All the Federation offices were there. That building belonged to the Jewish community, and we rented an office from them.

Unfortunately, my job did not work out very well with the OU. In the first few months, they did help out from New York and sent money for the office. But, after a while, they said, "Well, it's time that you are on your own and raise your own funds for your expenses." But, unfortunately, we did not have the cooperation of the Orthodox congregations to accomplish that.

As a result of this lack of support from New York and the lack of support locally, I gave up the OU position, and we made some compromise brokered by Rabbi Dolgin and Mr. Samson. I believe they paid me about $1,000 severance pay, and I left that position. However, I continued on with Yeshiva University teacher's college at night for about an additional year. I spent about four nights a week on that job. Sometimes I came in on Sunday to arrange things, and the main office in New York paid me directly.

At that time, the day school movement was also very weak. Hillel Day School was just about to finish its construction on Olympic Boulevard, where it is today. This past year, Hillel also dedicated an additional new building. Then, it was very small, and even the quality of the teachers was not the best, but it was better than the other day schools in the community. Hillel, the largest of the schools, was affiliated with the Beth Jacob congregation.

In the San Fernando Valley, they had just started the Emek Hebrew Academy, which probably had 60 to 70 students. It was affiliated with the Orthodox *shul* there, Shaarey Zedek. Rabbi Shoham was its rabbi. Yavneh Hebrew Academy was affiliated with Shaarey Tefilla. There was also Torah Emes, just a fledgling little day school supported by and affiliated with the Magen Avraham *shul* under Rabbi Issacson. It was a small school, but now it is the largest day school in the city, with close to 900 *talmidim*, students.

In those days, there was no Yeshiva Gedolah; today we have a Yeshiva Gedolah in Los Angeles, we have a Beit Yaakov, and we have a large *kollel*, the Lakewood Kollel, that came in around 16 years ago with Rabbi Fassman. Of course, there are many new *stieblach* (small neighborhood congregations) and *shuls*, also.

Los Angeles had a number of Orthodox *shuls*, although some were sort of modern. The traditional Orthodox rabbis included Rabbi Schroit at Bnai David and Rabbi Levine of the Judea Shul. Some of those *shuls* had mixed seating in those days, but today at least three or four of the *shuls* have put in a *mechitza* (divider between men's and women's seating), and now they are real Orthodox *shuls*.

When we first came to LA, we lived in a duplex at 924 North Gardner Street. We attended a *shul*, a little *shtiebel*, where we were called the *jungerlite* (young people). There were a number of rabbis, teachers, and professionals; it was a very nice group. It was on Melrose, near Gardner. Sometimes we would *daven* (pray) on *Shabbes* morning in the Young Israel of Los Angeles, where we met Rabbi Brissman, the librarian in the Jewish department at UCLA. We became friends, and we've stayed friends since that time. The Brissmans moved away, and they now live in New York where their daughter lives.

Just before we left Duluth, we bought a station wagon, which came in very handy for the trip. Later, it came in very handy when we got into the nursery day care center business. Mommy had a position as a preschool kindergarten teacher at Shaarey Tefila at Yavneh Hebrew Academy. Rabbi Spiegelman was the rabbi of the shul, and the principal was a Rabbi Goldberg. Mommy needed a car, so we bought a used convertible. It was very good and came in very handy, and Mommy loved the car. Sometimes she would take down the roof of the car and ride with it open. We bought it from Rabbi Schroit, the Rabbi Emeritus of B'nai David.

At that time, Orthodox Judaism was still very small in Los Angeles. There were two *kosher* restaurants, Hartman's and Tel Aviv, both on Fairfax, but both later folded. Today, if you added up all the *kosher* restaurants from the Valley to Los Angeles itself, you probably would have 35 to 40 *kosher* restaurants, so you can see the growth. The growth is more on the other side of town, the Hancock Park area. There, you have Hasidic Jews; you have children with *payot* (side curls), mainly Torah Emes children. It's a completely changed community from what it was 29 years ago when we arrived.

So, after I left OU, there was a problem about what I should do, how to make *parnassa* (a living). I considered, perhaps, going back into the *rabbanut*. I even contacted the New York office of the Rabbinical Alliance, where Rabbi Lifshitz was the director. No position was open here in Los Angeles or the Los Angeles area, although Rabbi Uri did ask me if I wanted to become principal of the Talmud Torah of Shaarey Tefila, which did not exactly appeal to me. So we were in a dilemma about what to do.

When we registered our children for Hillel Hebrew Academy, for the day school, we were speaking to Rabbi Gottesman, the principal, and I mentioned that the tuition was expensive, so he said, "Why don't you go and open your own kindergarten?" I'm not sure how he meant it, perhaps as an idea or perhaps as a joke, but it stuck in our heads, and we started thinking seriously about it.

Then Grandpa and Grandma came to visit, and we thought perhaps we could open up our own *shul* on the West Side near UCLA, in the Westwood area where there was no *shul*. So we looked for buildings, but everything was quite expensive. Besides, among Orthodox Jewry, there were very few *shomer Shabbes* (Sabbath observing) Orthodox Jews who would really attend a *shul* like that. Today, there is a *shul* there that does not yet have its own building. It has an Orthodox rabbi, and some of the UCLA faculty attend that *shul*.

Mommy was teaching at the Yavneh Hebrew Academy, and she had a co-teacher, Mrs. Fernly. She brought one of these throw-away newspapers, and it had an ad that a nursery school was for sale in the Valley.

We borrowed some money from Grandpa, because we didn't have much money. We didn't make too much money from Duluth, but he had saved up. He insisted that we borrow from him. And, of course, we paid back every penny. We just didn't want to take from Grandpa because he also had to save up for old age.

Thank God, he lived to a ripe old age and so did Grandma. And thank God they were not starving, they lived very well and, later on, they owned their own nursery school.

Now we will continue with what happened once we were able to purchase the nursery school. In July, 1963, we bought our school in the Valley. However, during the summer, the registration was very slow. The teachers and the students were leaving, so we were quite upset that summer because we didn't know what to do. But any way, July came, July 22, 1963, and we took over the school.

It's difficult to go into all the details of the school. We were a little bit inexperienced in the school business, but we were able to learn and get along. Thank God, we made quite a success of it. Some of the time things were slow, sometimes they were better, but, thank God, we made a nice living from the school.

We were able to provide our children with most of the things they needed. We were able to send them to summer camps and to *yeshivas* and Hillel, and then the girls went to Rambam and Myer went to Ohr Elchanon. And all of them went to Israel to learn, *baruch HaShem* (thank God), so we are very grateful to HaShem for all those things.

Once we acquired the school, it was easier for us to live in the Valley. So, we moved to an apartment in North Hollywood on Coldwater Canyon, about a mile from the school. This made it easier for us, especially for me and Mommy. Mommy didn't really teach in the school at first. For a while she did, but Elizabeth was born in 1965, and then she was busy with Elizabeth. She stopped teaching for a while to take care of the house and Elizabeth and all of the children.

The nursery school was not easy work. It was hard due to all the bookkeeping, the programming, and *schlepping* the children on trips. I also had to worry about maintenance, although we had a couple who opened the school in the mornings, and she taught there. When I was not there, they were. The husband had another job, also, but they used to do a lot of the maintenance work. I learned quite a bit from them. I also did quite a bit of the maintenance, fixing many of the smaller things that needed to be repaired.

The older children, Myer, Raizel, and Esther Sue, were going to Emek Hebrew Academy. Rabbi Shocham was there, and the day school principal was Rabbi Schlissel. He and his wife became close friends of ours and still are today.

The community itself—the North Hollywood Orthodox Jewish community around Shaarei Tzedek *shul*—was very close knit, and we had a lot of friends. We still maintain those friendships and see each other at various *simchas*. At the time, Shaarei Tzedek had an old building. They built the present *shul* in its place. Emek Academy's building was built around then also, and now it's a very large school.

But in those days, there were factions. The rabbi of the *shul*, Rabbi Shoham, opposed Rabbi Schlissel and me, both *shul* board members. Rabbi Schlissel and a number of others could not see eye to eye with Rabbi Shoham and others about the educational aspect of Emek. We didn't feel that the curriculum had enough Torah education in it.

For a number of months, the rabbis would meet with Rabbi Uri, the coordinator from the Bureau of Jewish Education, to work out a program. The matter came to a climax due to disagreements and *machlokot* (arguments) between the *shul* and Emek. And it gave me an ulcer, which led to an operation in 1967.

For a while we had a breakoff *minyan* from the *shul* in the home of a Mr. Pollack. By that time, Rabbi Schlissel had already left the principalship. He went into the spice business, his wife's family's business in New York, and he was very successful.

We took the kids out of Emek, the Valley day school, and moved them to Hillel in the city. We carpooled several times a week with the Schlissel children and Selma Schimmel, whose father was a rabbi in the Valley. Mommy mainly did the driving across the canyon, and it was quite a *schlep* (bothersome trip) to go to Hillel every day.

We did this for about two years, which was very difficult. First of all, the road through the canyon had many steep curves and the children would get dizzy and tired on the way to school. Then we had to go back and pick them up. It took at least half an hour. Sometimes, with traffic and rain, it would take more time. It was not very convenient at all.

So, we had made up our mind that we were going to move to the city.

But before I talk about the city, I would just like to go back for a minute to the Valley.

We lived in the Valley for about a year in an apartment at 6318 Coldwater Canyon Avenue, near Victory Boulevard. The manager of the apartment building was very bad and nasty to our children. It was terrible; the children couldn't walk; we couldn't do anything. It was just unbearable. It was very small, anyway, and there was no air conditioning, so in the summertime it was hot.

We decided to buy our first house at 12604 Tiara in North Hollywood. We bought it from the owner, and we lived there happily for close to five and a half years, starting in December, 1968.

The children enjoyed the house. We had trees on the side of the front yard, we had swings, and we could make a nice large *sukkah* (temporary shelter for the Sukkot holiday). In the Coldwater Canyon apartment, our first *sukkah* was very small because we didn't have our own back yard; the back of the apartment opened into the alley. So, we had to make it so that we walked from the kitchen door directly into the *sukkah*.

A nice family named Lorkas lived across the street from us. They were very friendly. Mrs. Lorkas worked for us in the school for about a year or so. They had three children, and two of them are married now. One of the boys, Mark Lorkas, lives in Detroit and was Myer's neighbor. He is a very *frum* fellow, and he learns in the *kollel* there.

In the Valley, we were very fortunate that Uncle Vel and Aunt Joanne and their children lived close by, so we were able to visit them on *Shabassim*. For quite a while, Mommy babysat for their son Jonathan on weekdays when Joanne was teaching in the Valley. We would see each other very often. They also had a swimming pool, and we used that swimming pool quite a bit in the summer. In the Valley, our children would take summer courses at Valley College before they were old enough to go to the summer camp run by B'nei Akiva.

We were also very close to the Schlissels, and most *Shabbes* afternoons either they would come to our house or we would go to theirs. We had many things in common. We had the same background, and our children had the same background. Even today Myer is very close to Gershon. We are still in touch with the Schlissels, although now they live in the Hancock Park area, and we live in the Carthay area near Beverly Hills. From time to time, we see each other at various *simchas* (celebrations), but unfortunately not too often.

Zeidy with his good friend Rabbi Akiva Schlissel at
the Bar Mitzvah of his grandson Baruch.

So, after all these years and the fights in the Valley, we decided to buy a house in the city. One Sunday afternoon, we were taking a ride around the area of Olympic and La Jolla, and we saw a house for sale by the owner. Mommy liked it. I liked it, too; it was very nice, much larger than the Valley house. We started negotiating with the owner, a Jewish interior decorator named Stein.

We negotiated on our own, but we did not get the oil rights. Oil rights are very important in this area, especially when the prices of gasoline are very high. It made quite a difference, but he was unwilling to sell the oil rights, so we just bought the house without the oil rights. We moved here at the end of December, 1968. Our children were settled in school here, so there was no problem with their school, the *yeshiva*.

Living in the city was nice. I visited several *shuls*, and I decided we would join the Young Israel Beverly Hills. At that time, it had a very nice young Orthodox crowd. The rabbi was Rabbi Uri, a part time rabbi. We knew him from before we moved to the city. I would contribute every year by leading *shacharit* (morning) services on the high holidays and blowing the *shofar* (ceremonial ram's horn). I did this, also, for many years in the Valley at Shaarei Tzedek.

When we settled in the city, the children were getting older. Raizel was probably in the seventh grade, Myer in the sixth grade, and Esther Sue in the fourth grade. Elizabeth did not go to school yet, so we would bring her to our nursery school.

Life in the city was more difficult for me because I had to travel every day to the nursery school early in the morning. I left home sometimes at 8 a.m. Sometimes I had to open up the school during vacation time, which was very hard. Then, I had to be there at 6:30 a.m.

The Roszlers in the 1970s.

I would come home usually around 7 p.m. because we closed the school at 6:00, and generally I wanted to be there to talk to the parents. Friday afternoon, I would leave at 1:00 or 1:30. That was not easy, but it was worth it because the children did not have to travel and Mommy didn't have to *schlep* to the Valley every day.

Here in the city, we made some new friends. We were friendly with the Brissmans. I knew Rabbi Brissman from New York, and he had become the librarian for UCLA's Semitic Department. We were very close.

Uncle Vel and Joanne moved to the city two or three years after we moved. At first, they rented a house, and then they bought a house in Beverly Hills. The Schlissels also moved into the city. It was very nice to have some of our close friends and relatives in the city.

When we lived in the Valley, Grandpa and Grandma would come very often. The airline they came on at that time was called PSA, and they flew into Burbank. They would come as often as possible to visit us and spend time with us for *Shabbes* and *yom tov* (holidays). Later on, as the area where Grandpa had his business in San Francisco was deteriorating, his business slackened. So, they decided to come live in Los Angeles. Grandpa and Grandma moved here approximately 23 years ago. At first, Grandpa, who was 62, thought he would retire. Then he figured he was too young. We suggested that he could look around at businesses, and he decided that perhaps they also would move into the nursery school business.

Fortunately, with *HaShem*'s help, the grandmother of a girl in our school was a real estate broker. One day, she came in asking if I knew of anybody who was interested in buying a school on Pico Blvd. in the city. At that time, Grandpa was already very actively looking to buy a school. He went out to Inglewood to look at one, and he also looked at many other outlying places, but those schools did not work out. It was fortunate they didn't work out, because he would have had to move there or to *schlep* from here all the way out. [They eventually bought the nursery school on Pico Blvd].

Looking back at that, we realize *HaShem* always manages things in His own way, and we always have to say thank you to *HaKadosh Baruch Hu* (the blessed Holy One).

Before we bought Playpen Nursery school, which we renamed the Gateway School, we were actually ready to buy a school out in El Monte, a drive of about three-quarters of an hour when there's no traffic or disruptions. When there's traffic, it could be an hour and a half. It's quite a way out of Los Angeles, and it was a much smaller school than the one we bought in the Valley. We were so upset when we didn't get that school, but it was all for the best.

Chapter 16

We were desperate when we almost bought that nursery school in El Monte. One Sunday morning, we decided that we'd call up the owner of that school, tell him that we're ready to go ahead, and we wanted to make a deal that day on purchasing the school.

But, fortunately, as I said, *Hashem* manages his own way, and the owner said she could not meet that day, that it would have to be tomorrow or the next day. It was that next day that Mommy's fellow teacher brought this newspaper she found to school, and Mommy found a school in the Valley which was a much better buy, much larger, in a better location, and with room for expansion.

At any rate, we ended up with the school in the Valley, not in El Monte, which was a much smaller school. It had a license for only 33 children, and it was very far away. Instead, we were in the Valley where we had a Jewish community. In El Monte, they eventually had an orthodox rabbi, Rabbi Fertig. He was a friend of Mom's since he had been a rabbi previously in San Francisco.

Remember, the main reason we left Duluth was to have a day school and an orthodox community. The hand of God guided us, and we were able to come here, so we could bring our children to the Emek day school, the *yeshiva* in North Hollywood.

When we bought our school in the Valley, it was licensed for 50 students. We expanded it to a license for 96 children. Mr. Landau, who later leased it from us, expanded the school even further, added additions, and remodeled. Now it is licensed for probably 130 to 140 children, because he changed around the number of children to go up as far as kindergarten, first grade, and so on. Now, it's one of the most beautiful schools in the Valley.

So as I say, we have *bitachon* in *Hashem* (faith in God). Sometimes we are doing our own thing, but God manages in His ways in such a way that it turns out better for us than we think. So it was with this school. During the time that we expanded, we were fortunate in having another building, which almost doubled the capacity of the school.

We also were fortunate in getting a loan for most of it from the Small Business Administration. For some reason, it was very difficult to get loans in those days. We went to a number of banks, and they were not willing to lend us the money. I had befriended a very nice man, Mr. Spivak, when I was the registrar of the Teacher's College of Yeshiva University of Los Angeles. He and his son were in the financing business with the Eastern Finance Company, I think. He was willing to give us a loan, but fortunately we didn't need it, because we got a better loan from the Small Business Administration.

Then, in 1973, there was a very severe earthquake in Los Angeles. It did a lot of damage, a number of people were killed, and many walls in different buildings cracked. We had some cracked walls both at the house and at the school. About a year or two later, we applied for money for damages to repair the school. Fortunately, about a year or two after that, the government forgave all these loans, which came to thousands of dollars. That helped with the building, and we paid off the loan to the Small Business Administration.

Grandpa George and Auntie Joanne bought a nursery school in Beverly Hills from a lady whose granddaughter attended our school. [Grandpa and Joanne managed the school for many years and eventually sold it to Chabad, which tore it down and built a large new school building that resembles 770 Eastern Parkway, the Chabad New York Headquarters]. So, all in all, God was good to us and to them, for which we are very grateful.

Over time, Raizel graduated from the Hillel Day School, and attended the Orthodox High School, which then was called Rambam. When Myer graduated from Hillel, he studied at a small local *yeshiva* under Rabbi Simcha Wasserman, whose father was a great *tzadik* (righteous man) and a disciple of the Chofetz Chaim, who was murdered during World War II. A number of very good boys attended school with Myer. Esther Sue went to Rambam, also. They all graduated in three years instead of four.

Myer then attended Yeshiva ITRI, a large yeshiva in Jerusalem for two years. Raizel attended Bar Ilan University in Israel for two years. Both were lonesome so far away from home, but they learned and matured there. Esther Sue attended Michlala, an excellent girls school in Israel, for a year. Afterward, in the 1970s, all three of them attended and graduated from UCLA, just like Grandma Maureen. [Grandma Sara was a student there, probably in the late 1920s].

When Elizabeth was ready for high school, Rambam had closed. It was replaced by Yeshiva University of LA. She also graduated in three years and attended Michlala. She started at UCLA, but she graduated from Yeshiva University's Stern College.

Raizel and Esther had jobs in college [Esther taught at Hillel] and Myer learned in the afternoons at Yeshiva University. [We all shared Grandma Sarah's old car, a 1966 Ford Mustang.]

Esther was an excellent student in Jewish Studies, and she won a full fellowship to graduate school at Columbia University in New York. After six months, she decided it wasn't for her. She came home, and eventually married Jeff Kandel, who grew up three blocks from us. He went to law school after they got married, and she worked at the Wiesenthal center in Los Angeles. She has three children, Jessie, Eliana, and Shimmy.

Myer attended medical school at Loyola in Chicago, and met Janis on a blind date. They got married right after medical school. Myer did his residency in radiology at the University of Pittsburgh, took a job in Detroit, and later moved to Miami. They have four children: Elisheva, Shira, Rachel, and Amichai.

Elizabeth graduated from Stern College and met Joshua Sunshine, a medical student at Yeshiva University's Einstein College of Medicine. When they first got married, they lived in the Bronx, and Elizabeth worked in computers in New York. They later moved to Cleveland, Ohio, where Josh did his residency in neurology and is now practicing. They have three children: Ahuva, Yoni, and Aryeh.

Raizel moved to New York City, where she worked in a number of different jobs, including at the Port Authority. She got a master's in communications from New York University. In 1993, Elizabeth met a doctor from South Africa, Brian Michelow, who was training in plastic surgery in Cleveland. She fixed Raizel up with him, and they got married in Cleveland where he is a plastic surgeon. They have two sons, Adam and JJ.

Top: Roszler family at Shira and Kivi's wedding in 2011.
Bottom: The Roszlers at Adam Michelow's Bar Mitzvah in Cleveland in 2014.

And we will stop here right now. Good *Shabbes*.

AFTERWORD

The El Maleh

Linz, Austria, 2016

On an early Sunday morning in September 2016, Amichai and I find ourselves in the city of Linz which is 120 miles from Vienna. Linz is the closest city to the Mauthausen and Ebensee Concertation camp memorials. It was also one of the most important cities during the Nazi regime. Hitler lived there during most of his youth and adolescence. He considered it his hometown. He wanted to turn it into the cultural center of Europe since he disliked Vienna. He felt there was Jewish influence in the city, and it had rejected him from admission to the Vienna Academy of Fine Arts (Hitler originally wanted to be an artist). The planned cultural center would have a university, library, hotels, concert hall and many other cultural and administrative buildings. But the crown jewel was to be the *Fuhermuseum* (leader's museum).

Hitler wanted to make a museum that was larger and had more and better art than the most famous museums in Europe, one that would become the greatest museum in the world. He and members of his regime would rank among the greatest art collectors in history, which they accomplished by confiscating art from captured territories, stealing from museums, raiding Jewish art collections and making private purchasing. He eventually accumulated more than 10,000 pieces of art and sculpture. He commissioned an architectural model of the cultural center and studied it frequently and fondly as the German Military was being defeated in 1945.

However the complex and library were never built. The confiscated art was kept in Munich and in storehouses in the Austrian countryside until Operation Dora in 1944, when Hitler had most of the collection moved to the Altaussee salt mines in rural Austria. As Allied troops were approaching, orders were given to blow up the mine. However, the Austrian miners refused the orders, saving more than 12,000 pieces of great and historic art.

Ebensee

From Linz it is 20 miles to the Mauthausen Concentration Camp and 55 miles to Ebensee. You can rent a car or hire a taxi, since taking trains and busses is very time consuming. Amichai and I took a taxi from the train station in Linz to the town of Ebensee, a beautiful town of 10,000 people on a lake ("see" in German means lake) in the Austrian Salzkammergut Mountains.

For many years Austria did not own up to its complicity with the Nazi's during world war. The Austrians saw themselves as victims rather than collaborators. However, after Kurt Waldheim was elected president of Austria in 1986, and his record of involvement in war time atrocities was publicized, the Austrian people went through a period of introspection. They started to take responsibility and memorialize their war time compliance and complicity. In 2001, the town of Ebensee turned its library into a museum of contemporary history.

Although the museum exhibit starts with material from 1918, a good portion is devoted to the history and workings of the Ebensee concentration camp. The exhibit includes multiple photographs, but the US army footage of the liberation is the most disturbing. In the records at the museum, Zeidy's brother Yitchak Shmuel is listed as perishing and Zeidy is listed as an inmate.

The next part of the exhibit, a short distance away by car, is called the Gallery. It is made up of remaining parts of the tunnels and quarries that the prisoners dug originally for development of A9/A10 intercontinental rockets, but that the Nazis used instead as a petroleum plant for producing fuel and manufacturing parts for tanks and other military vehicles. Within the tunnels, there is a very complete exhibit on the slave labor and work that was done there. Even during a summer visit, the temperature in the quarry was in the low 50s.

The third portion of the memorial is the cemetery near the tunnels. A mass grave was found on this site after liberation. However, the location of any individual person's grave is unknown, since there were other grave sites and a crematorium at Ebensee. This memorial includes tombstones, flags and plaques for the deceased, as well as the original entrance gates to the concentration camp. Here, Amichai—whose full name is Amichai Yitzchak Shmuel (after his great uncle, Zeidy's brother)—recited the *El Maleh* prayer in memorializing the dead.

Mauthasen

Mauthasen was the area's main concentration camp. Ebensee and some smaller outposts were classified as subcamps. Mauthasen was a processing camp for prisoners being shipped to the smaller labor camps. Zeidy and his brother spent a short time there. It was also the camp where the Nazis killed prisoners who could not work. Toward the end of the war, they evacuated many prisoners from other concentration camps and sent them to die in Mauthasen. The camp has been turned into a museum and memorial administered by the Government of Austria and its Research and Advisory boards. They also oversee the Ebensee Memorial.

For more information, see two excellent web sites: mauthausen-memorial.org and memorial-ebensee.at

Myer H Roszler
March 2021

APPENDIX 1

Zeidy's life from 1988 until 2017, the year of his passing

Aman named David Landau appeared out of nowhere in November of 1988 and asked to lease our nursery school, which Zeidy and Grandma Maureen had renamed Gateway Educational Center. It was a blessing from the Heavens; they had worked intensely there for 25 years. It was a very stressful business, since they were always worried about the safety of the children in their care and, of course, about getting home from Van Nuys in time for Shabbat and *chagim* (holidays).

Zeidy went in for a routine scheduled angiogram the day before he was due to sign the papers with Mr. Landau. However, things did not go as planned, and Zeidy required emergency bypass surgery the day after the angiogram. Prior to the surgery, the heart surgeon first tried do an angioplasty, but Zeidy coded. Grandma and Esther Sue stood in the hall murmuring *Tehillim* (Psalms) and watching as attendants rolling Zeidy's bed rushed him to an operating room. Thank G-d, he did well. He woke up in the Cardiac Care Unit of Kaiser Permanente on Sunset, and the first words he muttered were, "…sign those papers." Soon enough—by the end of November, 1988—the papers were signed, and Zeidy and Grandma were officially retired after working hard all their lives.

As the years went by, Mr. Landau repeatedly pestered Zeidy to sell the nursery school to him. Zeidy and Grandma wanted him to keep leasing it so they could hold on to it for the next generation, but Mr. Landau did not give them that option, so they sold it to him. Raizel, Myer, Esther

Sue, and Elizabeth were happy that their parents sold the school. They had worked there during many of their high school and college breaks, but they did not have fond memories of working there.

Zeidy suddenly had a lot of free time, but he found plenty to do. He immediately became a "*shul* Jew." He attended morning and evening *minyan*, the Tuesday night *shiur* (an in-depth Talmud class) at Beth Jacob, and daily *Daf Yomi* (a fast-paced lecture on a page of the Talmud, based on a seven-year cycle). He never missed a day unless he was sick, and then he caught up on the internet. He switched from the upstairs main *minyan* to his beloved smaller minyan, commonly known as Benny's minyan. He was the unofficial rabbi of that *minyan* and of the daily morning minyan. He was a fixture in the *shul* and became known as a revered *talmid hacham* (Torah scholar) there and in the LA community.

Daf Yomi became a phenomenon across the world, and Beth Jacob was no exception. Zeidy was asked to represent Beth Jacob and speak at the world-wide *Siyuum Hashas* (gathering upon completion of the seven-year cycle) which took place in the massive Hollywood Palladium. He received a standing ovation.

As soon as computers became all the rage, he dragged Grandma to weekly free classes for senior citizens in mid-LA. He asked so many questions, the teacher yelled at him. Zeidy responded, "You are the teacher, and it is your job to answer all my questions." He continued to bombard her weekly. Zeidy became quite a proficient computer user, particularly on AOL. Later he purchased the Bar Ilan *Sheelot Uteshusvot* disc of Responsa and Torah literature, which gave him great pleasure. He also found various Torah websites and multiple Israeli news sites. Arutz Sheva was a favorite.

Zeidy and Grandma helped Esther Sue tremendously by driving her carpools in the morning and afternoon when she had various pregnancy-related problems. They babysat Jessie very often when Esther Sue was on bedrest. Eventually, the pregnancies produced Eliana (December, 1989) and Shimmy (May, 1994). Esther Sue could not have managed without their help. They hosted Shimmy's *bris* in their home on 1064 S. La Jolla at a moment's notice, because Jeff was hospitalized after a major

Daf Yomi Siyum in Los Angeles—Zeidy represented Beth Jacob. He finished the Talmud almost four times at the Beth Jacob and later at Young Israel of Beachwood.

Shimmy Kandel (center) in the Israel Defense Force—Shimmy
served in the IDF Munitions unit as a Lone Solider.

surgery and released only two days before the *bris*. They had no time to
plan a big affair, but the *bris* was done beautifully, with the dining room
table serving as a handy place for the *mohel* to do his job, and Grandpa
George as *sandek* (the person who has the honor of holding the baby
during the bris).

Indeed, Zeidy and Grandma were a mainstay in Esther Sue and the
Kandel family's life from the time she and Jeff married and had children.
They had their family for *Shabbasim* and *chagim* (holidays) throughout
the years, the kids slept over constantly, and they took them out for pizza
after school, as well as on day trips and overnight trips to Santa Barbara,
the California Missions, and many other places. When the Roszlers and
Sunshines came to visit, Zeidy and Grandma took them on longer, more
extensive trips, sometimes by plane and often in their station wagon,
to Las Vegas, San Francisco, San Diego, Yosemite National Park, and

more. The grandchildren have memories of fighting over who got to sit in the "back, back seat" of the car, and eating bagels and American cheese, Grandma's go-to kosher food for travel.

The most popular trip by far that all the members of the family got to experience—including Raizel's children, Adam and JJ, who came along a bit later—was to the Santa Monica Pier, with a stop at the Coffee Bean. These trips and visits from all members of the family for *Shabbasim* and *chagim* at Zeidy and Grandma's home continued until they were in their late 70s. Then, Esther Sue picked up the mantel and started hosting them.

Aside from pinch-hitting for the Kandels, Zeidy and Grandma often flew to Detroit to babysit for Myer and Janis's children. They flew to New York to visit Raizel and Elizabeth when they were single. Later, they went often to Cleveland to help Elizabeth with her growing family. To supplement these trips and the more exciting ones they took, they took advantage of airline promotions that were available in those days allowing you to collect double or triple miles if you flew on various airlines. Zeidy would often fly to San Francisco or Las Vegas, short one-hour flights, in order to benefit from that month's bonus miles.

Zeidy and Grandma travelled to many exciting places, including Australia, Alaska, the Norwegian fjords, Scandinavia, Paris, London, and Italy. Zeidy went to the cemetery in Padua to try to find the *kever* (gravesite) of his great-great grandfather, the famous Maharam of Padua. The gates were locked, so he tried to climb over the fence, but, needless to say, he didn't succeed.

Possibly the best of their many trips was their voyage to China, hosted by Bar Ilan. They loved the dean of Bar Ilan, Professor Kaveh. The highlight was that Zeidy got to blow the shofar in The Great Hall. Before sounding the shofar, he uttered a *she'hecheyanu* (the blessing you make to mark special occasions or first-time happenings).

They tried to go to Israel every year or so. Once they went to Friday night services at the Great Synagogue in Jerusalem. Grandma was sitting way up in the women section, and she heard an interesting and familiar sounding *chazan* (prayer leader), who sounded like he was from Borgo

4 · HERITAGE SOUTHWEST JEWISH PRESS Friday, December 4, 1998

Tekiah! Once again, the shofar sounds in Beijing

Bar-Ilan delgation witnesses blossoming of Israel-China relations

By Gabe Levenson

Beijing, China (Special) — *Tekiah, teruah, shevarim* — the staccato notes of the *shofar*, not heard in this imperial capital since the time of Kublai Khan, were sounded recently by Los Angeles Rabbi Herman Roszler 700 years after Marco Polo first heard them in the same place.

The place was the gargantuan Great Hall — it seats 10,000 people — on Tiananmen Square, at a banquet celebrating a new milestone in China-Israel relations.

And the occasion marked the signing of an agreement that same morning between representatives of the Chinese Ministry of

Education and top officials of Bar-Ilan University to provide scholarships for 100 Chinese post-doctoral scientists and academicians to study at Bar-Ilan.

Each student will spend one or two years at the university, conducting research in a number of fields of science, from computer technology to agriculture to environmental monitoring through satellites. The students, 10 of whom have already begun their work at the university, plan to return to China after finishing their fellowship in Israel. Another 16 scholars have applied for entrance for the current academic year. Over the next four years, 100 Chinese students will have been enrolled.

The scholarship program has been funded by Fred and Barbara Kort of

SHOFAR IN BEIJING — Rabbi Herman Roszler sounds the ram's horn in the Great Hall.

Emek Hebrew Academy
invites
the entire community to a

Beverly Hills, who were guests of honor at the dinner (the first kosher event ever held there).

Kort, a man in his early 70s, is one of three living survivors of the Treblinka concentration camp, in which almost one million Jews were killed. He is president and chairman of Imperial Toy Co., an international enterprise he started in Los Angeles 50 years ago, shortly after arriving in the United States as a penniless

The item has earned Kort the title of "The Bubble King."

Kort's wife, Barbara, is a native of Hong Kong. On a trip to Israel last year — one of many the couple has made to the Holy Land — Barbara Kort told the Chinese ambassador to Israel: "As a native of China, I am personally moved by any initiative to expand relations between our countries. We are two unique peoples with great futures ahead of us."

Blowing the Shofar in the Great Hall in China.

BELOW: At the Kotel—Zeidy went to the Kotel every day when he was in Jerusalem. He is seen here with Myer and Amichai Roszler at his Tefillin party.

Prund. It turned out that none of the professional chazanim had showed up, so they asked Zeidy to lead the services.

In the early 1980s, they took an unusual and emotional trip back to Zeidy's hometown, Borgo Prund, Romania. Zeidy described what it was like to knock on the door of the neighbor he'd grown up with so long ago.

A man answered, and Zeidy asked, "Does anyone remember a boy named Hermann who lived here from birth, from 1929 until 1944?"

The man answered, "We don't remember a Hermann, but we remember a Heshu."

"I am Heshu," Zeidy said.

The man nearly shouted, "WE DIDN'T TAKE ANYTHING!"

Zeidy strangely seemed to enjoy seeing them again, despite his memories and his descriptions to his children remembering these neighbors as terrible anti-Semites. He told them he lived in Hollywood, and he was now a star. They seemed to believe him. They were still living in a very primitive way, with outdoor toilets. Zeidy had the last laugh. He made it out of that peasant hole, and they were still stuck there.

He also took Grandma to see the grave of his paternal grandfather in Vaslui and the burial site of his paternal great-grandfather in Bistritz. Romania was still under Communist rule, and they felt as if the Communist authorities were watching them. Zeidy knew to bring cigarettes and ballpoint pens to bribe Romanians to get things done on this trip, and he used everything he brought. When he described his trip, it sounded like he was talking about crossing borders in Eastern Europe just after the War.

The former Soviet Union collapsed in 1988 and travel to Eastern Europe became much easier. In 1997, Myer and Zeidy went back. They hired a driver with a beautiful Mercedes who picked them up in Budapest and drove them to Romania. The first stop was in the capital of Transylvania, Cluj (Klausenberg). Somehow Zeidy had the phone number of a neighbor with whom he grew up in Borgo, who was now the retired Minister of Culture for Transylvania. He invited the man to breakfast where he promptly ordered vodka.

Zeidy and Myer visited the graves of his maternal grandparents, Rav

Neighbor from Borgo—Zeidy with his neighbor, a childhood friend in Borgo Prund who became Transylvania's Minister of Culture.

Aryeh Leib Kahana and Henya Leah, who are buried in one of the Cluj cemeteries. They also visited the site of his Rav Kahana's former *shtiebel* (little synagogue). They went to Borgo, where they found his old rented house. It was occupied by the Guthska family, the town thieves. They told Zeidy they bought the house from his family, which wasn't true. Zeidy's family never owned it; another Jewish family did. Although the town still had outhouses and transportation by horse, Zeidy's former house had indoor plumbing. Old man Guthska told them he suffered pain from his wooden dentures and asked for medicine. Myer gave him aspirin, but he regrets not giving him Preparation H and telling him to take it by mouth twice a day.

From there, they went to Sighet and saw the graves of Zeidy's maternal great-great grandfather, who was famed for his renowned commentary, the *Kuntras Hasfekos*, and of Zeidy's Great-Great Uncle Rav Yosef Leib Kahana. A small community *kosher* kitchen was still functioning in Sighet.

Their next stop was Alba Ulia (Karslburg), the old capital of Transylvania, where Zeidy's maternal Great-Great Grandfather Yecheskal Panet, the *Maareah Yecheskal* and Chief Rabbi of Transylvania, is buried. The *shul* and the jail that the authorities authorized him to use still stand.

Then they went to Dinov, Poland, to visit the *kever* (gravesite) of
Zeidy's paternal Great-Great Grandfather Rabbi Tzvi Elimelech Shapira,
the Bnei Yissaschar, for whom Zeidy was named. Their final stop was
Aushwitz-Birkanau, where Zeidy prayed near the ashes of his parents,
brother, and sister, and those of the millions of Jews murdered there. It
was a very difficult trip for him. He returned to Los Angeles the week
before *Rosh Hashana*, which Esther Sue remembers as the first time she
knows of that Zeidy ever wept in shul.

In 1999, Zeidy and Myer traveled once again to Romania, to visit
Vaslui where Zeidy's grandfather Rabbi Chaim Ressler is buried. Even
though Vaslui had become a city of 100,000 people, the cab drivers still
knew which Jewish leader kept the key to the cemetery. From there, they
flew to the Ukraine and went to three graves: Zeidy's Great-Great Grandfather, the legendary R' Levi Yitchak of Berditchiev [see *yichus* chapter];
the great Baal Shem Tov, the founder of the Chassidic movement; and
R' Nachman of Breslov in Uman. More recently, R' Nachman became
the symbol of the resurgence of the Breslover Chassidim, whose members
make pilgrimages to his grave every year.

September 11, 2001, was an interesting day. Zeidy, Grandma, and the
Roszler siblings had all gathered the day before for Adam Michelow's bris.
Myer was on a plane headed back home to Florida as the terrorist attacks
were happening in New York City and Washington, DC. Esther was not
able to take off to get home to Los Angeles, and Grandma and Zeidy had
obliviously rented a car and driven happily off to Niagara Falls for a nice
vacation. (This was before cellphones were commonplace). At some point
that evening, they saw the news and knew what happened. However, for
some reason, they didn't realize that their children would be sick with
worry over them, since the entire country was in chaos that day, and even
the next. Myer called Auntie Joannie, Grandma Maureen's sister who
lived with her husband Vel in Beverly Hills, and asked if he should notify
the police. Finally Zeidy and Grandma called and let their children know
that Niagara Falls were still falling.

Although Zeidy always had back pain and other pains, they got out of control when he developed drop foot in Florida in 2003. He had surgery, but the pain never fully went away. He had to wear a cumbersome foot brace for the rest of his life, and suffered other forms of foot pain and persistent back pain. From then on, Zeidy suffered one health issue after another, visiting doctors on a weekly, then twice weekly, later thrice weekly, basis. Eventually, he had back surgery in December of 2009, but it failed and caused other problems, which led to yet another failed surgery in June, 2010. Eventually, doctors tried to control the pain by inserting a pain pump internally filled with strong narcotics. They were either too strong or not strong enough, and they never helped. Zeidy coped with pain all the time. He never slept, bled easily, and had constant problems with his dental bridge. He also developed wet macular degeneration, requiring a retina specialist to give him a shot every six weeks for years that miraculously kept him from going blind. And yet, somehow, he managed to get up every morning feeling happy to be alive and looking forward to his morning *minyan*, and his day in general.

Concurrently, Grandma began her battle with dementia. At some point, Esther Sue, who had gotten divorced and was the last of the Roszler siblings living in Los Angeles, saw that she was going to need more help caring for Grandma and Zeidy, so everyone decided it was best for them to move to Cleveland, where Raizel and Bryan (Michelow) and Elizabeth and Josh (Sunshine) lived.

In July of 2015, Zeidy and Grandma sold their house. His beloved *minyan* threw him and Grandma a beautiful goodbye *Kiddush*. Jessie and Shimmy spoke. Benny, the founder of the *minyan*, tried to speak to wish Zeidy a *tzeitchem leshalom* (fond farewell and good wishes). Each time he tried to talk he choked up. Finally he gave up. Zeidy had spoken numerous times in Benny's minyan over the years, sometimes for *yahrtzeits* (memorial commemorations), but mainly on happy occasions. He always started with, "If 60 years ago (plug in any number of years) anyone would have told me that I would be standing here, celebrating my (birthday,

At Shira Roszler Steinberger's wedding—Zeidy blessed
Shira during the Bedekin ceremony, 2011.

anniversary, etc), I would have said impossible, that simply could not be, yet here I am, thanks to Hashem." He also got *naches* (joy) from hearing his children and grandchildren speak. He asked Esther Sue to speak on his 80th and 85th birthdays.

Zeidy and Grandma moved to Cleveland in October of 2015. While everyone helped take care of both of them, and they hired caretakers, Josh was Zeidy's personal physician and oversaw everything he did. Elizabeth watched over him and Grandma daily. Zeidy, who became weaker soon after he got to Cleveland, still attended daily *minyan* and *daf yomi* (Talmud study) at the Young Israel next door. He went to the Green Road Synagogue with the Sunshines and Michelows every Shabbat. Zeidy earned quite a following in the short time he lived in Cleveland. About three months before he died, he *davened* for the *amud* (congregation) and, as always, received many compliments from people of all ages.

Dancing with Grandma
at Shira's wedding.

Zeidy and Grandma attended Elisheva Roszler's wedding in Florida in 2017 and went to New York for the *bris* of Shira's son Gideon George, even though Zeidy wasn't well. The trips weren't easy, but they always loved family celebrations and enjoyed themselves anyway.

Zeidy with his cousin Eddie Kahn at Shira's wedding.

Roszler family at Elisheva and Harris's wedding in 2017—
Zeidy's great-grandson Gideon Steiberger was the ring bearer.

Zeidy passed away on the sixth of Elul, *Taf Shin Ayin Zayin* (August 28, 2017). He was buried in Beit Shemesh, Israel. When the Roszlers were sitting shiva for him, a man came who spoke of how much he loved Zeidy's davening. In fact, he said, "I recorded your father's davening from about a half year ago on my phone, because I love it so much, and I thought maybe the family would want to have it one day." Then he gave Myer a flash drive with his father's davening.

Esther Roszler Kandel

Grandma Maureen Bloomberg Roszler

Zeidy's history would not be complete without Grandma Maureen Bloomberg's history, even though they were from opposite sides of the Earth. One grew up in modern America, and the other lived in a faraway world of horse-drawn carts and outhouses. Yet, they grew together to become almost one person. Zeidy's tragic European saga always far overshadowed Grandma's all-American life story, but we loved hearing her stories. We took pride in knowing that, through her, we were third-generation Americans.

Grandma's father, George Edward Bloomberg, was born in Des Moines, Iowa in 1907. He had one brother and two sisters. His father, Morris, was born in Poland in 1869 and his mother, Yenta (or Yetta) Katz, was born in 1878, in Russia. Elizabeth's Hebrew name is Yetta in her memory.

Grandma's grandparents, Morris and Yenta, were single when they arrived in the United States before the turn of the 20th century, and they married

Grandma Maureen Bloomberg Roszler in the 1970s.

in New York around 1898. Yetta's marriage license refers to her father, Grandma's great-grandfather, as Max, but her tombstone shows his name as Shmuel. He was from Pogost (pronounced "Pohost"), Russia. Grandpa George once told Esther Sue that the Czarist government gave Shmuel (perhaps called Max later) an important job drafting men into the military, and he tried not to draft Jews. He ran afoul of the government, perhaps for this reason, though we will never know. We do know that he fled Pogost, but the rest of his story is lost in time.

Pohost is also meaningful to the family because Grandpa George used to regale his nine grandchildren with made-up stories of his childhood growing up in the peasant town of Pohost. Knowing he was born in the USA, we mistakenly believed that Pohost was a fictional village. Much later we learned that a town called Pogost really did exist, and we wondered if he had heard about it as a child.

Morris died in 1924 when Grandpa George was 17. By that time, Morris and Yetta had been living in El Paso for about ten years. They moved there because doctors told Yetta that she had pleurisy due to TB, and she needed to live in a dry, warm climate.

Family legend has it that when Yetta was a young mother, she had her fortune told at a country fair. The fortune-teller said her husband would die young and she would go blind. Morris died of a burst appendix at 55, and glaucoma left Yetta blind at a relatively young age. George did not get to go to college because he had to work to support himself and his mother, and to help put his older brother, Samuel, through dental school.

After Grandpa George married Grandma Sarah, Great-Grandma Yetta lived with them for around seven years. George was hired to be a traveling salesman for Hayman Krupp shoes, and he was always grateful for that job, since selling shoes kept him employed throughout the Depression. He traveled throughout the southwest, as well as to the east coast.

Grandma Sarah's story also starts overseas. Her parents were both born in Russia. Her mother, Esther Adelman, was born in 1881, and she married Joseph Ackerman, born in 1877. They had Sarah in 1912 in Nowo-Selitz, Bessarabia (now the Ukraine).

Joseph's brother, Max, first made the long journey to America, arriving in Galveston, Texas, sometime before World War I. He went to Texas, not Ellis Island in New York, via the Galveston Project, an initiative designed to divert some of the massive flow of immigrants from New York City. Max brought his brother Joseph to America in 1913.

Joseph planned to bring Esther and his family over quickly—as soon as he could afford it. The two brothers lived in El Paso, where they eventually owned a dry goods store. Needless to say, keeping a store in Texas closed on Saturday (as well as on Sunday due to the Blue Laws), exacted a great financial cost, but they were *shomer Shabbos* and kept the store closed on Shabbat their entire lives. Aside from the store, they also peddled their wares on the Mexican border, just across from Ciudad Juarez.

The outbreak of World War I derailed Joseph's plan to bring Esther and their children to the United States in short order. Instead, Joseph and Esther were separated for seven years, leaving Esther alone to support the family in Bessarabia. She smuggled cigarettes and other contraband across borders to eke out a meager living. With a lot of hard work, Joseph finally was able to buy tickets for the family after the war. They arrived through Ellis Island and reunited in El Paso in 1920.

Joseph and Esther Akerman were deeply Zionistic. Joseph attended the 1927 Zionist Organization of America (ZOA) Conference, traveling by train all the way from El Paso to New York City. We have a picture of him among the throngs of attendees. Esther attended meetings of the Women's Auxiliary Zionist Organizations in Los Angeles in the mid 1930s. They had three daughters, Bella (later Hirsch), Sarah who was five years younger, and Annie, who was younger than Sarah. When Grandma Sarah was a girl, she attended *cheder* and her family hired a Hebrew tutor so she could learn the Hebrew language and its poetry.

Grandma Sarah met Grandpa George at a B'nei B'rith social when she was 15, and he was 19. Knowing the Ackermans had three daughters, Grandpa asked her, "Which number daughter are you?" She said, "Number 2." He said, "Then I won't have to wait so long."

But Joseph and Esther did not approve of their *shidduch* (match).

They felt Sarah was too young, and they worried that George was poor and still had to support his blind mother. So they packed Sarah off with Bella to study at UCLA. Sarah lived with a Jewish family in Los Angeles, and missed George desperately. Eventually, she came home, and they got engaged. Joseph and Esther hosted the engagement party in their new home. The society section of the local newspaper wrote up the event and noted that George's stylish married, older sister, Mary, arrived with much fanfare.

Great-Grandma Sarah was 19 and Great-Grandpa George was 23 when they got married in 1930. Grandma Maureen was born on August 7, 1933, in El Paso. Sarah took pleasure in dressing Maureen like a little doll. Even in her very earliest pictures, Maureen is dressed in adorable clothes. In fact, Sarah could have been a great stage mother. When Maureen was

Great Grandma Sarah and Great Grandpa George's wedding picture, 1930—
Grandpa George was known as the "handsomest man in Texas."

At a wedding of one of their grandchildren around 50 years later.

12, Sarah entered her in a Hollywood photo contest. The prize was an audition to play Merle Oberon's daughter in a movie. Maureen won the contest and was invited to come to LA for the audition, but it was held on Shabbat, so Maureen missed her chance to become a movie star. A colorized photo shows Maureen in a pink pinafore dress, with olive skin, dark eyes, rosy cheeks, and curly hair. Sarah got Maureen's pictures published in *The Ladies' Home Journal* and other publications.

Perhaps Grandma Maureen developed her amazing fashion sense due to Great-Grandma Sarah. Photos taken in New York and San Francisco show her as a very stylish young woman. Much later in her life, people always said Maureen was the most stylishly dressed woman in *shul* or wherever they happened to see her. Shopping in "vintage" stores was one of her greatest joys, because she could narrow in on cast-off couture clothes that she wore with a shawl, or brooch, or hat to make her outfit "pop." Always ahead of her time, she shopped in used-clothing stores many years before buying "vintage" became the huge trend it is now.

Maureen's younger sister, Joann, was born in June, 1939, in El Paso Texas. They were very close, and remained so until Grandma died. They never fought. Maureen read to Joann every night, especially poetry. (Grandma continued to read poetry, two generations later, and recited it by heart to her Kandel granddaughters, Jessie and Eliana. Her favorite was Edgar Allan Poe's "Annabelle Lee," which she could recite even when her memory waned.)

Great-Grandpa George and Great-Grandma Sarah Ackerman kept a kosher home. Maureen remembered going to the *shochet* (ritual butcher) in El Paso and seeing the chickens. The *shochet* had a son, Jack Erlich, who was an actual giant. He ran away and joined the circus, but Maureen recalls him lifting her up high so she could touch the Sukkah in her backyard. However, while living in Texas, Maureen encountered some incidents of racism. She inherited dark olive skin from Grandpa George. While the local Jewish community considered him "tall, dark, and handsome," Maureen's dark coloring worked against her. When she was a little girl, people told her she had to use the segregated water fountains and public facilities set aside for "Mexicans and Negroes." This made a permanent impression on her. She never understood the 1970s ad campaigns for tanning lotions or the "Black is Beautiful" slogan.

Grandma Sarah's parents, Joseph and Esther, moved to Los Angeles so the last of their three daughters, Annie, could meet a nice Jewish boy—as she did. She met and married Roy Gelberman. Later, when Maureen was 10, George and Sarah also moved to California. World War II was underway, and the US government gave married men the choice of being drafted or doing some kind of national service. George opted for the latter and decided to build ships in San Francisco, the home of Sarah's older sister Bella and her husband, Sam Hirsch.

One of Grandma Maureen's favorite stories from her childhood concerned her first day of school in San Francisco. The teacher introduced her to the class and told her where to sit. Being a polite Texan, Grandma replied, "Yes, Ma'am." The class burst out laughing, and Grandma was so mortified she dropped her Texas accent that minute.

Grandma Maureen was lonely in San Francisco, since she was *shomer Shabbes* (Sabbath observant) and the town then offered only limited opportunities for a Torah education. She ended up spending many adolescent summers in Los Angeles with her Grandma Esther, her Aunt Annie, and her cousins. Her Auntie Bella and San Francisco cousins often came to Los Angeles, as well.

The Ackerman, Bloomberg, and associated families sometimes rented a house in Lake Elsinore or Venice Beach. Maureen remembered going to the beach alone when she was only five. A generation later, when we biked around Venice and walked on the Santa Monica Pier, she reminisced about her happy summers with Great-Great Grandma Esther and her aunts and cousins on the beach, the Pier, at the "plunge" (the pier's public swimming pool), and at Lake Elsinore, where Esther visited the hot springs to ease her rheumatism.

When Grandma Maureen was 19, she went by train from San Francisco to Texas to say goodbye to Great-Grandma Yetta, who by then was not only blind, but also deaf and suffering from dementia. When Grandpa George's sister, Mary, picked her up from the train station, she warned Maureen that Yetta wasn't the same person she remembered. When Mary brought Maureen into Yetta's bedroom, she yelled into Yetta's ear, "Maureen is here. Do you remember Maureen, Sarah's little girl?" and Yetta said, "Sarah was such a sweet little girl."

Starting when Grandma Maureen was 12, her parents sent her to B'nei Akiva's summer camp, Moshava. She took the train alone from San Francisco to Union Station in Los Angeles. She adored camp and attended for five years. Moshava instilled in her a great love of Israel and Torah, and made a huge impact on her life. She always remembered that one Friday night at camp, a doctor diagnosed a case of polio among the campers. The camp closed, and the kids had to leave that night. Maureen made lifelong friends at camp. Many years later, women who had known her there would tell Esther Sue in *shul* in Los Angeles that Maureen was the most beautiful, popular, sought-after girl in camp. When Esther Sue repeated this to her modest mother, she would look surprised and say, "Who, me?"

Maureen graduated from Lincoln High School a semester early as an outstanding student and the class speaker. She was a bookworm until her last years when sadly she could not read anymore due to the tragedy of dementia. Maureen instilled a love of reading in her four children. Every Friday afternoon, she took them to the library in the Pico-Robertson neighborhood of LA, where they grew up. She loved reading so much that sometimes she would bring one of her books to the *Shabbes* table, "forgetting" that Zeidy didn't approve. We often did the same, but we always put them away after we got a quick warning glance from him.

Grandma Maureen attended a semester of college at the University of California at Berkeley, with her cousin Ida Hirsch (Bick), but as much as she enjoyed the beautiful campus and her studies, she knew that she needed to be with other Jewish singles. She was determined to go to New York, but she met with some resistance from Great-Grandma Sarah who eventually gave in. This was during the Korean War, so before Maureen went to New York—and when she would come home to visit—she went out with many Jewish soldiers who passed through San Francisco on their way to war. She turned down many marriage proposals.

Grandma Maureen spent about three years in New York, living in Borough Park and other Jewish neighborhoods, working as a nursery schoolteacher and as a secretary for an absent-minded professor. She took classes at the Teacher's Institute and at Brooklyn College, all the while keeping an eye out for her future mate. Ironically, she met him while she was at home in San Francisco on vacation.

Grandma and Zeidy would never have met if he hadn't taken that cross-country trip with his maternal first cousin Eddie Kahn. They stayed at the home of Grandma's Auntie Bella Hirsch, Grandma Sarah's older sister. Bella and her husband, Sam Hirsch, were well known among the local Orthodox Jewish community. Their name was also well known in Lakewood, New Jersey. In 1941, during World War II, the Hirsches became very close to Rav Aharon Kotler, who escaped from Europe to San Francisco. Sam Hirsch's father and grandfathers had been prominent rabbis in San Francisco in the early 1900s, and he donated their fine library to the fledgling *yeshiva* that Rav Kotler started in Lakewood, New Jersey. Now more than 7,000 students use it.

In the 1950s, as a gesture of *hakarat hatov* (repayment of a favor), the Kotlers invited Sam and Bella's daughter, Ida Hirsch (later Bick), and her first cousin, Maureen—then both single women living in New York—to spend the Passover *sedarim* (seder dinners) at the *yeshiva*. Grandma Maureen said later that she never experienced longer *sedarim* in her life, and though they invited her again, she never returned.

She was so happy to marry Zeidy, and she was thrilled that he was a rabbi. Grandpa George and Grandma Sarah also were bursting with pride that their daughter was marrying a rabbi. Their wedding took place on New Year's Day at the Chevra Tehillim *shul*. Maureen was delighted to be the first San Francisco bride to bring in Israeli songs for the chuppah (marriage ceremony) and the dancing afterward.

Grandma Maureen went on to have a very happy, fulfilling life with Zeidy. She wrote letters to her parents telling them how happy she was in each place where Zeidy served as a pulpit rabbi. After living in Hornell, New York, where Raizel was born, and in Duluth, Minnesota, where Myer and Esther Sue were born, they made their way to Los Angeles, where Elizabeth was born and where they lived for 55 years.

Buying the nursery school in Los Angeles was Grandma Maureen's idea, and she taught the three-year-olds for 25 years. Yet, somehow, she made her four children feel as if she were a stay-at-home mother, since she was present for every carpool, doctor's appointment, and school play. She made dinner at home every night and hosted lovely *Shabbosim* and *Yom Tovim* (Sabbaths and holidays) filled with guests.

Maureen was ahead of her time as a female business owner who worked outside the home. She took salads and vegetables to a whole new

After 50 years of marriage.

level before anyone else. Today, people pay outrageous sums of money at upscale vegan restaurants for salads just like her original avocado, mango, papaya, and spinach salad. Despite this gift for making healthful salads, Grandma Maureen kept a private reserve of Rollo chocolate-covered caramels and Hershey's Kisses. She also had a secret stash of cake and cookies in the freezer, and woe unto the person who decided to sample them without her permission. She relished having those treats with a hot cup of Lipton tea. She must have consumed eight cups of tea a day right up until the end of her life.

Maureen felt that education was extremely important, and she was determined to complete her bachelor's degree. She had attended many colleges, but her studies were constantly interrupted by marriage and the arrivals of four children. She finally received her bachelor's degree in history from UCLA, graduating *magna cum laude*, when Elizabeth was two years old. She dreamed that one of her children would attend an Ivy League university, a vision that was fulfilled first when Esther Sue won a full fellowship to Columbia University's Graduate School of History. However, she attended for only a short while before returning to Los Angeles to marry. Myer and Janis Roszler's son, Maureen's grandson Amichai, did her proud by graduating from the University of Pennsylvania law school.

Grandma and Zeidy were very much products of their times, even though she was Zeidy's business partner, and they wanted all their kids—the girls as well as Myer—to receive a college education. First and foremost, though, they wanted their daughters to marry. They saw this as the highest accomplishment Raizel, Esther Sue, and Elizabeth could attain, and they thought it would guarantee their security at a time when women's professional avenues were still limited. By the time Elizabeth went to college, they urged her to study something practical, so she majored in computer science.

Grandma Maureen worked hard preparing for family road trips, including weekends in Palm Springs, San Diego, Laguna, Ventura, Santa Barbara, and many other places in the vicinity. She also made the preparations for their longer adventures to San Francisco, the Grand Canyon, Las Vegas, Oregon, and Yosemite National Park, one of her favorite places. Grandma would pack Igloo coolers with *kosher* food for a week—including *Shabbos*—for a family of six, no easy task. Her children did not appreciate how much work went into these trips until they became parents.

These trips always incorporated Maureen's love of nature and animals. The family walked, hiked, biked, swam, rode horses, and saw all kinds of wildlife. Grandma and Zeidy drove to many of the national parks with Elizabeth. As the baby of the family, she benefited from being alone with them, and she had an especially close relationship with her mother, from childhood until Maureen's death. They even took some trips on their own. Many of the grandchildren in the next generation went on lots of the same road trips with Grandma and Zeidy, who both had remarkable energy through their late 70s.

The Roszler family spent many Thanksgivings and various other holiday weekends in Palm Desert. The vacation towns in the California desert—Palm Springs, Desert Hot Springs, and Rancho Mirage—became almost homes away from home. Later on, Montecito supplanted all of them. As part of our daily routine there, Grandma insisted that we take an evening walk on the beach and along the train tracks. She loved walking, and literally stopped and smelled the roses. Her family nickname was "The Yellow Rose of Texas," after the song. Zeidy talked about his Yellow Rose at every birthday, anniversary, and Mother's Day celebration. We would bring her yellow roses and sing her signature Texas song.

We used to ask her how she managed all the hard work that went into making Pesach while working at the nursery school and handling weekend trips to Palm Springs. She would shrug and say, "I think of Daddy's (Zeidy) mother, and I know how much harder she had it with a wood-burning stove, no electricity, or running water, and I can't complain."

She also found time to perform many *mitzvot* (good deeds) that no one knew about, such as taking cancer patients to their chemo appointments and, for many years, doing *taharot* (the ritual of preparing a body for burial). She was one of the few in LA who did this *chessed shel emet* (ultimate good deed). Later she taught the ritual to her sister Joann, who also carried it out for many years. Aside from this recurring service, she was president of the women's division of the Orthodox Union, and she was active in her children's Jewish day school, the Hillel Hebrew Academy. She and Zeidy were both intellectuals who liked classical music, and they often went to concerts at the Hollywood Bowl.

Grandma also sewed, including making dresses for Raizel that became hand-me-downs for Esther Sue and then Elizabeth. She knit beautiful sweaters for her grandchildren, crocheted, and did needlepoint. She needlepointed a stunning *atarah* (collar) for Zeidy's tallis. She used to scold Esther Sue, asking her, "Why don't you do things with your hands? It will make you more creative."

Grandma was closest to her immediate family members, including Joann, who had married Walter (Vel) Hulkower and had five children. When she and Zeidy traveled, Auntie Joannie and Uncle Vel always opened their home to their children. Maureen also stayed close to her first cousin,

Nathine Gelberman Benyowitz, who lived nearby. Her oldest childhood friend, Hedy Alperin Gouraie, remained a life-long friend. Their parents had been friends in San Francisco, so Maureen and Hedy met when they were young and cemented their friendship at Camp Moshava. Grandma had many other friends in Los Angeles and other places across the United States and in Israel.

Grandma and Zeidy were fortunate to be able to retire when they were still under 60. The proceeds from selling the school gave them an income for many years. They traveled all over the world, always bringing their own food. They took an Alaska cruise, visited Scandinavia, and went through most of Europe and Australia. Grandma particularly enjoyed their trip to China, where they traveled with a group of Bar-Ilan University supporters. Zeidy even blew the shofar in the Great Hall of China. However, Israel was still their favorite destination, no matter how many times they went. They enjoyed it with all of their children and many of their grandchildren on numerous occasions.

Grandma loved being with Zeidy, and making sure he was always safe, comfortable, and well fed. In addition to traveling, Grandma and Zeidy would visit their adult children and take care of their grandkids. When Myer and Janis went to explore the world, Grandma and Zeidy would stay with the kids. The Kandel family also spent many *Shabbosim* and *chagim* (holidays) at Grandma and Zeidy's, their second home. Elizabeth brought her kids to LA very often, and Grandma also went to Cleveland often to spend time with them and, later, with Raizel, Bryan, and their children. When Raizel and Bryan were adopting J.J., Grandma spent a month in Kentucky in a residential hotel with Raizel. Grandma never forgot it because the weather was so cold.

When the time came, Joannie and Maureen took wonderful care of their parents in their old age. In this way, as in many others, they were role models for their children, who later took care of them. As Zeidy and Grandma's health declined, they moved from LA to Cleveland, where Elizabeth and Josh and Raizel and Bryan formed a strong team to take care of their multitude of health issues.

When Grandma and Zeidy moved from Los Angeles to Cleveland, they built a wooden deck onto their house so they could sit outside. Grandma got joy from watching the deer and listening to the birds. Toward the end of her life, when spring and summer were in full bloom in Cleveland, she always quoted her favorite phrase, *"Hodu Lashem Ki tov, Ki le' Olam Chasdo,"*—"Give thanks to God, because He is good, for His kindness is eternal"—from Tehillim, 136:1.

In 1998, Great-Grandma Sarah and Great-Grandpa George passed away within two weeks of each other. They were buried in the Mount Carmel Cemetery in the *barrio* (region) of East Los Angeles, in the same cemetery as Sarah's parents, Joseph and Esther Ackerman. Grandma had an important realization at her parents' funerals. She looked at the cemetery's surroundings, and decided that she did not want her eternal home to be East Los Angeles. She and Zeidy decided that they wanted to be buried in the bucolic Eretz Hachaim cemetery in Beit Shemesh, Israel.

Grandma's whole goal in life was to make Zeidy happy, to try to make up for the traumas he suffered in his youth. She lived to please him. When he passed away in 2017, a huge part of her passed with him. Though her memory faltered, she always asked about him, even after he was gone. Two years after he died, Grandma passed suddenly and without warning in Cleveland on the second day of *Rosh Hashanah*. The family buried her alongside Zeidy at Eretz Hachaim Cemetery, as they had wished. Her family and her many friends attended her funeral and shiva in Israel, Cleveland, and Los Angeles. Everyone loved and respected Grandma Maureen, who lived a quiet but very fulfilled life.

Esther Roszler Kandel

APPENDIX 3

A Brief History of Ebensee

Background

Lack of manpower was one of the most pressing problems of the German wartime economy. After the Nazis' unsuccessful *Blitzkrieg* against the Soviet Union in the winter of 1941, weapon manufacturers were increasingly interested in using the labor of foreign civilians, prisoners of war, and concentration camp inmates. In March 1942, the SS and the armament industry jointly agreed to build dedicated labor camps near the weapons factories. Between 1942 and 1944, they also opened numerous concentration camp outposts in Austrian territory. In particular, the Nazis focused on using this labor for their missile program. This focus became even more acute after they lost the Battle of Britain in 1941.

Germany's main missile factory was the Peenemünde Army Research Centre on the island of Usedome in the Baltic sea. On October 3, 1942, the Nazis successfully launched the V-2 rocket (also known as the A4 rocket) from Peenemünde. Realizing the significance of the missile program, the British bombed and partially destroyed the facility on August 17 and 18, 1943. Adolph Hitler, Heinrich Himmler, and Albert Speer, the minister for Armaments and War Production, consequently decided to relocate the missile's production to an underground plant near Nordhausen, Germany, and to supply it with labor by building an outpost of Buchenwald there, the Mittelbau-Dora concentration camp.

They likewise wanted to move the Peenemünde research facilities to underground galleries, but lacking any existing facility, they started constructing a new underground missile development installation at Ebensee, Austria, in September 1943. They selected Ebensee because of its favorable geological and topographical characteristics. The site's thick forests, existing quarry, and efficient traffic links to railway lines and roads offered excellent conditions for the secret construction project.

Underground tunnels in Ebensee—The inmates dug dirt and rocks in the quarry under cold, harsh conditions to create these tunnels, which the Nazis planned to use to develop and produce secret missiles and rockets.

They named the undertaking "Project Zement," and set out to relocate the production of the V-2 rocket and the A9 intercontinental missile to Ebensee by late 1944. The plan called for creating two units, "A" for housing and "B" for testing the missiles. However, technical problems delayed the plan. As a result of Allied bombings of fuel production facilities, they came to use "Unit A" for petroleum refining. Because Allied troops were approaching, the Nazis moved the production of Steyr-Damiler-Puch AG tank engines from Hungary to galleries four and five of "Unit B" at Ebensee. They installed more than 200 machines to produce engine components for tanks. Shortly before liberation, another division took up production in galleries one and two.

Creating Ebensee

At first, the Nazis used Mauthausen primarily to murder their political and ideological opponents. In the period before 1942, they put people to work more as a form of punishment or humiliation than because they needed the labor. Forced labor became a central element of imprisonment at concentration camps only when the Nazi leadership was unable to overcome Germany's labor shortages with either POWs or foreign forced labor. The SS could no longer be the only monitor of industry and construction projects, so the Nazis brought in civilian workers to supervise and instruct prison laborers.

In November, 1943, Germany transferred more than 500 prisoners from Mauthausen to build a "labor camp" intended to last for the duration of the project. Ebensee, the first concentration camp set up for the purpose of building a new subterranean set of tunnels for storing armaments, was constructed outside town in densely forested terrain and surrounded by electric fences. By the spring of 1944, the SS began building a crematorium next to the infirmary barracks and the so-called "rest blocks." These facilities were less for healing sick prisoners than for separating out those so sick, malnourished, or injured they could no longer work. They erected administrative buildings in a semi-circle around the camp's main square.

After completion of the first barracks blocks in January, 1944, the camp gradually increased in size until, by July, 1944, it held more than 6,000 prisoners. Nevertheless, the construction site faced a shortage of manpower which, together with other factors, prevented the project from being completed as rapidly as planned. When the *Jägerstab*, a commission directing the war economy, decided to "pump in" more inmates to work on construction of the underground facilities, the number of prisoners at Ebensee increased dramatically. At the end of 1944, more than 9,000 prisoners were held there. In the final period of the camp's existence, the population reached 18,509 prisoners.

Conditions at the Camp

The SS, which administered the camp, leased the prisoners to the construction companies under contract. The companies submitted their "requirements," and the SS allocated prisoners to them accordingly. The companies paid the SS on the basis of the prisoners' professional skills and ability to work. If a prisoner became ill or unable to work, the company returned him to Mauthausen and replaced him with someone who could work. Most of the prisoners who were sent back died of exhaustion or illness, or were murdered.

The prisoners were guarded by SS units and, after the summer of 1944, by members of the *Wehrmacht*. Only the camp commandant, the *rapportführer*, SS medical personnel, and the *blockführer* were allowed to enter the camp itself. They coordinated the deployment of labor and monitored the number of prisoners who turned up for work, as well as the prisoners who were ill and unfit for work. The notoriously brutal heads of the camp tortured and murdered prisoners.

The Germans also delegated prisoners as *kapos* for internal administration and supervision of the camp, a system created deliberately to prevent any sense of solidarity among the prisoners. They summoned the prisoners to the main square in the camp several times a day for roll-call and grouped them in "work brigades" according to the construction companies' "prisoner requirements."

Most Ebensee prisoners worked in the tunnels under appalling conditions. Weakened by malnutrition, they had to perform under utterly inadequate safety precautions and often without the appropriate tools or technical resources. In addition, the prisoners had to march two kilometers daily to and from the camp. Some of the most strenuous labor included producing prefabricated concrete parts for the tunnels, which had been specially manufactured by German companies. Prisoners regarded less strenuous work in camp administration as a privilege.

Ebensee concentration camp prisoners belonged to more than 20 different national groups. Prisoners from Poland, Russia, Hungary, France, Germany, Italy, Yugoslavia, Greece, Italy, and Czechoslovakia constituted the largest national groups. Some 30% of the inmates were Jewish, and some 40% of Jewish inmates died. A prisoner's living conditions and chances of survival were determined by how Nazi racist ideology categorized his nationality. The Nazis' treated German "political" and "criminal" victims better than individuals of western or southern European nationalities. Citizens of the Soviet Union and Poland ranked lower, and Jews and *Romani* (gypsies) of all nationalities were at the bottom of the scale.

Prisoners died from bad hygiene, inadequate food and clothing, and exposure to the snow, damp, and cold. Around 27,278 prisoners passed through the camp between 1943 and 1945, and 8,500 to 11,000 prisoners died at Ebensee, mostly from starvation. Conditions became even more critical after January, 1945, when transports of prisoners arrived from evacuated concentration camps. Amid catastrophic overcrowding, the supply system broke down. The camp's administration tried to solve the problem by deliberately causing death through cruelty and deprivation, particularly among Jewish prisoners. At this time, they gave sick Jewish prisoners no food at all. The camp authorities became increasingly nervous as they received news of Allied victories. The SS officers began looking for ways to destroy any trace of their actions.

Liberation

The approach of Allied armies meant hope of liberation and increased the prisoners' resistance. National and political groups developed within the camp, In May,1945, they began to fear the SS would carry out mass murders of the prisoners, so they made preparations to prevent it. On May 5, the camp commandant tried to get the remaining prisoners to enter one of the mountain tunnels, but the prisoners refused, and the camp staff left. On May 6, 1945, the US 80th Infantry Division liberated Ebensee and found that the tunnel was full of explosives.

The SS guards fled after destroying documents about the camp's administration. The American military police captured 400 people, but most received light punishments. However, American military courts sentenced the SS camp doctor, SS *Rapportführer*, SS medical orderly and SS *Blockführer* to death and sentenced a few other guards to life in prison.

A few weeks after liberation, US authorities arranged to erect the first camp cemetery in Steinkogel. Three years later the Lepetit Monument was inaugurated in the former area of the camp. Beginning in the 1950s, Austria removed all remains of the former camp, except the main gate. Since that time, they've built a village with about 120 family homes to cover the camp's location. However, in 2012, a new memorial was created. The Museum for Contemporary History Ebensee has archive including a photographic display and a list of 8,500 prisoners' names.

Amichai Isaac Roszler

[The majority of this history is abridged from the book Ebsensee Concentration Camp: The "Zement" Project *(2014) published by the Zeitgeschichte Museum Ebensee.]*

APPENDIX 4

Yichus (Lineage)

FROM MY FATHER'S SIDE

I am named for my great grandfather, Chaim Ressler's father, Tzvi Elimelech. He moved from Galicia to small town in Romania called Mureşenii Borgo and bought a large tract of land. He is buried in the nearby city of Bistritz. His wife Sarah, my great grandmother, is also buried in Bistriz. She descended from the Chacham Tzvi and the Baal Halevushim.

To complete the picture of my father's ancestors, discussed below, Tzvi Elimelech's great grandfather was Rav Tvi Elimelech Spira of Dinov, Galicia. He was known as the Bnai Yissachar. Other ancestors include Tzvi Hirsh of Zidichov, the Kedushat Levi of Berdichov, and the Ramah on the *Shulchan Aruch*.

The Bnai Yisschar (1783–1841): My Namesake

Rabbi Tzvi Elimelech Spira was born in Dinov, Galicia, now Poland, in 1783, and he died on the 18th of Tevet in 1841. He is also known as the Rebbe, Reb Hersh Melech, or the Dinover. He is named after his popular book, the *Bnai Yissachar*, which is a commentary on

Refurbished matzeva of the Bnai Yissachar—This is the tombstone of Rabbi Tzvi Elimelech of Dinov, whose book is in the library of every chasid. Zeidy was named after him.

Shabbes and Jewish holidays, and is a main staple for any Chassidic library. It has recently been translated into English. Rabbi Spira, a prolific author, wrote many other *sfarim* (books) as well. He is the subject of many legends and stories, including how he chose the name of his book.

בעז"ה איגרת יהוס מצד סבא משפחת רעסלער רומאניא נאונגארן

חיים מאיר ריזל, אסתר, שרה, יטה רבקה בן (בת) הרב צבי אלימלך רעסלער און ראזלער (מלפנ"ס רב בתהארנעצעל גיו יארק נבדולנטה מינאסאטא) בן מוריר מאיר זצ"יל שנהרג באנישוניטץ עי"י הגרמאנים, בן מוריר חיים רעסלער זצ"יל בן מנריר צבי אלימלך ז"ל בן מוריר בנימין זצ"יל חתן מוריר שמואל שאפירא זצ"יל בן מוריר צבי אלימלך ז"ל מדינוב. בעל בני ישכר: מוריר שמואל שאפירא הנ"יל הי' חתן מוריר הערציל זצ"יל חתן מוריר צבי הירש מזידזטשוב בעל עטרת צבי.

מוריר בנימין רוסלער הנ"יל הי' בן מוריר חיים זצ"יל חתן מנריר מאיר זצ"יל בעל כתר תורה בן מורינו ורבינו ר' לוי יצחק זצ"יל מברדיטשנב בעל קדושת לוי מנריר מאיר בעל כתר תורה הנ"יל היה חתן מנריר אליעזר זצ"יל ראש ישיבה בפינסק חתן מנריר ישראל זצ"יל איסר זצ"יל אביד פינסק בן מוריר אבא זצ"יל נארדאק, חתן מנריר ישראל איטריל זצ"יל אביד קאליש בן מוריר משה זצ"יל מלנבלין חתן מנריגנ נרבינו ר' שמואל אליעזר הלוי אידליש זצ"יל בעל מהרשיא על השיס: מוריר ישראל איטריל הנ"יל היה חתן מוריר אברהם זצ"יל בן מוריר ליטמאן זצ"יל חתן מנריגנ נרבינו ר' מאיר זצ"יל מלנבלין בעל מהריים על השיס: מוריר משה מלנבלין הנ"יל הי' בן מנריר יצחק זצ"יל מלנבלין חתן מנריר בנגם זצ"יל חתן מורינו נרבינו ר' משה איטרליש זצ"יל בעל רמיא.

מוריר צבי אלימלך רעסלער הנ"יל הי' חתן מנריר מאיר זצ"יל מפאליק בן מנריר משנלם זלמן זצ"יל בן מוריר משה אפרים זצ"יל בן מנריר מרדכי זצ"יל בן מנריר נתן זצ"יל בן מנרינו נרבינו ר' צבי אשכנזי זצ"יל בעל חכם צבי.

מנריר לוי יצחק מברדיטשנב הנ"יל הי' חתן מנריר ישראל זצ"יל בן מנריר פרץ זצ"יל בן מוריר ארי' לייביש זצ"יל חתן מנריר יצחק מאיר פרנקל תאונמים זצ"יל אביד זלקנוא, סלנצקי נסיבעקי, בן מירונג נרבינג ר' ינגה תאנמים זצ"יל בעל קיקירן דיננה חתן מנריר מאיר נואהל זצ"יל אביד בריסק בן השר ר' שאנל ננאתל זצ"יל בן מנריר שמנאל יהודה זצ"יל בן מנרינו נרבינו ר' מאיר זצ"יל בעל מהריש פדגנא: מנריר פרץ זצ"יל הנ"יל היה חתן מנריר שמנאל זצ"יל בעל בית שמנאל על אה"יע חתן מנריר אריי: לגיב פישל זצ"יל אביד קראקע חתן מנריר ענסרים פישל זצ"יל בן מנריר צבי זצ"יל בן מנריר פישל זצ"יל מבריסק חתן מנריר נרבינו ר' שלנמה לנריא זצ"יל בעל מהרש"יל על השי"ס:

Yichus brief of Zeidy's paternal family

Apparently, he always felt a special affinity toward the holiday of *Chanukah*. Once, when he went to his Rebbe, the Seer of Lublin, he told him that he didn't understand this affinity, since he could not be a descendent of the Macabbi's because they were *Kohanim*, and he was not. His Rebbe told Rabbi Spira that he was a descendent of the tribe of *Yissachar*, the scholars of the *Sanhendrin*, the Rabbinic ruling body that established the holiday of *Chanukah*. In Moses' blessings to the Jewish people, he promised that the tribe of *Yissachar* would be the scholars and rabbis in Israel. The Bnai Yissachar's sons and grandsons established the Munkatzcher Chassidic dynasty.

Zvi Hirsh Eichenstein of Zidichov (1763–1831)

Zvi Hirsh Eichenstein was a great kabbalist and founder of the Zidochover Chassidic dynasty. He is known for his books on the Zohar, the Ateret Tzvi, and the Pri Kodesh Hillulim. He claimed that his soul was that of the martyr Rabbi Yishmael Kohen Gadol.

The Kedushat Levi (1740–1809)

Levi Yitchack Derbarmdger, also known as the Berditchever Rebbi, was born in 1740 and died in 1809. He wrote a classic work, the *Kedushat Levi*, a commentary on the weekly Torah readings encompassing Chassidic and Kabbalistic thought. He was also known as the defender of the Jewish people, since he often engaged G-d in dialogue in defense of individual or groups among his Jewish brethren. Indeed, many people among the Chassidim have the custom of saying his name, Levi Yitchak ben Sarah Sasha, when they hear bad news. They ask him to intercede with the heavens for salvation.

The Kedushat Levi descends from the great commentators on the Talmud, the Maharam, Maharsha, and Maharshal. His family tree also includes the Ramah; the "king for a day" Saul Wahl; and Rabbi Meir Katzenellebogen, the Maharam of Padua, Italy. The Maharam descended from Rashi, Rabbi Shmuel Yitchaki (1040–1105), the great author of the commentary on the Bible and Talmud. And Rashi could trace his lineage to King David.

The Chacham Tzvi (1658–1718)

Rabbi Tzvi Hirsch Ashkenazi was born in Moravia, Czechoslovakia in 1658 and died in 1718. Though born in Moravia, he studied in Sephardic cities, including Salonika, Greece, and became a rabbi in Constantinople, Turkey. He was given the honorable Sephardic title of *Chacham* (the smart leader). He later was a rabbi in a number of cities in Germany, and then served in Amsterdam and London. He was an ardent foe of the Shabbatian movement. His *Sheilot utushuvot* (responsa) still are held in high esteem.

The Ramah (1530–1572)

Rabbi Moses Isserles was a rabbi in Krakow, Poland, where he led a large *yeshiva*. He wrote the Askenazic laws in the *Shulchan Aruch* (Jewish Code of Law—literally, the name means the set table), which was called *Hamapah* (the tablecloth). His tombstone states that from Moses and the Rambam, to Moses (Iseerles), there was no one like Moses. His synagogue is still in use today in Krakow.

Ba'al Halevushim 1530–1612

Rabbi Mordecai Yoffe of Posen wrote a 10 volume codification of Jewish law that emphasized the customs of Eastern European Jews.

Saul Wahl (1541–1617)

According to Jewish folklore, this member of the Katznellbogen family was King of Poland for a day. He ruled while the Polish rulers were trying to decide who would become the permanent king. The name Wahl in German means election.

The Maharam of Padua (1482–1565)

Although he was Ashkenazi by birth, Rabbi Meir Katzenellenbogen became the rabbi of Padua in Venice, Italy. His *responsa* is famous, and he was a very popular rabbi. He has thousands of descendants, many of whom also became famous rabbis. He traced his ancestry to Rashi, who in turn could trace his lineage to King David.

Therefore, we descendants of the Roszler family also can claim lineage from King David.

YICHUS FROM MY MOTHER'S SIDE

The Tosfos Yom Tov Hagaon Harav Gershon Shaul Yom-Tov Lipmann Heller (1578–1654)

Arieh Leib Kahana, z'l, my maternal grandfather—the father of my mother Raizel—was a descendent on his father's side of the Tosfos Yom Tov. The Tosfos Yom Tov's daughter, also named Raizel (d. 1819), married Jacob Joseph Kahana. He was a great-great-great grandfather of Judah Kahana Heller, who wrote the *Kuntras Hasfekos* (and was referred to by its name) and who was the great grandfather of my grandfather Arieh Leib Kahana. The brother of the *Kuntras Hasfekos*, Aryeh Leib Kahana, published the world-famous book *Kzotz Hachoshen*.

The Tosfos Yom Tov wrote the classical commentary on the *Mishna*, the *Tosfos Yom-Tov,* and he was thereafter known by its name. The commentary is printed in every edition of the Mishna and is essential to the understanding it. He was the chief rabbi of Vienna, Prague, and Krakow.

In 1629, the Tosfos Yom Tov was arrested in Prague, probably at the behest of some wealthy members of the Jewish community who were upset

Megillas Eivah—The story of the tribulations of the Tosfos Yom Tov from 1629-1644. As his descendants, we decided to name this book *Megilat Tikvah,* similar to the title *Megillas Eivah,* which also describes loss, redemption, and faith.

that he levied the government tax load disproportionately on them. The charge they conceived of was that he insulted Christianity in his writings. He was imprisoned in Vienna, exiled, fined, and not allowed to return to a major city for 15 years, after which he returned to Krakow. He wrote about his travails in a book called *Megillas Eivah,* the *Scroll of Animosity.* He had 16 children, including Raizel, who married Jacob Joseph Kahana and who is the ancestor of Zeidy's mother Raizel. The Tosfos Yom Tov declared that his thousands of descendants should fast on the fifth day of Tammuz, the day he was arrested in Prague, and celebrate a day of feasting and joy on the first day of Adar, when he was restored to glory as the chief Rabbi of Krakow. Many of his descendants still commemorate these days.

The Kuntras Hasfekos, Rabbi Yehuda Kahana Heller (1743–1819)

Although he was a Kohen and his last name was Kahana, the *Kuntras Hasfekos* also took the last name Heller, since he was a descendant of the Tosfos Yom-Tov. He was just a tutor for Talmud students when he published his book, the *Kuntras Hasfekos,* which discusses cases in the Talmud regarding monetary disputes. His scholarship immediately made him

Matzeva of the Kuntras Hasfekos in Sighet, Romania—Rabbi Yehuda Kahana Heller was the great-grandfather of Zeidy's grandfather, Aryeh Leib Kahana.

famous, and he served as a rabbi in a number of cities. His last post was in Máramarossziget (Sziget or Sighet in Romania), where he is buried.

His grandson Yitchak Isaac married Chava, the daughter of the Maareah Yecheskal.

Rabbi Yehuda Kahana's brother, Rabbi Aryeh Leib Kahana (1745–1813), was also a Talmud tutor. He wrote the *Ktzos Hachoshen*, a book on monetary laws which was published with the *Kuntras Hasfekos*. He also became instantly famous and became rabbi in a number of cities. His other books, which include the *Avnei Meluim* and *Shev Shmetai,* are revered and studied in modern day *yeshivas*. They are classic works of the *pilpul* learning method.

The Maareah Yecheskal, Rabbi Yecheskal Panet (1783–1845)

My grandfather's mother Chava was the daughter of the Maareah Yecheskal, whose name was Rabbi Yesheskal Panet. He was a rabbi in the small town of Tarcal, Hungary, when the Chasam Sofer recommended him for the post of chief Rabbi of Transylvania. The government gave him broad powers, including the authority to arrest people. He had a small prison in his shul. He brought *chassidus* to Romania and would travel throughout the country to strengthen Jewish observance.

After the death of Yitchak Isaac Heller, Chava married her brother-in-law Yosef Leib Kahana. He was her sister's widower and her husband's first cousin. She was widowed again and married Yitzchak Berger. They moved to Tzfat in Israel, where she died and is buried.

Famous Haggadah from the Maareah Yecheskel—The vision of Yecheskel is taken from the Haftorah for the first day of Shavuot in which the prophet Ezekiel issued a prophecy including four Angels in human form.

[While in Tzfat in 1998, we went to the Rabbanut of the city who had a record of where she was buried. We went to the cemetery, but the tombstones had been damaged by weather, so we found only the one marking the kever (grave) of her stepson.]

One of the Maareah Yecheskal's children became a Chassidic rebbe in Dej, Transylvania, and he founded a dynasty. There are Dej *shtiebels* (small synagogues) in many cities throughout the world, including in Miami Beach. He has thousands of descendants, many of whom are listed in books about his life.

[The names Yecheskal and Chava appear commonly in all generations of Zeidy's family including our own.]

Aryeh and Henya Leah Leib Kahana

My maternal grandfather Aryeh Leib was raised by his uncle Yosef Leib Kahana in Sziget. He was a well-known singer and a very wealthy man. There is a story that on Friday nights he would gather people from the *shul* around him to eat and sleep in his house, and he would practically give away his own bed. He was held in very great esteem, and people loved him. He also was a big *baal tzedakah* (philanthropist) and was a big *talmid hacham* (Torah scholar).

My grandmother was Henya Leah aleya hasholem—I believe her family name may have been Richtman. She was also related to Rabbi Richtman, who is now an old man in New York. I lived with him when I first came to the United States. My grandfather died in 1943, I believe, about two days before my Bar Mitzvah, so my parents couldn't come.

My grandmother was a very big tzadekes (holy woman). She was a wonderful mother and a gracious hostess. She strived her whole life so my grandfather could learn Torah yomam va'lelea (day and night).

Matzeva of Yosef Leib Kahana— An important dignitary in the town of Sighet, he was the uncle and stepfather of Aryeh Leib Kahana.

This was her mission. She loved her children and her grandchildren; when we came there, she didn't know what more she could do for us. She loved all her children, of course, but especially my mother, who was her mizinkele (youngest) daughter.

She also extended great love to my cousin Eddie Kahan who was left alone, an orphan. His mother died in childbirth when she gave birth to his sister Channa (Helen), who married Sam Baum. When Eddie's father remarried, Eddie was sent to my grandparents' house in Klausenburg, and my grandmother loved him more than her own child. She was always worried about his eating and his sleeping and his growing up. He lived with them for many years. She hoped that her children would be religious Jews and talmidei hachamim and Bnei Torah (scholars).

APPENDIX 5

My Immediate Relatives

DESCENDANTS OF ARYEH LEIB AND
HENYA LEAH KAHANA (Maternal Grandparents)

And now I'm going to start enumerating the children of my maternal grandfather (Aryeh Leib Kahana) and grandmother (Henya Leah):

Rav Itzhak Ayzik Kahana

Rav Kahana, the eldest son, moved the family to Klausenburg from Apahida after the first world war. In the early 1930s, or perhaps the late 1920s, he decided to come to the United States. But after seven years, he came back to Klausenburg, to his daughter and son-in-law the Richtman family. I don't know exactly what he did when he was in the United States, but he was some kind of a businessman. He was such a good-hearted man, and when he could, he would send money back to the family and to my grandparents. He would send clothes for us to my mother, his sister. When he later returned to the United States, going there for a second time, he also brought the Richtmans, his daughter and son-in-law with him to America.

Rav Kahana was a big *talmid hacham;* he also served on a voluntary basis as a synagogue rabbi in Williamsburg, Brooklyn. He spoke for that congregation for many years. After many years, he asked the synagogue for a favor. He wanted them to issue him an affidavit he could use to bring his family to America after the Second World War. He needed an official certificate that the congregation would accept him as a rabbi.

Family of R'Yitzchak Aizik Kahana—STANDING: Chaim (son), Mrs. Richtman (daughter), Raizel (his sister and Zeidy's mother), and Chavitza (daughter). SITTING: Joe Kahana (son), Rivkah (wife), and R'Kahana. Chaim, Chavitza, and Raizel perished in the Holocaust.

Actually, it was only a matter of a guarantee, just paperwork which really didn't mean anything for them, but they would not give it to him. He parted company with them at that time, and he felt they were not being nice to him after all those years.

He was a big *baal tzedakah* (man of charity) and a *baal hessed* (always doing kind deeds). The first time I met him in the United States was the day I arrived by boat.

After the Second World War when the *Klausenberg Rebbe* came to the United States, Rav Kahana was a big *macher* (official) for him. And when the *Satmar Rebbi* came, my uncle became his righthand man and would sit next to him to hand out the *Tisch* (food blessed by the rabbi at a meal). He was also the *Satmar Rebbi's* confidant. At that time, the *Satmar chasidim* were not as numerous as today. Their *beit hamidrash* on Bedford Avenue in Williamsburg drew a very small group.

The *Rebbi* lived upstairs, and the *minyan* (prayer session) was in the basement, with maybe 40 to 50 people, altogether, maybe 70 people. I spent *Yom Kippur* with them in 1947, when the *Satmar chasidut* was very small. Of course, it started growing later, and now thousands of *Satmar Chassidim* live in New York, Williamsburg, Borough Park, and all over the city.

I went to my uncle's house in Williamsburg many times for *Shabbes* during my early years in the United States. By that time, he'd married his third wife, whom he met at a very old age. (My uncle's first wife died in Klausenburg, before he came to the United States. Then he married his second wife, a very nice person whom I knew as a child and still remember. She gave birth to the other children.)

At the time I visited my uncle, Williamsburg was the center of Orthodox Judaism. It had a couple of *yeshivas*, Torah Vodass and Chafetz Chaim, and maybe two or three more. Yeshiva University was in Washington Heights in Manhattan, but Orthodox Judaism was centered in Williamsburg. It was very nice for me to go there on *Shabbes.*

In the summertime, when my dormitory at Yeshiva University was closed, I would leave my suitcase at the home of my uncle and his wife. For many years, I built their *Sukkah* for them on the second story of their house. The *Sukkah* wasn't very big, just enough for two or three people, and it was on top of the roof of the first floor, outside his window.

I remember a funny thing my uncle said. In 1950 or 1951, I had bought a car. It was nice looking, but, of course, the engine was very old and very used. One time I took my uncle *alav hasholem* to a wedding, and when we were coming home it was already one or two in the morning. All of a sudden, the car decided not to work; it was broken. I was very angry, naturally, that it broke at such an hour. And my uncle said to me, "What are you so angry about? It is a sentence in the Torah that it doesn't have to work. It says that a *zaken lephi kovodo* (an old person according to his honor) should not have to work so hard." In other words, the old car should not have to do so much work.

This is just one little thing, but he was a big *talmid hacham* and always said *divrey Torah* (Torah insights). Many times when I acted as a rabbi for different towns during the High Holidays, I would come to him for a *dvar Torah*, and he would always have something at hand.

Joe Kahana

My uncle's eldest son was my cousin Joe Kahana, who came to the United States as a young man before anyone, the first in the family to go to America. He was a watchmaker, a jewelry man. And he eventually married here. His wife was Esther Cohen, who came from a very *choshuva* (important) family in New Rochelle, New York, a half an hour from New York City by train. Her father was a big *talmid hacham* (scholar), and a *machnes oreach* (known for inviting people to his home), and one of her brothers learned in R Yizchak Elchanon (present day Yeshiva University). Her family had a big men's store in New Rochelle.

Joe had a very nice home, a big house on a big lot. Of course, for the city people who lived in Manhattan and Brooklyn, at that time in the early 1940s, a house like that was a tremendous thing. When I came to America, I didn't know anyone who had a house. My other relatives lived in apartments or they lived in brownstones, attached houses in Brooklyn. A large single-family house with a yard was quite a revelation.

I visited Joe and Esther a number of times. He was a choshuva person, president of the orthodox shul. They had only one child, Howard (actually, Yecheskal, named after Maareah Yecheskal). I haven't seen him for a number of years, but occasionally I hear about him. He married and lives somewhere in New Jersey, I believe. But he is not in close contact with the family.

Cousin Joe had a jewelry store on the Lower East Side on Canal Street in Manhattan. He manufactured and sold gold watches. He did very well, and he had a number of people working for him, including his father Ayzik Kahana, who was a salesman and also worked in the factory. I believe Joe gave him a salary.

Rabbi Shlomo and Hanna Richtman

My uncle's daughter Hanna Richtman, was married to Rabbi Richtman. She was a very nice person, and she looked so much like my mother. She and her husband worked very hard for many years. They lived on Hart Street, in the Bedford Stuyvesant section of Brooklyn, a nice Jewish area with brownstone houses. He was a rabbi and a *talmid hacham*, a *Talmid* of the old *Satmar Rabbi*.

He bought a brownstone and converted part of it to a wedding hall. They would cook downstairs while weddings parties were in the wedding hall on the middle floor. The shul, where he also had *huppas*, was upstairs. They both did very well financially, especially during the war years, since many young people who went to the Army got married. After the war years, I worked there as a waiter on *Shabbes* nights and sometimes Sunday afternoons, to make some extra money to support myself.

The Richtman children were very nice. They went to yeshivas and got a good Jewish education. Their sons, Lazer Dovid (Herbie) and Chezky, got *smicha* (rabbinic ordination). They first went to Torah Vadaas and then to Yeshiva University. Of course, I was very close to them since I was about their age and I grew up with them. I would stay with them on *Shabbes* and holidays.

The Richtman's daughter Elizabeth *aleya hasholem* died a number of years ago. She was married to a fellow who now lives somewhere in New York. Their daughter Eva married Bob Khlar, a very fine person, a *talmid hacham* with *smicha* (ordination). He is in the diamond business, and I'm very close to his wonderful children. Of course, they are also close to cousin Helen, Eddie's sister, and so are we. I will come back to Helen a little bit later. The Richtman's youngest daughter was Rifka, whom I loved very much. When I came to the United States age 17, she was a tiny baby, six months old, a very sweet beautiful baby. Today she is married to Aaron Weiss, they live in Ashdod, and they have wonderful children, three boys and a girl. We see them often when we go to Israel. When they visited the United States, they would come to Los Angeles and usually stay with us.

My uncle's next daughter was Chavi, a very beautiful woman. She was married to a distant cousin, Yishay Kahana. They lived in Klausenburg in the complex I described which my uncle had bought many years before he moved to the United States. Yishay was the secretary or the executive director of the *Sfardic Kehila*. It was not truly Sfardic, but that was what the *Chassidic* community was called. Yishay and Chavi had three children, but the whole family perished in the concentration camp. Nobody was left from that family at all.

The head of the *Sfardic Kehila* community was Rav Halberstam, the Klausenberger Rebbe, *zay gezunt* (he should be well), who lives today in Union City, New Jersey. He also lived for many years in Israel where he established in Israel many wonderful institutions, including a Kollel. He also established the *Mif'al ha-Shas* (a daily learning program) and the Laniado hospital, a very fine institution in Netanya.

My uncle's son, Chaim Kahan, was a very fine *talmid hacham*. As noted earlier, he was like a controller, bookkeeper, and overseer of the Hellman bakery. In the early 1940s, my brother Yitzchak Shmuel went to live in Klausenburg in order to learn the techniques of bookkeeping and accounting from him. Chaim was a solid man and a *baal abatesh* (respectable) person. He and his wife and their three or four children also perished in the concentration camps.

Rav Yehezkel Kahan

I had another uncle, Rav Yecheskal Kahan, who lived in the Hellman bakery apartment complex. I remembered coming to visit him often when I was in Klausenburg. He would come to *daven* (pray) with my grandfather on *Shabbes* morning, and when they came home, he would make the eggs and onions, that was his task on *Shabbes*. He was a very pleasant man, a very fine person, with a very nice family. They also perished, killed by the Germans *yimach shmann* in a concentration camp.

My uncle had another son, Yossef Leib, who died before he could be married, during the terrible flu epidemic at the end of the first world war.

Many, many people died. *[In fact between 50 and million people died of the Spanish flu.]*

Yidditz (Yehudit) and Rabbi Hillel Michali

I believe my aunt Yidditz (Yehudit), was the second oldest of my grandparents' children. She was married to my uncle Rabbi Hillel Michali, a big *Talmid Hacham* (scholar), and also a nice-looking man with a big white beard. He came to the United States a bit earlier, I believe, in the 1930s. He was a rabbi for many years in Baltimore. At the time that I lived in New York City, he was still alive, and I visited him three times, or so, on *Chol Hamoed Succos* or *Pesach*.

They had a nice home, and they had a little elevator with a seat going up the stairway. To me, it was a revelation.

His eldest son had *smicha* (ordination) from Yeshiva University. Unfortunately, he did not turn out the way his parents and grandparents would have liked. He left the Orthodox *Rabbanut* (clergy), married a wealthy woman, and became a Reform rabbi, although he is a big *talmid hacham* (scholar). He is an influential man in Cincinnati at Hebrew Union College [the rabbinical school for Reform Judaism]. I saw him only once in the United States, when he also was visiting his parents and his family in Baltimore. The only thing he asked me was what size shirt I wear. Of course, at the time, I barely had anything because I had just come from Europe. [When Zeidy told him what size, he said, "Too bad, my shirts don't fit you."] He is a very bright person but, unfortunately, he left the fold of orthodoxy, and I don't think that our grandparents would be very proud of his actions.

His next daughter was Chavi, a very fine, very *frum* person, who married Rabbi Rothenberg. He comes from a *Chassidic* rabbinical family. When I visited, he was very pleasant to me. Later on, he served as a rabbi part-time and taught Hebrew and English subjects (he had a secular college degree) in the public school system in Baltimore. Afterward, for many years, he was a principal at day schools in Pittsburgh; then he was a principal in Ohio. He and his wife live now in Miami Beach. He and Chavi had one daughter who is married and lives in New Jersey.

Their other daughter, Susan, is married to a man named Tarogan who also comes from a fine family. His father was a *rav* (rabbi) in Baltimore for many years, I still recall him. I believe when he died, he was more than 100 years old. He had a *shul* in Baltimore, where they lived. Susan and her husband have very fine children, religious children. Of course, I haven't seen them since they were very young, very little actually. One of them is an accountant, now, and the other works for his father's business. His name is William, and he visited here several years ago. He is Rosalie Zalis's uncle, so he came to one of their weddings. He came to our house and stayed with us. He, too, was a very fine person. He is very well known in Baltimore. This was the family of my mother's older sister, my aunt.

Chaya Rochel and Rabbi Binyamin Alter Ruttner

My grandparents in Klausenburg had another daughter, my aunt Chaya Rochel *aleya hasholem*. She was married to Rabbi Binyamin Alter Ruttner, and they were the parents of the Ruttner family who live in New York. Before the war, they lived in Transylvania. The city was called Vásárhely in Hungarian and Targu Mures in Romanian. The name means the marketplace of Mures, a big river flowing through that city. It was a very fine city, and they were very *chashuv baal abatesh* (an important family). Rabbi Ruttner was a *shochet* (ritual slaughterer) and *chazan* (cantor); he was very respected. They were a very good family; he had an open house, and their children were wonderful children, religious children.

The eldest son was Moyshe, who lived in the city of Margareten. He was a *shochet* and, later, he became also a *Rav*; he was a big *Talmid Hacham*. I believe he was the *Talmid* of the Satmar Rebbe Yoel Teitelbaum. He had a family, I think, six children from his first wife, but his wife and children were taken to a concentration camp and were all killed. Later on, he remarried his second wife Razel. She was a very fine person, and they built a second family and had several children. One of them was named after Moyshe's father and [his grandfather] Binyamin Alter. I believe he sells jewelry. He had a daughter who died when she was about ten, and two other daughters, Chaya Rochel and Leah. My cousin Moyshe died a number years ago, and it was a great loss to the family and to everybody; he was very well liked in the *shul*.

When Moyshe first came to the United States, he became *rav* in Wilmington, Delaware. He was very well-liked, and he lived there with his family for a number of years until the children got older, and then he and his family moved back to Brooklyn. Later on, he had his own shul in Queens. Our daughter Raizel used to visit them frequently on *Shabbes*.

In 1945, when I returned from concentration camp and lived in Klausenburg, I spent about four weeks with him. I went to Margareten and spent *yamin noraim* (High Holidays*)* and *Sukkes* at his house. At the time he lived with his sister Devorah, since he had not yet remarried. Anyway, Moyshe was a very fine person. I always liked him very much, and he always thought very highly of me. When I was at their house, they treated me with great *kavod* (honor) and were very nice to me. Of course, I had no family, and they didn't know what to do for me. Their daughter Leah is a very fine, humorous person, but, unfortunately, she was married to a *Breslov Chassid* who did not treat her very well, and consequently they were divorced. So far, she has not remarried.

The Shomkuter Rav, Yecheskal Ruttner

The next member of the Ruttner family is the Shomkuter Rav, Yecheskal Ruttner *alav hasholem*. He was a very nice little person, a very fine and kind person. Originally, he was a *talmid* (student) of the Uyvar Rav, who later came with him to the United States. Uyvar is a small town in Transylvania. He married his first wife, the Shomkuter Rav's daughter. He may have already served as the city's rav before the war. And he had a number of children and a wife who all perished, killed by the Germans *yimach shmann* (may their names be erased) in Auschwitz.

After the Second World War, Yecheskal was liberated at Feldafing, and came into the Displaced Person Camp where there were 4,000 Jews. He became the chief rabbi, with the Klausenberger Rebbe (who moved later on to another DP camp, Föhrenwald, where he was again chief Rabbi). He performed marriages for a number of survivors in the camp.

Anyway, at the end of 1945, Yecheskal Ruttner's brother, Tzalel, who lived with him in DP camp, went back to Romania, and he made a *shidduch* (found a wife) for him, a woman named Hindi. She was the daughter of the Uyvar Rav. When he was a *talmid* at her father's *yeshiva,* she was a baby, and he used to carry her in his arms. In 1946, he married her. Their first daughter Rifki was born in Germany in the DP camp. They later moved to the little town of Wilhelm, Germany.

When the Ruttners came to the United States, Yecheskal opened a *shtiebel* (small synagogue) with his father-in-law, the Uyvar Rav, at 119 Penn Street in Williamsburg. He later on moved to Flatbush and opened one of the first *shtiebels* there, while his father-in-law stayed in Williamsburg. Yecheskal was very successful and very well loved. He gave a *shiur* (class) in the Young Israel of Flatbush, and he had a very nice *minyan.* He was also instrumental in building a beautiful *mikve* (ritual bath) right across from the *shtiebel* on 16th Street.

Yehezkel and Hindi had several children, four daughters and a son: Rivke, Chaya Rachel, Leah, and Sarah, and the son was Binyamin Dovid. Three or four years ago, at the elevated train or at a subway, Yehezkel fell down and had a heart attack. It was a great loss, a terrible loss, too young, of a very fine person, a big *talmid hacham* who learned *yomam va'lelea* (day and night). He was beloved, and he had a very fine personality. This was a tragic thing. His son Binyamin Dovid who had learned in the Stoliner Yeshiva succeeded him.

Mendel Ruttner, another son of the Ruttner family, was older than Yecheskal *alav hasholem.* He was a businessman who got married in the town of Shimlo. His wife's name is Chaya. He is a big *talmid hacham,* but not a rabbi. He used to wear a modern jacket rather than a *kappatta* (rabbinical robe).

The first time I met Mendel was after the Second World War. I went to visit my cousin Moyshe, his brother, in Margareten, and I stopped in Shimlo. I knew someone from the concentration camp who was in the beverage business who went to live there after the war. I spent a few days with my cousin who did not have children at that time. Later on, he came to Klausenberg for a business trip, to shop and buy textiles and clothes. He spent Shabbos with me and Eddie.

Later, Mendel and his wife had several children. I do not know their names, but we met some of them when we visited Israel. He made *aliyah* to Israel, where he lived many years. He also went through a tremendous amount. Mendel was not in a concentration camp, but—just like his older brother Moyshe—he was drafted during the war years until 1944. They drafted Jewish people into the labor force and sent them to the Russian front.

Mendel acted "melancholy" for a while, as if he were a mental case, and his sister Devorah went with him to a mental hospital. He acted really mentally imbalanced to avoid being sent to the labor camp and then being sent to Russia, to the front. And, of course, many people who were sent there died.

Also, at that time, in 1944, I believe he was drafted into the labor force. But after the war, the Russians took him as a prisoner, and he came back to Romania only several months after liberation.

He was very fortunate in one way in that he found his wife, who also survived the concentration camp, but their children got killed by the Germans, their first children. After the war, when they got back together, they started a business again in Shimlo. They were there for a short period, and after a few years they made *aliyah* (moved to Israel) and had another family, but he died of a heart condition. If he'd had open heart surgery, he could possibly have been saved, but at that time open heart surgery was not as common as it is today.

My first cousin Devorah is one of Ruttners' other daughters. Devorah was a pretty girl, very nice, a very fine person. She spent one summer with us in Borgo Prund, when she came on a vacation.

She was saved and survived the concentration camp, and after the war she lived with her brother Moshe in Margareten. Then she came to the United States with him. She married Lippa Margolis, head of Yeshiva Torah Temema in Flatbush, New York. He built it from scratch, and today it is one of the largest *yeshivas* (schools) in the United States. It's a very fine *yeshiva,* and they have a waiting list. You'd find it very difficult to get into that *yeshiva* today. They're a very fine family. One of their sons, Mendel, was married to Mindy Halberstam in Los Angeles and had six children. [Unfortunately, he died of the coronavirus in 2020.]

[There was another Ruttner brother named Tzalel. He survived the war and lived in Germany with Zeidy after the war. Zeidy was somehow instrumental in Tzalel meeting his wife, Shifra. They later moved to America, and Tzalel opened a *shtiebel* (small synagogue) in Brooklyn. He and Shifra could not have children, but they managed to adopt a baby. They named her Rifka. They never told her she was adopted; they pretended that she was their natural child to all their neighbors and acquaintances. When it came time for a *shidduch* (a match) for her, she had a lot of trouble because of the rumors that she had been adopted. This was a big negative in the Chassidic world where your *yichus* (lineage) is very important

She managed to find and marry a young man from the Scranton Yeshiva. At the time of her wedding, in 1984, Shifra, her mother, was dying of kidney cancer. During Rifka's second pregnancy, she was diagnosed with inoperable metastatic ovarian cancer. She and her husband moved to Los Angeles where doctors at the City of Hope Cancer Hospital carried out surgery for her cancer and also delivered her second child. The greater Los Angeles religious community embraced the family. Her father, Bzalel, stayed with Zeidy and grandma. Poor Rifka passed away around two years later.

But her husband eventually found a happy ending. He got remarried to a widow who was part of the Richtman family of Toronto. This family is among the wealthiest Jews in the world.]

My first cousin Freida was another Ruttner sister. She was married to her uncle, Chaim Betzalel. An uncle marrying a niece is permissible—a *mitzvah* (good deed)– but an aunt cannot marry a nephew, *al pi haTorah* (it says this in the Torah). Freida died in childbirth. She left a son they called Zeydele [literally "grandfather;" this must have been in relation to his mother dying in childbirth or a reference to him being an only child]. He was about my age, but he, too, *nebech* (a pity), was taken to a concentration camp and killed.

I had another Ruttner first cousin named Shmiel who had a beautiful voice and who also died in the Holocaust. That concludes the Ruttner family.

Hannah and Zamalay Leib Kahana

Hannah was my mother's sister, another daughter of my grandparents. She was married to a cousin Zamalay Leib Kahana. I'll just give a little bit of background. My grandfather Arieh Leib Kahana, *alav hasholem*, had a brother Wolf Kahana. He lived in Borgo Prund, and he had a number of children, who I will enumerate later on, perhaps, if I have a chance. One of the sons was called Zamalay Kahana in Yiddish; his Hebrew name was Yekusial Yehudah. Hannah was his first cousin. [The Jews in Eastern Europe often married their relatives, partially out of being located next to each other and also because they knew one another's lineage.]

Hannah had three children. The oldest was Yecheskal, whom I will refer to as cousin Eddie. She also had two daughters, Freida and Hannah (called Helen). She was named after her mother who died during her birth.

[Zamalay Kahana remarried a woman who did not want his children from his first wife around]. So he sent Eddie to live with my grandparents in Klausenberg. Freida grew up with the other grandfather Wolf Kahana in Borgo and eventually moved to Budapest where she was killed by the Nazis. My Uncle Itzhak Ayzik Kahana adopted Hannah (Helen) and took her to America in the 1930s. His daughter, Mrs. Richtman, raised her, and she married Sam Baum. They live in New York and have two daughters, Marsha and Sharon.

Two years ago, some family members visited Eddie, Freida, and Helen's mother Hannah's grave in the old cemetery in Klausenberg. She's buried not far from my grandparents, Aryeh Leib Kahana and Henya Leah. Actually, they were buried near the fence because they were Cohens. This way the children could go outside the fence and still see their graves.

[Cousin Eddie lived as colorful a life as Zeidy. He had a beautiful voice and sang in choirs in Cluj and in the choir of the Vishnitzer Rebbe. He also learned with the Klausenburg Rebbe and the Satmar Rebbe. He was drafted into the Rumanian army and became an officer because he brought his own horse. He was in a labor camp during WW2 and was reunited with Zeidy after the war, when he looked after him. They were very close before and after the war, and Zeidy considered him more of a brother than a cousin.

Eddie moved to the United States after the war and married Edel. He opened up a very successful estate jewelry business in Chicago and Palm Beach. He recently passed away at age 103 (he was officially 108 according to his immigration papers) and was still going into work every day. On High Holidays, he would lead his congregation with his *chaznut* of *Uneta Tokeph*. He was really a remarkable person, always well dressed, polite, and smiling. He never dwelt on or talked about his difficult life before he came to America. He had three children: Nina (Tyger), who is a psychic in Seattle; Tobina, who runs the House of Kahn Estate Jewelry in downtown Chicago; and Todd, who is the CEO of Coach clothing, a Fortune 500 company.]

Chaim Tzalel Kahana

My uncle, my mother's brother Chaim Tzalel Kahana, was the youngest of my grandparents' children. He was a big *talmid hacham* (Talmud scholar). For a while, he was Rav in one of the *shuls*, I believe it was the Poalei Tzedek shul in Klausenberg. He married the daughter of the Satmar's *shochet*. He lived not far from my grandparents, and after my grandfather's death, he became the official rabbi.

He was very *frum* (observant) and wore a *shtreimel* (round fur hat) and *kaftan* (Rabbinic robe). I can still see him; he had a red beard and he was a very fine person. And he, too, was killed by the Germans.

Yosef Hezkel

Then I had another uncle who was older than my mother, Yosef Hezkel. He was married and they lived in a very fine house. He was a very *frum* person; he had a beard, but a trimmed beard, and he was a businessman. During the Romanian period, he was very successful financially. He dealt in foreign currency. He would exchange currency for people who came to visit Klausenberg from different parts of the world. His currency exchange made a very fine living. He lived in a very beautiful apartment by the standards of the time, a nice apartment with indoor plumbing. Of course, he would mostly *daven* (pray) at my grandfather's shul.

He had two children. Baruch Shamshim was a big *talmid hacham* (Talmud scholar) who went away to learn with the Vishnitzer Rebbe. He would pass by Borgo Prund from time to time. During the war, he went to a labor camp, and he died somewhere in Yugoslavia, which was occupied at that time by the Germans.

My uncle also had a daughter, Chava—they used to call her Baba. Sometimes during vacation time, she would come to visit my parents and us in Borgo Prund.

In 1940 and 1941, the Hungarians occupied our part of Transylvania, and it affected my uncle Yosef Hezkel's business very badly since few foreigners came to visit the Hungarian part of our country during the war years. As a result, he was out of the money exchange business, and he went into the bottle business. He would go by bicycle and collect bottles with his son and recycle those bottles. So he struggled to make a living, having done very well before in business. Still, he kept his dignity. That was his personality. As I said, they were a very fine family.

Their whole family was killed by the Nazis; nobody in that family survived.

This concludes the immediate family that I recall from my mother's side. There are other cousins and so on, but I cannot remember right now who they were.

Descedents of Chaim and Rifka Roessler (Paternal Grandparents)

My father was the eldest of the children of my grandparents, Chaim and Rifka Roessler.

The next child was my aunt Henya, who also was killed by the Germans in the concentration camp in Auschwitz. She died with her husband, my uncle Leifer. Some of their children also were killed by Hitler, their sons Yossi and Zissu. Thank G-d, two of their daughters are alive. One lives in Israel and is also married to a man named Leifer. A Hasidic rebbe in Petach Tikva, he is in the *Olamos Elyonim* (ethereal world). He later moved to Bnei Brak, and had a *shtiebel* at 9 Kutler Street. He had at least nine children. [Many of the Leifers are known as the Nadvorna Rebbe's—more than 100 around the world.]

I went many times to visit them in Petach Tikva. The last time was about six weeks ago, and Elizabeth came with us. It was a *motzaey Shabbes,* (Saturday evening after the Sabbath), so Mommy and Elizabeth couldn't see the Rebbe at this time, because men sat separately, but they visited my cousin and his wife, Sarah.

The other Liefer sister, Bracha, lives in New York. She lived in Vienna for a number of years and in London, and now she is in New York, married to her second husband. She had a number of children—all named Lerner—with her first husband. She doesn't have children with the second husband. I met one of her sons in Williamsburg in a dry goods store. Her other son is a *Rosh Yeshiva*, in a *Satmar Yeshiva*. One of the sons-in-law is a Belzer-Chasid, so he lives in Belgium. And, another of his wife's sons lives in Manchester, England. My cousin was here, visiting with her second husband; they are nice people.

Rachel Ressler

And today I will start with my father's sister, Rachel. She lived in the city of Bistritz, not far from Borgo, about 20 kilometers. She was married to a distant cousin by the name of Meir Ressler, and *lo aleichem ve lo aleynu* (not on us, not on you), they didn't have any children. She would come quite often to visit us at Borgo, and she would stay with us for a few days. This Meir Ressler was a big *talmid hacham* (Torah scholar) and tried to do all kinds of things—whatever he could—to make a living. I don't know how rich he was, not very rich actually, but he made a living, and they were a happy couple, very nice people. As children, we were always glad to see relatives, especially when she came to visit us in Borgo. From time to time, Rachel and Meir would also visit my grandparents at Mureşenii, or Marosborgó, and I would see them.

Unfortunately, I don't remember very much about them, but I recall that he came from the city of Vásárhely. He was, I believe, either a first cousin or a second cousin to his wife and to my father. It was customary in Europe, in many families, for cousins to get married. Marrying a cousin was not a problem because you knew the *yehuss* (family background), and it is still like that in many *chassidishe rabeishe* (Hasidic dynasty families); cousins often get married.

Yankal Ressler

My uncle Yankal Ressler, one of my father's brothers, was a *shem davar* (a great man). He was a brilliant man who also lived in the city of Bistritz. I do not recall exactly at which *yeshiva* he learned, but it may have been the Satmar Yeshiva. When he was a young man, a *bachur* (still unmarried), he was brilliant in every facet of life. He never had a real secular education—though perhaps as a young child he went to the public school in Marosborgó for the primary grades—but his wisdom in learning *Gemarah*, *rishonim*, and *achronim* (commentaries), and astronomy was unprecedented.

He also married a cousin, a woman from a city called Marosvásárhely in the Hungarian language; in Romanian, it is called Târgu Mureș. His wife's name was Sasha, and she was very pleasant and very *frum*, of course. They had several very small children whose names I cannot recall.

Uncle Yankal would come often, not so much to Borgo Prund, but to visit his parents in the 1930s, and I remember him from when I was a young child. I remember once he was visiting his parents, and I was there for a *yom tov, Hoshana Rabba, Shmini Atzeret, Simhat Torah*. I don't remember if he was married at the time. He was a *moreah ve gadush* (uncertain meaning, possibly a teacher), a big *talmid hacham*, and he knew hundreds of pages of *Gemarah* by heart.

In the Second World War, in the early 1940s, he also struggled to make a living. He tried to do everything he could, selling and buying here and there. He also was a *Rosh Yeshiva,* he had a *yeshiva,* where he had *metzuyanim,* outstanding *bachurim* (students), who would come and learn from him. He would give *shiurim* (classes). He also studied astronomy and he would go to various communities and make out the *luach* (Jewish calendar) and include crucial calendar entries, such as candle lighting times for Shabbos. In those days, towns did not have a weather bureau to furnish the times of sunset, sunrise, and so on, which we needed for prayers and for *Shabbos.*

Various communities such as the city of Gross Vedain or Oradia in Romanian [where the Visnitzer Rebbe lived between the wars] asked him to come. For Oradia, he made a *luach* showing a thousand years of the right dates of various Jewish festivals. He was very well known among *rabbanim,* and everyone who spoke of Yankal Ressler had high praise for his learning, his *anivus* (humility), and his wisdom.

In 1943, they drafted the Jews to go to work camps, which were established before the concentration camps. They drafted *goyim* to go into the army and Jews to go to work camps and labor camps.

They sent many Jews to work in Hungary, building railroads, doing difficult, hard manual labor. They sent many other Jews to the Russian front to serve as labor for the German army. The armies didn't give them any clothes. They had to bring all their clothes and food from home.

The Germans sent my Uncle Yankal to a labor camp, which is where he died, apparently of starvation or cold. But while he was alive, the survivors who knew him say that he was an unprecedented man. They were touched by his extraordinary behavior. He would say *tehillim* (psalms) while he worked, and he learned with people, studying the *Gemarah* by heart. They say that his sacrifices for *Yiddishkeit* (Jewish tradition) were incredible. The survivors who came back could not praise him enough, for his life was devoted to *Yiddishkeit* and to the Jewish people. He died somewhere in Ukraine, on the Russian front. I don't know how. Was it due to starvation, or was he killed by the Germans? I don't know exactly. His wife and children also were sent to the concentration camps, and they all perished by the hands of the Germans *yimach shmann.*

Binyamin Ressler

Next, my father's next brother was Binyamin Ressler. He was, of course, also a very *frum* man, and they were all tall actually by standards of height in Europe at that time, both my father's brothers, Binyamin and Yankal.

An interesting episode I recall about Uncle Binyamin is from the time he spent at my grandparents' house with my uncle Yankal in Mureşenii for *yontif, yamim-tovim* (holidays).

There are certain strange things you recall. In this case, I remember he had a very nice overcoat. In those days it cost a fortune to buy good clothes. He married someone from the city of Piatra Neamţ, I believe, somewhere in deep Romania, which was considered quite a distance in those days. Normally people would marry someone from their own area, but he married someone from either Târgu Neamţ or Piatra Neamţ, two different Romanian towns or small cities. And for some reason, he divorced his first wife. I don't know why and how, or what happened. Either his first wife's family had a flour mill or, possibly, it was his second wife's family. Later on he remarried in one of those two cities.

In 1939, or the beginning of 1940, the Romanians drafted people from this part of Transylvania, sending Jews and non-Jews to the army.

Somehow Uncle Binyamin ended up in the state of Bukovina, near the city of Chernivtsi. People told stories of him, about his sacrifice to *Yiddishkeit*: he never drank *chalav akum* (gentile milk); he would not drink any milk unless he saw a shepherd going by and could stand by him and watch him milk the sheep or cow. That's the kind of *meseros nefesh* (sacrifice) he had for *Yiddishkeit*. But then, all of a sudden, we lost contact after our part of Transylvania became Hungary, and we received only one postcard from him as now he was in a different country. That was the last thing we've heard about him…he was killed by the Germans, or the Romanians, or Russians, or maybe, somehow, by the German or Romanian anti-Semites.

When Grandma and I took our first trip to Israel—I believe it was in December 1967—we visited our cousin Leiffer, the Rebbe in Petach Tikva. And it was *motzaey Shabbes* (Saturday night), and while we were there, a very young couple was there, too. I asked our cousin who they were. He told me that the young man was the son of my Uncle Binyamin.

Apparently just prior to being drafted into the Romanian army, he remarried, and his wife was pregnant. I don't know if he ever saw the child. The young man's name was Shalom Sigler, the surname of his mother's family. The reason he has the name Sigler is because his uncles on his mother's side adopted him in order to be able to bring him out of Romania to Israel. I believe he came to Israel in the 1960s. It was very interesting, because we had lost contact and didn't know anything about his family, and here he appeared at my cousin's house.

Since that time we established close contact with him and tried to help him financially, and we visited him in Israel many times. He is today a *Rav* in Bnai Brak, in Kiryat Herzog. He is the *Rav* of the Beit Haknesset Oley Russia *shul*, whose members are people who came from Russia in the last few years. He has many children and, of course, he is very *frum* (religious); he's a *Hasidic Rav*. He is a Sadegera *Hasid,* and his wife is a very frail person, physically, but she's very nice.

They were very cordial, very nice, and very happy to see us. We also saw some of their children. They are all in various *yeshivas*; one is married now. The girls are in Beit Yaakov, or I'm not sure at what school they learn. *[One of his sons decided that he is a Hasidic rebbe and calls himself the Bizstratzer Rebbi; he has a small place in Bnai Brak.]* Rabbi Shalom Sigler was studying to become a *dayan* (judge) in Israel, but it requires taking a very hard, complicated test.

Feiga Ressler Friedman

My father's youngest sister was Feiga, a very talented woman in many aspects, especially a talented businesswoman. She lived with my grandparents in Mureşenii, six miles from us. So, she ran a story with my grandmother, and they lived in the very big building where there was an inn and a store, though the inn was not used. The inn means a bar, a very common business among Jewish people, religious people.

Feiga was a very hard worker. For years she would travel every Tuesday to the big city, to Bistritz, where the wholesale stores were. She came to visit us in Borgo on Tuesday mornings. She would spend a few hours with us and get the train to Bistritz, which took an hour because Bistritz was 20 kilometers away from Borgo. She spent the day shopping and sent back all the merchandise with a man who had a sort of minor freight company. He was a very poor man, but he had a horse and wagon, and this is how he made a living, carrying freight from Bistritz to Mureşenii, maybe for some other merchants, too. Feiga did this trip practically every week, going to buy from wholesalers and bringing goods to the retail store she managed with my grandmother's help.

In 1943, when she must have been in her late twenties or early thirties, through a *shadchan* (match maker) she met this wonderful man, a very pleasant person, a Vishnitzer *Hassid*, but you would call him a modern type of a *Hassid*. He had a beard, of course, but he wore a short jacket that was considered modern among *Hasidic* Jews. His name was Sholem Friedman, and the reason I remember this is because I was at the *bashow*, the sit-in or showing. *[This practice has been called "a chaperoned quasi-date," a meeting that was held so we could look at each other.]*

They would bring together members of the families from both sides, and they would meet and look at each other, and see if the couple liked each other, and if the families like each other, then it would become a *shidduch* (match). This *bashow* took place in my uncle's house, Uncle Yankal Ressler's apartment, in early 1943. Then my father *alav hasholem* paid for the wedding, I believe. Because the families on both sides did not have a sufficient amount of money for the wedding, but for my father, despite the anti-Semitism and persecution in Hungary, business was quite good. He was known as well-to-do, relatively speaking.

The wedding took place at my grandparent's house in Mureşenii. As I said, it was a big house with a huge inn, which is where the wedding took place. Since there was no transportation from Borgo to Mureşenii, about six miles or ten kilometers away, my father rented a truck and a driver. The truck belonged to people who had farms with cows and milk, so this was the transportation.

It was a very beautiful wedding, a big wedding, a very happy wedding, and they were both very happy. Many people came to the wedding from Klausenburg because his family was from Klausenburg. His family had a big printing company, the Iparon printing company.

There was a problem however, because he could not be seen; he lived in hiding. As I mentioned, before that time, they already had drafted the Jews to go to labor camps, and they would send Jews also to the Russian front. Some of them were able to hide because they had false papers. Sholem Friedman was one of the people who were able to hide. He hid because going to the Russian front, as my uncles were forced to do, was almost certain death.

Before his marriage, he was hiding at Gross Vidane, now called Oraadia, in Rumania, which is where the Vishnitzure Rebbi had his court. When he asked the Rebbe about a *shidduch* with our family, the Rebbe told him to not ask any questions, but to make the *shidduch* immediately. So after the wedding, he went back into hiding. My Aunt Feiga is the relative that I went to help before she gave birth; I got the doctor when she went into labor.

These are the members of my immediate family that I remember.